THE PATH OF AMERICAN
PUBLIC POLICY

THE PATH OF AMERICAN PUBLIC POLICY

Comparative Perspectives

Anne Marie Cammisa and Paul Christopher Manuel

LEXINGTON BOOKS

Lanham • Boulder • New York • Toronto • Plymouth, UK

Published by Lexington Books
A wholly owned subsidiary of Rowman & Littlefield
4501 Forbes Boulevard, Suite 200, Lanham, Maryland 20706
www.rowman.com

10 Thornbury Road, Plymouth PL6 7PP, United Kingdom

Copyright © 2014 by Lexington Books

British Library Cataloguing in Publication Information Available

Library of Congress Cataloging-in-Publication Data Available

Cammisa, Anne Marie.
  The path of American public policy : comparative perspectives / Anne Marie Cammisa and Paul Christopher Manuel.
     pages cm
  Includes bibliographical references and index.
  ISBN 978-0-7391-8659-6 (cloth : alk. paper) — ISBN 978-0-7391-8661-9 (pbk. : alk. paper) — ISBN 978-0-7391-8660-2 (electronic) 1. United States—Politics and government. 2. Political planning—United States. 3. Comparative government. 4. Great Britain—Politics and government . I. Title.
  JK276.C35 2014
  320.60973—dc23
                                                                            2013038915

∞™ The paper used in this publication meets the minimum requirements of American National Standard for Information Sciences—Permanence of Paper for Printed Library Materials, ANSI/NISO Z39.48-1992.

Printed in the United States of America

To our daughters

Maria Teresa & Rosa Caterina

Contents

List of Images   ix

Preface   xi

Acknowledgments   xv

1 Of Ideas and Institutions: The Foundational Tension of
   American Democracy   1

2 The Path of Political Development in Great Britain and the
   United States: A Brief Comparative History   47

3 Agenda Setting and Agenda Control: Case One: A Legislative
   History of the 1994 Republican Contract with America   85

4 Agenda Setting and Agenda Control: Case Two:
   The 2008–2010 Battle over Healthcare   117

5 What if American Democracy Were on a Different Path?   153

6 Conclusion: Ideas and Institutions Matter   189

Bibliography   201

Index   215

About the Authors   221

List of Images

1.1 President Woodrow Wilson addressing Congress,
2 December 1918 — 16

1.2 Cohabitation: French Prime Minister Jacques Chirac and
President Francois Mitterrand at a press conference, 27 June 1986 — 21

1.3 Portuguese chief executives, 25 April 2011 — 22

1.4 Leaders from around the world gather at the L'Aquila
G8 Summit, 9 July 2009 — 30

2.1 The Houses of Parliament in London—the birthplace
of parliamentary democracy — 51

2.2 The United States Capitol Building in Washington, D.C. — 75

3.1 House Republican leader Newt Gingrich presents the Contract
with America to the American people, 27 September 1994 — 88

3.2 First Lady Hillary Rodham Clinton offers a toast to Speaker
of the House Newt Gingrich, 20 January 1997 — 107

4.1 President Barack Obama escorts Senator Ted Kennedy into the
East Room of the White House, 5 March 2009 — 124

4.2 House Speaker Nancy Pelosi speaks at a healthcare news
conference on Capitol Hill, 2 October 2009 — 125

4.3   Republican Senator-elect Scott Brown of Massachusetts
          celebrates at his victory rally in Boston, 19 January 2010   136

4.4   President Barack Obama waves after signing comprehensive
          healthcare reform legislation during a ceremony in the
          East Room of the White House, 23 March 2010   144

5.1   A woman reads a copy of the *Washington Star-News*, with
          "Nixon Resigning" as the headline on the front cover,
          8 August 1974   162

5.2   President Franklin D. Roosevelt prepared to throw the first
          pitch of the opening day game between the Washington Senators
          and the Boston Red Sox, 16 April 1940   174

5.3   Election workers hand-check ballots for hanging, pregnant,
          or dimpled chads at the Miami Dade County Government
          Center, 20 November 2000   182

6.1   *Washington as Statesman at the Constitutional Convention*
          (1856), by Junius Brutus Stearns (American, 1810–1885)   198

Preface

Along the Bumpy, Cobblestoned Path

A MONG ALL THE WORLD'S DEMOCRACIES, the American system of government is perhaps the most self-conscious about preventing majority tyranny. The United States still functions under a governmental system of checks and balances designed in the eighteenth century, purposively arranged to limit the reach of government and, therefore, to expand individual freedom. To help illustrate the enduring legacy of this governmental blueprint of the framers, the cover of this volume features Acorn Street on Beacon Hill in Boston, an eighteenth-century cobblestoned pathway. Just for fun, imagine if the contemporary American interstate highway system still relied on a network of eighteenth-century pathways modeled on Acorn Street. One can only imagine the mess when trucks, cars, and buses all tried to navigate their way down one narrow, bumpy, cobblestoned pathway. The result would be slow-moving circulation throughout the country, constant gridlock, and generalized frustration. The highway system would certainly not be large, well maintained, and orderly, with well-marked lanes. To the contrary, interstate transportation and commerce would be at a standstill, and nothing much would ever get accomplished. Such a road system wouldn't prevent traffic from getting from one point to another, but it would certainly slow things down.

Does this sound anything like the process of policy formation in Washington today? It should: the American constitutional system is designed to constrain innovative policy development, and therefore, contemporary policy formation in the United States continues to take place along such a bumpy, narrow, eighteenth-century cobblestoned path. Broad, sweeping reform is not common in the American presidential system, nor is it what the framers intended.

Our argument is not that comprehensive change can never occur in Washington, but that it is exceedingly difficult to make it happen. We acknowledge that there were several time periods in American history when comprehensive change did occur. The social program of the New Deal in the 1930s, adopted in response to the Great Depression, is a case in point. In his classic work *Bureaucracy: What Government Agencies Do and Why They Do It*, political scientist James Q. Wilson has argued that one of the reasons government grows is due to majoritarian surges—the public demands new goods or services, and, at various times in our history, government has expanded to meet the new demand (New York: Basic Books, 2000; see especially chapter 10).

This book will give an example of when comprehensive change failed (the 1994 Contract with America), and an example of when it succeeded (the 2010 Affordable Care Act). While 2010 illustrates an exception to the rule about comprehensive policy change in the United States, 1994 is an apt example of how our system of checks and balances usually works to stymie expansive, far-reaching legislative initiatives. A comparison of the two cases will shed light on how and why Obama's healthcare overhaul was shepherded to law under Nancy Pelosi, while Newt Gingrich was less successful with his Contract with America. The contrast between the two cases highlights the balance between majority rule and minority rights, and illustrates how these kinds of constraints impact the formation of public policy. We will argue that coalition building occurs in our system around single policies (e.g., healthcare reform), and that parliamentary-style coalition building (i.e., forming a government that will then act on a predetermined list of legislative priorities) is not a major part of the American system.

President Obama's healthcare reform effort serves as an example of broad policy change in the United States. While Obama was unable to "change the way Washington works," he was still able to see healthcare reform—the type of comprehensive, far-reaching reform that our system usually thwarts—be enacted as law by Congress and upheld as constitutional by the Supreme Court. Thus, the Affordable Care Act provides an exceptional case to illustrate the tension between majority rule and minority rights in the American constitutional system. We will examine the kinds of constraints that existed to limit the actions of policy entrepreneurs, why healthcare reform was so difficult to pass, and how its final passage illustrates the relationship between the three branches of government.

We ask a number of questions derived from the comparative public policy literature: How and why do countries differ in policy choices, processes, and implementation? What are the determinants of public policy? How do policy and politics interact? What are the causes for variation in policy formation and implementation in different countries? How might constraints and influences on policy making—including ideas, institutions, issue framing, agenda control and agenda setting, and path dependence—limit the range of options available to policy makers in some countries, but not others? What does the resistance to change in Washington teach us about the American system of checks and balances? Why is it so difficult (though not impossible) to make sweeping policy changes in the United States? How could things be different? What would be the implications for policy formation if the United States adopted a British-style parliamentary system?

The book also examines the broader debate in the field of political science over the advantages of a parliamentary system versus a presidential system, applies these questions to the case of the United States, and asks students to consider whether it is better for a democracy to function under a British-style parliamentary system (which enables a legislative majority to dominate politics, and thereby facilitates rapid change) or an American-style presidential system (which provides for stable government, a complex balancing of powers, and incremental change). In the face of a parliamentary alternative to the American presidential system, the book illustrates how the constitutional system of checks and balances functions, including the separation of powers, the role of political parties and elections, and the legislative process.

This book was originally published by Westview Press in 1998 under the title *Checks and Balances: How a Parliamentary System Could Change American Politics*. Like the first edition, this updated and revised edition explains how the institutional dimension of the political equation—sometimes overlooked by politicians and scholars alike—is of vital importance to a proper understanding of American politics. This book does not advocate that the United States adopt a parliamentary system; it simply makes the case that ideas and institutions matter to policy formation. We hope that this book will help American students better understand their own form of government, while expanding their knowledge of other governments. We also hope that it may explain the American system to those who are more familiar with parliamentary systems.

Acknowledgments

THE ORIGINAL MANUSCRIPT for this book started as a discussion between two professors, one of whom teaches comparative politics and government; the other teaches American politics and government. Both found that their students in some ways lacked a context when discussing American democracy. Both professors—the comparativist and the Americanist—often drew comparisons between the British parliamentary system and the American presidential system in order to provide a context for their students, a framework through which they could expand their concept of democracy and their understanding of various political systems. In discussions with each other, the two professors wondered what the United States would be like if it had a parliamentary system. And since the two professors are married to each other, the discussions continued on a daily basis, and the idea for this book was eventually formulated.

There are many people who made this revised and expanded edition of this book possible. We are grateful to our colleagues at Georgetown University and Mount St. Mary's University for providing supportive and intellectually stimulating environments. We are especially thankful to Bill Gormley, Kent Weaver, and Clyde Wilcox. Anne Marie Cammisa presented a draft of the chapter on healthcare at the 2012 Annual Meeting of the New England Political Science Association in Portsmouth, New Hampshire. She is grateful to the members of her panel for their very useful comments: William G. Mayer, Garrison Nelson, and William Crotty. An earlier version of chapter 5 was presented at the 1996 Fall Meeting of the Northeastern Political Science Association in Boston. We would like to thank all of the participants on the panel "History and Structure of Party Systems" for their very constructive commentary, including Eileen McDonagh, Arthur Paulson, and John Berg. We are indebted to the anonymous reviewers of the original proposal for the book for their very useful comments.

Anne Marie Cammisa would like to thank her students at the McCourt School of Publc Policy at Georgetown University for their energetic classroom debates and discussions about the intricacies of policy formation in the United States. Special thanks go to Stephen Green, who witnessed the thirty-seventh vote to repeal healthcare reform, and obligingly offered the details of what the House felt like that day. In particular, she would like to thank all of her Policy Process Institute students for their insight on the agenda-setting process of healthcare reform: cohort VIII, Section B, you know who you are!

We are most grateful to Rachel Keeler, who was Paul Manuel's classmate at the Weston Jesuit School of Theology in Cambridge, Massachusetts, for her masterful copyediting job. Carole Sargent, the founding director of Georgetown University's Office of Scholarly Publications, provided valuable insight on the publishing process. We would like to express our appreciation to Justin Race and Alissa Parra of Lexington Books for their support of this project. Archer O'Brien, who is a member of Mount St. Mary's University class of 2016, offered very useful comments and observations on the manuscript. Jim Cammisa ably prepared the tables. We also recognize the help and support of the administrative staff of the Institute for Leadership at Mount St. Mary's University: Katherine McDonagh, Kathryn Price, and Bobby Rudd.

At Saint Anselm College and Suffolk University, we had the able assistance of several students, including Janice Camara, Michael Guilfoyle, Michele O'Connor, Laurie Silverio, and Jennifer LaPierre. The staff at both Saint Anselm College's Geisel Library and Suffolk University's Sawyer Library were quite helpful in finding obscure documents through interlibrary loan. A 1996 summer research grant from Suffolk University provided support for the research. Additional research for the book was carried out at Harvard University's Widener Library, Georgetown University's Lauinger Library, and at the Library of Congress in Washington, D.C. The Montrose Spa on Massachusetts Avenue in Cambridge, Massachusetts, provided much-needed nourishment during the preparation of the original draft.

Finally, we would like to thank our daughters, thirteen-year-old Maria Teresa and eleven-year-old Rosa Caterina, for all of their goodness, understanding, and love. *We dedicate this work to them.*

Anne Marie Cammisa and Paul Christopher Manuel
Washington, D.C.

1

Of Ideas and Institutions

The Foundational Tension of American Democracy

The United States of America may be said to be the only country in the world founded in explicit opposition to Machiavellian principles.

—Leo Strauss

In framing a government which is to be administered by men over men, the great difficulty lies in this: you must first enable the government to control the governed; and in the next place oblige it to control itself.

—James Madison

Right now, what I'm trying to do is create an atmosphere where Democrats and Republicans can go ahead, get together, and try to get something done.

—President Barack Obama

THE AMERICAN CONSTITUTIONAL SYSTEM is predicated on an inherent ideational and institutional tension dating back to the foundation of the nation, which constrains innovative policy development. Namely, the framers designed a system that simultaneously seeks to protect the rights of the minority out of power and provide for majority rule. These opposing goals are based on the idea that limiting governmental power will guarantee individual liberty. We contend in this book that this foundational tension has been, and remains, a significant constraint on American policy makers, from the founding to the present day.

Pick any time period in American history, and you can see how this tension has made it difficult to adopt new public policies in Washington. That is, just as the nature of the American separated system made it difficult for the Obama administration to implement its 2010 Healthcare Law, or for the 104th Congress to pass the Republican Contract with America into law in 1994, previous Congresses have also been unable to pass many items supported by a majority of Americans, including the many earlier attempts at healthcare reform, gun control, campaign finance reform, and term limits. Even as political commentators and the general public lament the lack of bipartisan cooperation—some even suggesting that the lack of congressional action in these areas is symptomatic of a dysfunction in American democracy—things may actually be working according to the original plan of the framers. Let's take a look at that question in some detail.

Why Does American Government Appear to Be Spinning Its Wheels?

Thursday, 16 May 2013, was a bright and sunny day in Washington, D.C. As the country absorbed news of a devastating tornado in Texas, and revelations that the IRS had targeted conservative and Tea Party groups for auditing, the Republican-led House of Representatives was holding a vote to repeal healthcare reform, formally known as the Patient Protection and Affordable Care Act, but commonly referred to as the Affordable Care Act (ACA). Michelle Bachmann, the repeal bill's sponsor, stood in the well of the House with a poster of Democrat Max Baucus and the words "train wreck" behind her. "We're all sworn to protect and defend the Constitution, and that's why today we have to end this horrible piece of legislation," she announced before the vote began.[1] Republicans lined up to speak in favor of the measure, Democrats against. Bachmann's remarks reiterated her opposition to the measure in light of current events:

> [W]ith the recent news that the IRS, the agency tasked with enforcing Obamacare, has targeted groups based upon their political beliefs, there is more reason than ever to get rid of Obamacare. Under Obamacare, the average American will pay more, get less, and worry that big brother may punish them because of their beliefs. It's time to repeal Obamacare and replace it with real free market solutions for healthcare.[2]

As Bachmann returned to her seat, she fist-bumped her Republican colleagues. The repeal bill passed, 229–195, with all of the Republicans and two Democrats voting for it. Did this mean Obama's healthcare plan was about to be dismantled? In fact, no; far from it. In the first place, the vote occurred in the House; a similar bill had no chance of Senate passage. Even if the Senate did pass a bill repealing healthcare, the president would most certainly veto it. 16 May marked the thirty-seventh time Republicans had voted to repeal healthcare reform.[3] President Obama anticipated the vote in his Mother's Day remarks in the Rose Garden the week before:

> It has been more than three years since Congress passed the Affordable Care Act and I signed it into law. It's been nearly a year since the Supreme Court upheld the law under the Constitution. By the way, six months ago the American people went to the polls and decided to keep going in this direction. So the law is here to stay.[4]

If, as the president said, "the law is here to stay," why thirty-seven separate votes to repeal it? Why is the Congress continually spinning its wheels? Why isn't the passage of healthcare reform enough to stop the "politics" around it? Alternatively, why couldn't a Republican majority repeal the law? And why, despite the fact that the Affordable Care Act was passed in 2010, was it at the center of a controversial government shutdown in late 2013?

One answer to these questions may be located in the framers' institutional design for the American republic. Fearful of the tyranny of a despotic ruler, or of a majority of the citizens, the framers designed a system of government characterized by complex checks and balances and divided power arrangements. These institutions were predicated on a foundational idea: that the preservation of individual liberty requires strong limits on governmental power. Consequently, the framers designed the new system of government to protect the rights of the minority of citizens out of power, and as such, thwart the ability of any elected government to quickly pass and implement sweeping changes. In this case, the word "minority" is a bit misleading, as Republicans actually held the majority in the House in 2013. But they were the "minority" party, in that Democrats controlled the Senate and the White House. (And as to public opinion on healthcare reform, in April 2013 it was split: about 35 percent of the public had a favorable opinion of the Affordable Care Act, while 40 percent had an unfavorable opinion.[5]) In any case, the system is structured in such a way as to allow a minority in Congress not only to stop passage of authorizing legislation, but also to use other legislative means to obstruct the will of the majority in government. In other words, even though the majority party may win the day, that doesn't mean the minority has to make it easy for them.

To illustrate the impact of American government's foundational idea and institutional design, consider what could have happened in 2008–2010 if the United States functioned under British-style parliamentary rules. The British parliament is composed of two legislative houses: the House of Commons

and the House of Lords. The rules of this system accord the legislative majority in the House of Commons the necessary tools for effective and responsive
governance, and enable the House of Commons to dominate the House of
Lords on most legislative matters. Further, in this parliamentary system, the
majority party in the legislature selects the prime minister and the executive cabinet officers. So if the United States functioned under British-style
parliamentary rules, legislative and executive powers would be combined
in the powerful House of Commons (the British equivalent to the House
of Representatives). The 2008 election resulted in Democratic domination
of government (Democrats held the presidency, the House, and the Senate). Under our presidential system, this was not enough to ensure passage
of healthcare legislation, as Democratic leaders had to build coalitions and
bargain for votes—even among their own rank-and-file party members. In
addition, the president was removed from the legislative process, leaving
House Speaker Nancy Pelosi and Senate Majority Leader Harry Reid to craft
the bill and broker the compromises. Under a parliamentary system, there
would not have been three leaders (president, Speaker of the House, and
Senate majority leader); rather, the majority party in the lower house would
vote for a leader to be both head of the legislature and head of the executive
branch. This leader would likely have been "Prime Minister" Barack Obama,
who would have had broad powers not only to pass his legislative agenda, but
also to immediately implement it.

Legislative and executive functions are not separated in a parliamentary system; meaning that first, the prime minister leads the legislature in ways that a
president does not, and second, the legislature controls the executive branch in
ways that Congress does not. So not only healthcare reform, but *all* of Obama's
initial legislative priorities would have been passed immediately in 2008, without all of the political maneuvering and deal making that became necessary (see
more details in chapter 4) for passage of the healthcare law. A broad, comprehensive legislative initiative could have been passed and implemented easily
and seamlessly. Furthermore, in a parliamentary system, if the public became
unhappy with governmental action, a new election could bring in a new majority party, which could then quickly and seamlessly implement its own legislative
changes. So the election of 2010, which brought a Republican majority to the
House, could have, under a parliamentary system, swept in Republican control of government. In such a case, healthcare would have been immediately
repealed.

The possibility of American politics functioning under a parliamentary system, in which a governmental majority would be able to dominate the political
system, is ripe with promise, challenges, and perils. At least initially, many
Democrats would have been happy to have Barack Obama as their prime min-

ister, championing liberal solutions to America's problems through a compliant Congress. On the other hand, most Republicans (and probably some Democrats) would have shuddered at the thought of Obama having that much power. However, Republicans might relish the thought of giving the authority of a prime minister to some of their favorite leaders—Ronald Reagan or even Newt Gingrich (see text box 1.1) come to mind. Of course, Democrats would see a "Prime Minister Gingrich" as an unmitigated disaster. In short, neither side would be particularly enthralled with a parliamentary system during that time when their political opponents formed the legislative majority.

And therein lies one difficulty with a parliamentary system. A Prime Minister Obama could have easily passed and implemented sweeping healthcare reform; a Prime Minister John Boehner in 2011 or Mitt Romney in 2013 could just have easily repealed the law. Swift change has its own drawbacks, not least of which is instability in the governmental system.[6]

TEXT BOX 1.1
Prime Minister Newt Gingrich?

The 1994 midterm legislative elections marked a watershed event in American political history. Running on a ten-point legislative agenda known as the "Contract with America," the Republican Party gained control of both the House of Representatives and the Senate for the first time since 1954. When the 104th Congress convened in January 1995, all eyes turned to the new Speaker of the House, Newt Gingrich, who had played a leading role in the design of the Contract. In a flurry of activity over the Congressional session's first one hundred days, Gingrich's leadership resulted in the approval of nine of the Contract's ten proposals by the House of Representatives. In spite of this rapid legislative work, however, most of the Contract's legislative initiatives had not been enacted into federal law as Congress adjourned for summer recess.

If the United States had a parliamentary system, the 1994 legislative election would have resulted in Republican domination of the legislative body. When it came time to elect the political executive (i.e., the prime minister), the Republican majority in this fictional American House of Commons would have selected their leader, the conservative Republican Newt Gingrich of Georgia, to be prime minister. In that capacity, Gingrich would have had the power not only to steer the Contract with America quickly through Parliament, but also to immediately implement it as the law of the land. Since the chief executive is chosen by the parliamentary majority and not elected separately, Gingrich would not have had to deal with a Democratic president who had two years of office remaining from his 1992 election. Rather, he would be free to reform the system in even more profound ways. Of course, Gingrich would also face a perilous danger, as at any moment he could lose a parliamentary vote of confidence, which would topple his government.

The Foundational Tension: Majority Rule versus Minority Rights

Asking how American politics would function under a British-style parliamentary system reveals an inherent dilemma of American democracy, dating back to the formation of the nation: *How can we provide for the effective rule of the majority and still protect the rights of the minority out of power?* That is, just as the nature of our separated system placed many obstacles in the path of President Obama's healthcare reform, and made it difficult for the 104th Congress to implement quickly the Republican Contract into law, past and present Congresses have been unable to pass many items supported by a majority of Americans, including gun control, campaign finance reform, immigration reform, tax reform, and term limits. Many good explanations have been offered to account for the failure of the government to respond quickly in these areas, including the power of lobbying groups, insider corruption, and the insulation of politicians from the voters.[7]

While we acknowledge the wisdom of these other explanations, this book offers an institutional reason for what we perceive as the tension between majority rule and minority rights. In our view, an understanding of the institutional design of a government is of vital importance to a full and proper understanding of comparative public policy: the way we frame our political debate and representative institutions may just be of central importance to legislative and public policy outcomes.[8] In that respect, one of the reasons why the American Congress appears to take so long to enact and implement legislation may be found in the Constitution itself. The framers designed an institutional structure that, in order to block majority tyranny, impedes majority rule. That is (as we will discuss later in this chapter), the American system of checks and balances allows for the possibility that a minority in Congress can hold up or block passage of legislation, even if a majority in the full Congress, or among the population, supports that piece of legislation. The framers specifically thwarted the rule of the majority, reasoning that impassioned public opinion should be tempered by deliberative processes.

Specifically, and drawing on the insights offered by R. Kent Weaver and Bert Rockman in their seminal contribution, *Do Institutions Matter?: Government Capabilities in the United States and Abroad*, this book asks whether the current American institutional framework continues to be useful in the twenty-first century.[9] As indicated in figure 1.1, Weaver and Rockman suggest that since an analysis of the relative impact of various institutions in politics can become quite complex and unwieldy, it is useful to focus the analysis on three tiers, or levels, of explanation. The first level examines the differences between presidential and parliamentary systems. Presidential systems rely on a separation of powers (that is, executive, legis-

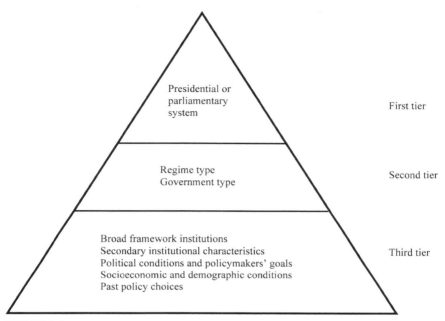

FIGURE 1.1
Tiers of Explanations of Differences in Government Capabilities
Do Institutions Matter? Government Capabilities in the United States and Abroad, ed. R. Kent Weaver and
Bert A. Rockman (Washington, DC: Brookings Institution Press, 1993), 10.

lative, and judicial powers are placed in separate institutions), while parliamentary systems rely on fused power arrangements. The second tier looks at variations within the two systems, making comparisons among the types of presidential models and the types of parliamentary models. The third level focuses on secondary institutional characteristics that may impact either a presidential or a parliamentary system, including whether a country is federal (divided into a central government and other subdivisions such as states) or unitary; the role of the judiciary; and other relevant social, cultural, and historical factors in a given country. This work is interested in all three tiers, but will focus its explanation on the first—examining the differences between presidential and parliamentary systems.

If the political structures in the United States were modified according to a British-style parliamentary system, would American government become more responsive to its citizens? Alternatively, would a parliamentary system in Washington be less respectful of minority rights than the current system? This chapter introduces the dichotomy between majority rule and minority rights. It will first look at the problem of gridlock, examine the thoughts of Bagehot and Wilson, discuss six common misperceptions about democracy—

perhaps better understood as cognitive locks, as we shall discuss—held by many Americans, and then revisit the dilemma.

Is American Government Really Unresponsive?

It is not uncommon to hear people refer to the president as ineffective, or to describe the Congress in even more negative terms. Many Americans are frustrated when Congress is slow to pass legislation that is supported by a majority of people. Although understandable, their frustration also indicates a troubling unfamiliarity with the complex system of checks and balances in American government. Since American government has been designed to be more concerned with protecting the minority out of power than with facilitating the rule of the majority in power, the very institutional design of American government may be seen as partly responsible for a perception among our citizens that the political system is sluggish, unresponsive, and distant.

The framers realized that one of the greatest threats to democracy comes from its very reliance on the people. In general, majority rule is viewed positively by proponents of democracy. It does, however, have its drawbacks. The framers were primarily concerned with mob rule, or what Madison termed the "tyranny of the majority." An impassioned mob might call for governmental action that in the long run would be detrimental to the public good. The majority might have selfish or irrational motives for its espousal of particular policies, and might overlook the interests of the minority. The framers believed that one role of government was to protect the interests of the minority against the passions of the majority. To do so, the framers put in place a series of brakes on majority power. Thus, American democracy is indirect (representatives are elected to debate and pass public policy), there are two houses in Congress (either of which may check the other), power is separated into three branches at the national level, and the system of federalism divides power between the state and federal governments. The power of the majority is dispersed and therefore diffused. These brakes on majority rule also serve to slow down the policy-making process, leading to criticism of government as ineffective or inactive.

Much of that criticism has focused on divided government in Washington, which has been a pronounced feature of American government in the postwar period.[10] It occurs when the president is of a different party than the dominant party in the legislative branch. Although the framers of the Constitution could not have predicted the evolution of the party system, they might approve of divided government, in that it conforms to their desire to disperse power. If the president is of one party and the majority in Congress of another, then each branch has strong incentive to act as a "check" on the other. On the other hand, critics have held divided government responsible by for a myriad of governmental problems, including obstructing the government's ability to get legislation passed.

In particular, critics have argued that divided government inextricably leads to *gridlock*, which may be defined as a stalemate in government over legislative priorities. Gridlock can function at many levels, including between the president and Congress, between the Senate and the House, or between the two parties within Congress, and it prevents Congress from moving on legislative programs. Critics have argued that the net result of gridlock has been governmental movement without significant legislative accomplishments. Like a caged gerbil on an exercise spinning wheel, governmental gridlock generates a lot of motion without any forward progress.

In Defense of Gridlock

Not everyone thinks that divided government or gridlock is antagonistic to good government. To the contrary, several observers have argued that divided government itself has resulted in the stability and longevity of the constitutional system. Seymour Martin Lipset, for example, has suggested that governmental gridlock is the very definition of responsive government, in that it exists because the people, by splitting the ticket in the voting booth, have, in effect, voted for gridlock. In his view, American voters since 1946 have used the midterm elections as a means to signal displeasure with certain policies of the sitting president, but have still been ready to reelect him two years later.[13] As such, gridlock has resulted in stability more durable system, because it has enabled voters to express their displeasure with the sitting administration without challenging its fundamental stability. Similarly, former Congressman Bill Frenzel (R-MN) has lavishly praised the system of separated powers for its ability to filter out the temporary passions of the public from good public policy:

> There are some of us who think gridlock is the best thing since indoor plumbing. Gridlock is a natural gift the framers of our Constitution gave us so that the country would not be subjected to policy swings resulting from the whimsy of the public. And the competition—whether multi-branch, multilevel, or multi-house—is important to those checks and balances and to our ongoing kind of centrist government. Thank heaven we do not have a government that nationalizes this year and privatizes next year, and so on ad infinitum.[14]

Further, David Mayhew convincingly demonstrated that a divided government is not necessarily an unresponsive one. In a rigorous study of congressional legislative production from 1947 to 2002, he found that were no significant differences regarding legislative policy outputs under periods of divided or unified government. Mayhew disputes the very notion that divided government and our separated system produce gridlock or an undesirable form of government, arguing that unified and divided governments do equally well in terms of getting important legislation passed.[15]

The Problem with Gridlock

So why do so many people think that gridlock is such a bad thing? How can an electoral mechanism that simultaneously enables citizens to signal displeasure with a sitting administration and protects the government from the temporary passions of the electorate possibly be considered in negative terms?

James Sundquist sheds some light on this question. Noting that even though Mayhew's research correctly shows that legislative output can be as high during periods of divided or unified rule, Sundquist contends that gridlock produces a poorer quality of legislation, without much governmental accountability.[16] In his view, it is extremely difficult to hold a particular political leader or party accountable for his or her actions during a period of divided powers and competing legislative agendas. Indeed, if there is more than one center of power, it becomes quite easy for a particular elected official to place the blame for failure somewhere else when a popular bill fails. The president can always blame Congress, even if his administration did a poor job. Alternatively, even if Congress had previously denied the president the requisite tools to do the job well, congressional leaders can always blame the president for, among other things, poor preparation, poor leadership, and obstruction. The problem with divided government, then, is that citizens are unable to pinpoint one branch of government as the source of the problem. Neither the president nor the Congress is completely accountable to the public, and yet each has the other as an easy scapegoat. In a system of separated powers such as the American system (in which the legislative power is in Congress and the executive power rests with the president), divided government is a real and serious problem.[17]

A Case of the Lack of Accountability under Divided Government

In late April 2013, Americans watched in disgust as air travelers faced massive delays and cancellations of flights, throwing a wrench into travel plans and wreaking havoc at major airports. What was the cause of these delays? Well, bad weather may have had something to do with them, but the main reason was a furlough of large numbers of air traffic controllers. This furlough (air traffic controllers were forced out of work because the government could

TEXT BOX 1.2
The Blame Game in Washington, circa 1980

Shifting blame for budgetary woes, including spending cuts and deficit spending, is nothing new. Consider, for example, the case of the national deficit increase in the 1980s under a divided government. Although all sides have acknowledged that the national debt rapidly increased during the Reagan presidency, they differ strongly over whose fault it is. Republican Ronald Reagan defeated the incumbent Democratic President Jimmy Carter in the 1980 election on a campaign that promised to accomplish five legislative goals: to build up America's defenses, to cut taxes, to cut the bureaucracy, to cut social spending, and to balance the federal budget by 1983. In the 1980 congressional elections, the Republican Party also won control of the Senate, which supported the president's legislative agenda. The Democrats, on the other hand, retained control of the House of Representatives, and were opposed to the president's program. As Reagan started his first day at the job, the new president faced a hostile and confrontational House of Representatives, and the problem of divided government became the source of intense legislative battles.

Tip O'Neill, the liberal Democratic Speaker of the House, did not support the president's legislative package. However, after several meetings with Reagan, O'Neill agreed not to block the president's legislative program to increase defense spending, and to support a tax cut, as long as Reagan agreed not to veto the Democratic budget, which maintained spending increases for some social programs, including Social Security. A bargain was reached, and a budget was passed that both cut taxes and increased spending. The net result of this deal between the president and the House of Representatives was that the federal government started to take in less money and to spend more in the early 1980s. Revenues went down, at the same time that spending was going up. As one might surmise, when President Reagan left office in 1988 (he had been reelected in 1984), the national debt had significantly increased, despite the use of budgeting "tricks" to make the debt look smaller.[11]

So, who was at fault for the increased debt? The Democrats blamed President Reagan, and pointed out that the president had violated his 1980 campaign promise to balance the budget by 1983. In addition, they contended that the tax cuts and increases in defense spending that took place under his administration swelled the national debt, and faulted him for never having submitted a balanced budget. The Republicans, on the other hand, blamed the Democratic-controlled House of Representatives for the increase in the national debt. They pointed out that since the Constitution grants Congress the power of the purse, the legislative branch is ultimately responsible for every federal dollar spent. Further, Republicans pointed to the record of House-approved bills in the 1980s as one that simultaneously increased social and defense spending and decreased taxes. Republicans claimed that Speaker O'Neill and the House acted irresponsibly, and that the House Democrats were to blame for the debt predicament. The Democrats, according to Republicans, took the easy way out, by both approving President Reagan's tax decreases—which were very popular with the public—and insisting on increases in social spending, also popular with the public.[12]

not pay their checks) was itself the result of "sequestration," a budgetary maneuver involving automatic, across-the-board spending cuts. Republicans protested that the Democrats were just playing games, that the Democratic administration could have found something else to cut in the Federal Aviation Administration's budget, other than air traffic controllers' salaries. Democrats, Republicans contended, were using these particular cuts for political gain, to turn the public against sequestration and budget cutting. Republicans also insisted that massive budget cuts were necessary to offset the yearly deficits that contribute to a growing national debt. For their part, Democrats vociferously reiterated their position that sequestration had been a bad idea all along, that Republicans were willing to cut vital government programs in pursuit of political gains. Each side claimed that the other was ultimately responsible for the air traffic controller furlough.[18] So who was responsible? Were Republicans correct in asserting that Democrats were playing political games? Or were Democrats right that it was Republicans' fault to begin with?

Perhaps a look at sequestration itself can shed some light on the situation. In late 2011, Republicans and Democrats were wrangling over both how to deal with the debt limit (Congress has to pass a law to increase the amount of debt that the federal government can hold) and how to cut spending. Given that the federal government owes much of its debts to foreign governments, defaulting on the debt would have both national and international consequences. Democrats, afraid of those consequences, were anxious to increase the debt limit. Republicans, who wish to reduce the size of government by reducing spending, wanted to focus on cutting government spending. Democrats and Republicans could agree on some spending cuts, but they needed to make more. So the Budget Control Act of 2011 was born. Republicans agreed to increase the debt limit, in exchange for further spending cuts at a future date. Those cuts were to be determined by a bipartisan panel. To encourage the panel to make tough cuts, a very large stick was put in the legislation: if the panel could not come to agreement, there would be automatic, across-the-board spending cuts, a procedure known as sequestration. No one thought this would actually happen, of course, and politicians of all stripes were dismayed when the panel could not agree to spending cuts and sequestration went into effect. Imagine if you had to cut your personal budget equally across all spending areas: that would mean that housing, transportation, mobile phone costs, and basic groceries would be cut by the same percentage as clothing, eating out, other electronics, and entertainment. Wouldn't it be more logical to decide the areas where spending is less flexible and more important, and cut more from the areas where spending might be more flexible or less crucial? The same idea holds true for sequestration.

Where did the idea for sequestration come from? Its immediate provenance was Obama advisor Jack Lew, who thought it might be a way to force the Republican Party's hand. But Lew himself got the idea from the Gramm-Rudman-Hollings Act, a Reagan-era attempt to force budget cutting. So, in the end, whose fault are the automatic spending cuts? Blame can be equally distributed among Democrats and Republicans, Congress and the executive, past and present politicians. Such a wide distribution of blame means that no one person, party, or branch of government is held accountable, and finger pointing becomes the order of the day. The public was left frustrated with delayed and canceled airline flights, and confused as to whose fault the delays actually were. No one in government took responsibility for the debacle.

In fact, even though *both* the executive and legislative branches had a hand in sequestration and the consequent air traffic controller furlough, neither side accepted responsibility, and both could plausibly deny their role. Each branch had ample evidence to blame the other for unpopular budget cuts. R. Kent Weaver and Bert Rockman have argued that this type of poor policy making and lack of accountability are inherent problems in the institutional design of American government. According to former Treasury Secretary C. Douglas Dillan, "the president blames the Congress, the Congress blames the president, and the public remains confused and disgusted with government in Washington."[19]

Critics of the separated-powers system point to this lack of governmental accountability as a significant problem for American government. The system should be reformed, they say, in order to correct this problem, which impairs the government's very ability to govern. For example, Theodore Lowi has observed that although there is nothing necessarily sinister about a democratic government needing to run up a big deficit now and then, there is a serious problem when governmental spending outpaces revenue over a period of years, regardless of economic conditions. Lowi suggests that a constitutional system of divided powers leads directly to an institutionalized incapacity to govern. Such a system prevents elected officials from taking charge and, simultaneously, accords them with the means to deny any responsibility for government action.[20] In Lowi's view, presidential democracy in the United States is currently in "a pathological condition we must seek to heal."[21] Is Lowi correct? Has divided government led to an institutionalized incapacity to govern in the United States? What solutions are available to address these problems?

A Possible Solution? Enabling Majority Rule

The Englishman Walter Bagehot, writing in the nineteenth century, found fault with this problematic constitutional relationship between the legislative and executive branches. In his 1867 work, titled *The English Constitution*, Bagehot argues for a fusion of executive and legislative powers.

Placing executive and legislative powers in the same branch, according to Bagehot, avoids altogether the problems of divided government. The government will never be divided if the legislature chooses the executive. The American system, in which both the president and members of Congress are chosen by popular election, creates the possibility that the majority in Congress will be at odds with the executive branch. In addition, Bagehot argues that the separation of powers makes it more difficult to pass legislation, since it must be approved not only by two houses of Congress, but also by a separately elected president.

Bagehot castigates the American system for its fixed and inelastic nature, which, in his view, imperils its citizens. The long and protracted procedures necessary to pass legislation make it difficult, according to Bagehot, for the United States to respond quickly to any unforeseen crises. Further, he contends that the division of legislative and executive powers leads to the problems of stalemate and lack of accountability:

> The executive is crippled by not getting the law it needs, and the legislature is spoiled by having to act without responsibility: the executive becomes unfit for its name, since it cannot execute what it decides on; the legislature is demoralized by liberty, by taking decisions of which others [and not itself] will suffer the effects.[22]

Bagehot argues in favor of a parliamentary arrangement, in which the elected representatives select the national leader. In contrast to a system of divided powers, citizens in a parliamentary system are able to hold their leaders accountable for governmental action, in that the prime minister and the cabinet (both chosen from the legislature) are exclusively charged with the responsibility to govern. If they are found to be incompetent before their term is over, they can be forced from office: a vote of no-confidence in Parliament can bring down a government, and new elections can be quickly arranged. This characteristic flexibility of a parliamentary system enables the government to rule authoritatively and effectively, well able to adapt to the changing times.

Writing a few years later, and before he entered the political arena, Woodrow Wilson found himself to be in essential agreement with Bagehot's analysis. Wilson, who was elected president in 1912 and reelected in 1916, was the only American president to hold a PhD in political science. Wilson argued in 1879 that the changing times at the end of the nineteenth century favored a more centralized form of government.[23] The national government faced a host of problems related to the Industrial Revolution, from how to protect workers to how to deal with a rapidly expanding economy. The national government, called on to regulate new and changing areas of the national economy, was designed when the United States was still quite agricultural. Although he acknowledged that the system worked reasonably well in the eighteenth century and for most of the nineteenth century, Wilson insisted that the demands of the late nineteenth and early twentieth centuries required that American institutions be redesigned. In his view, the constitutional system of separated powers devised by the framers was no longer useful, precisely because it enfeebled the national administration, generating a leaderless government and a weak executive:

> Why is it that this leaderless character of our government did not disclose itself to an earlier generation as it has disclosed itself to us? The government has the same formal structure now that it always has had: why has its weakness been so long concealed? Why can it not serve the new time as well as it served the old? Because the new time is not like the old—for us or for any nation. . . . For one thing—and this can be no news to any man—the industrial revolution separates us from the times [before].[24]

Pointing out the many changes to American society brought about by the Civil War and industrialization, Wilson suggests that a form of parliamentary government should replace what he saw as an antiquated system of government. In particular, he criticized the committee system in Congress, where most of the work was done out of the public view. He preferred a parliamentary system, in which the cabinet, rather than congressional committees, would be dominant:

> I ask you to put this question to yourselves: Should we not draw the Executive and the Legislature closer together? Should we not, on the one hand, give the individual leaders of opinion in Congress a better chance to have an intimate party in determining who should be President, and the President, on the other hand, a better chance to approve himself a statesman, and his advisors capable men of affairs, in the guidance of Congress?[25]

An executive-driven cabinet government would be preferable to a legislative-steered committee government, according to Wilson. It could better concentrate political power, address the nation's problems, and be held accountable by the citizenry. In his view, American government needed to be able to authoritatively cope with the many new challenges posed by industrialization, as well as be directly held accountable for its actions by the electorate. The best way to do this would be to centralize, rather than separate, powers.

IMAGE 1.1
Before he entered the political arena, President Woodrow Wilson argued in favor of a parliamentary system for the United States. He is pictured here addressing Congress on 2 December 1918. © CORBIS.

How the Foundational Ideational Tension Limits Innovative Policy Development: Ideas Conceptualized as Cognitive Locks

Although the critiques of the American presidential system offered by Bagehot and Wilson ring true to some observers today, many people do not have a proper context to evaluate their views. For that matter, many do not even have a clear idea about what democracy really is. In the United States, Americans are so used to the presidential system that many often mistakenly think that it is the only form of government a democracy can take. Further, it is ironic that many Americans today are prone to think almost piously of the Constitution, ignoring that it, similar to any other legislative outcome in a democracy, was the result of political settlements among various factions at the Constitutional Convention.

This brings us to the concept of cognitive locks in comparative public policy.[26] Mark Blyth has persuasively argued that ideas do matter to policy formation, "in that they are simultaneously the media through which agents understand the world and the material that constitutes it." Extending this notion, he usefully defines the notion of "ideas conceptualized as cognitive locks" as follows:

Ideas conceptualized as cognitive locks is an approach that . . . seeks to explicate how new ideas, once successfully institutionalized, can affect policy outcomes. Historical institutionalists have generally argued that once ideas have become institutionally embedded, policy-making becomes possible only in terms of these ideas. As such, ideas can produce outcomes independent of the agents who originally developed them.[27]

Applying this concept to the case of the United States provides useful insights about how the foundational ideational tension limits both innovative policy development and the way Americans think about how democracy ought to work. Such pre-set ideas, or cognitive locks, can lead to the development of profound misperceptions, and impede any thoughtful consideration of proposals advocating the reform or even the replacement of the American presidential system with some form of a parliamentary regime. Very schematically, we can identify six broad areas:

- Misperception 1: The American Constitution defines modern democracy.
- Misperception 2: Democracies must always function in a federal system.
- Misperception 3: A democracy requires a national bicameral legislature.
- Misperception 4: The chief executive must be both the head of state and the head of government.
- Misperception 5: There can only be one winner in an election and only one representative per electoral district.
- Misperception 6: The American constitutional system would work anywhere.

Let us now examine each one of these in turn.

Misperception 1: The American Constitution Defines Modern Democracy

Many Americans associate the political structure of government created by the Constitution with the very definition of modern democracy. That is, many consider the separation of powers of the government into executive, legislative, and judicial branches; the checks and balances among and between these three branches; and judicial oversight (the power of the courts to invalidate actions of the other two branches) to be necessary and sufficient conditions for a democratic regime. The truth is, however, that the American Constitution has created what is only one form of democracy, and these three features are not present in all of the world's democracies.

To begin, let us define *democracy*. Joseph Schumpeter provides us with a useful starting point. According to Schumpeter, any political regime can be called a democracy if it meets at least the following three fundamental conditions. First, there must be broad and authentic competition among individuals, organized political groups, or political parties for all effective positions of power in the government, including the position of chief executive. Second, a high level of citizen participation, in which no major adult groups are excluded from the political process, is required. Finally, basic civil and political liberties, such as the freedom to compete for political office, as well as the freedom of assembly, of speech, and of movement, must be guaranteed. If these three components are present in a political system, it can be considered a functioning democracy. This definition builds on the very simple premise that although a democratic regime does not involve a particular concoction of institutions, it is founded on a basic respect for civil and human rights.[28] Philippe Schmitter and Terry Lynn Karl remind us that democracies are not necessarily more economically successful, administratively efficient, or even more stable than nondemocratic regimes. Rather, in their view, democracy is properly understood as an ongoing process in which the representatives of the people peacefully settle disputes and establish public policy objectives.[29] As long as these conditions are met by a political regime, we can safely call it *democratic*.

Having defined democracy, let us now examine the three main institutional forms that it may take: presidential, parliamentary, and semipresidential.

Presidential democracy is the system currently operating in the United States. Giovanni Sartori has identified three characteristics of the modern presidential system.[30] First, a president must be elected by a form of direct popular election, for a term of office usually ranging from four to eight years. Remember that this is a necessary but not a sufficient condition for a presidential regime. Even though a country may hold national and direct elections for president, that does not necessarily imply that the president has real power. Second, in a presidential system the chief executive can neither be appointed nor dismissed by a legislative vote—executive power derives from a popular mandate, not from the legislative branch.[31] Third, the president is in exclusive charge of the executive branch, and faces no competition from senior policymakers or from cabinet officials.[32]

Further, Juan Linz has observed that one of the most important features of a presidential system is the concept of *dual democratic legitimacy* for the executive and legislative branches of government. That is, under the rules of presidential democracy, both the executive and the legislature are elected independently of one another by the people, and therefore enjoy separate bases of legitimacy. This leads to a certain inflexibility of the system, because, criminal behavior notwithstanding, no matter how ineffective or incompetent a president or representative may be, the legislative branch does not have the right to remove him or her.[33] Impeachment is one way in which a presidential system might eliminate a president who has broken the law, although it is a difficult and lengthy process. In addition, executive and legislative branches of government compete with each other over legislation under a presidential system. The legislative branch subdivides its membership into several committees, and charges each with gathering relevant information on the issue over which it has jurisdiction. Once obtained, that information will enable the legislature to vie with the president over legislative items and priorities. This can lead to the problem of gridlock discussed earlier.

Parliamentary democracy stands in contrast to presidential democracy. Although there are several variations of this system in the world, the parliamentary system used in Great Britain is the world's most renowned form. Arend Lijphart has referred to the British system as the majoritarian-confrontational system,[34] and it is also known as the Westminster parliamentary model (named for the county in which the British Parliament is located).[35] As we will discuss in chapter 2, this system provides for a close connection between the executive and legislative branches. Further, the British prime minister, who is the political executive, is also the head of the majority party in the House of Commons.[36] The prime minister chooses a cabinet from members of the majority party in the legislature, and the cabinet is collectively responsible to the House of Commons. As long as the legislative majority is maintained, the prime minister can expect to have all of his party's legislation passed without any revisions from the opposition. The prime minister is responsible to Parliament, and must maintain the support of the governing party. Variations of the Westminster parliamentary system are used in many countries, including Greece and Ireland.

The dual-executive or semipresidential regime is an amalgamation of presidential and parliamentary systems. It features both a president and a prime minister. Concocted by French leader Charles de Gaulle, it was first introduced in the 1958 Fifth Republic Constitution. De Gaulle sought to create a strong presidency able to respond to major threats to national security. At that time, the institutional problem for France was, in de Gaulle's estimation, a weak chief executive—the parliamentary French Third Republic (1870–1939) had simply collapsed when the Germans invaded, and for a variety of reasons, the parliamentary French Fourth Republic (1947–1958) disintegrated when Algeria demanded independence from French colonial rule. De Gaulle argued that a strong executive was necessary to lead the country though these types of crises, but also understood the need for the legislature to continue to function under parliamentary rules that it had more or less followed since 1870. The 1958 Constitution provides for a parliamentary legislature, and grants the president a number of important emergency powers to deal with a crisis.

TEXT BOX 1.3
Key Characteristics and Variations of Democratic Regimes

Key Characteristics of Any Democratic Regime
- Competition for office
- A high level of citizen participation
- Guarantee of basic civil and political liberties

Key Variations of Democracy
- Presidential system
- Parliamentary system
- Dual executive (semi-presidential) system

Key Characteristics of Presidential Systems of Democracy
- Separation of legislative (congressional) and executive (presidential) powers
- Direct popular election of the president
- The chief executive may neither be appointed nor dismissed by a legislative vote
- The president is in exclusive charge of the executive branch
- Separate elections (and separate bases of legitimacy) for the president and legislature

Key Characteristics of Parliamentary Systems of Democracy (Westminster Model)
- Legislative and executive functions are fused
- Prime minister is also head of the majority party of the parliament
- Cabinet members are chosen by the prime minister from members of the majority party in the legislature
- As long as the legislative majority is maintained, the prime minister can expect to have all of his or her party's legislation passed without any revisions from the opposition

Key Characteristics of a Dual-Executive (or Semi-Presidential) System of Democracy
- Powers are both fused and separated
- Directly elected president with constitutional powers
- Prime minister chosen from majority party in the parliament

---

The French dual-executive system created a unique mélange of the American and English systems, in that executive and legislative powers are separated and fused at the same time: analogous to the United States, there is an elected president with constitutional powers; similar to the United Kingdom, there is a prime minister who is both the chief executive and the head of the legislative chamber. Following a parliamentary system, the prime minister is selected by the majority party in the legislature, and following a presidential system, according to the constitutional referendum of 1963, the president is directly elected by the citizens.

Critics have pointed to a number of dangers created by a system that has institutionalized executive rivals, conceivably leading to a battle for control of the government between the president and the prime minister. Under a dual-executive system, divided government is called *cohabitation*, defined as that situation when the president is of a different party than the prime minister. In France, cohabitation first occurred from 1986 to 1988, when the Socialist President François Mitterrand had to deal with a rightist Gaullist majority in the National Assembly, led by Prime Minister Jacques Chirac. The system worked well for a number of reasons, notably because President Mitterrand sought only to criticize the prime minister, not to obstruct his government and force a constitutional crisis.

There is a presidential-parliamentarian crossbreed in Portugal as well. In contrast to the French case, the Portuguese dual-executive model is more of a parliamentary system with a president. Although the president has independent authority and legitimacy outside of the National Assembly, the law-making function rests with the prime minister and the National Assembly. Further, the president is expected to monitor the activities of the government,

IMAGE 1.2
France operates under a dual-executive arrangement. In this image taken during the period known as cohabitation, French Prime Minister Jacques Chirac (at left) smiles as French President Francois Mitterrand answers a question at a 27 June 1986 press conference. © Thierry Orban/Corbis.

IMAGE 1.3
The Portuguese constitution provides for a dual-executive democratic system. Here
the president of the republic, Cavaco Silva (2-L), is accompanied by his predecessors
in office since 1974: Mario Soares (L), Jorge Sampaio (R), and Ramalho Eanes (2-R)
during the celebrations marking thirty-seven years of the revolution, at Belem Palace,
in Lisbon, Portugal, 25 April 2011. © INACIO ROSA/epa/Corbis.

and he can veto legislation. In the event of a stalemate in the National Assembly, the president has the power to dismiss the prime minister, appoint a
new prime minister, or call for new elections. This moderating role has been
very important for Portugal during its transition to, and consolidation of, a
democratic regime after forty-eight years of dictatorial rule. The president is
elected by universal suffrage to a five-year term, and no president may serve
more than two consecutive terms.[37]

The institutional structures of France and Portugal have each attempted to
find an appropriate fit between the presidential and parliamentary models of
democratic government in terms of each country's particular historical development and national characteristics. In each case, this has led to lengthy and
enduring periods of democratic stability.

As the above review of presidential, parliamentary, and semipresidential
systems clearly indicates, there is no one set of institutional patterns for contemporary democracies. As table 1.1 shows, there are many different types of
institutional arrangements operating in contemporary democracies. Some

TABLE 1.1
A Sample of Contemporary Democracies Using Different Constitutional Arrangements

Country	Separation of Powers	Judicial Review	Presidential or Parliamentary
Brazil	Yes	Yes	Presidential
Canada	Yes	Yes	Parliamentary
France	Yes	Yes, of administrative, not legislative acts	Semi-presidential
Germany	No	Yes	Parliamentary
India	Yes	Yes	Parliamentary
Israel	No	Yes	Parliamentary
Italy	Yes	Yes, under certain circumstances	Parliamentary
Japan	No	Yes	Parliamentary
Portugal	Yes	Yes	Semi-presidential
Spain	No	Yes	Parliamentary
United Kingdom	No	Non-binding	Parliamentary
United States	Yes	Yes	Presidential

Source: U.S. Central Intelligence Agency, *The World Factbook*. www.cia.gov/library/publications/the-world
-factbook/geos/xx.html. Accessed 13 May 2013.

parliamentary systems fuse, rather than separate, the executive and legislative branches. In some cases, the legislative branch is even sovereign over the judicial branch. In short, there are political systems elsewhere in the world that significantly deviate from the American constitutional system, but are nonetheless democratic.

Misperception 2: Democracies Must Function in a Federal System

The framers of the American Constitution devised the system of intergovernmental relations known as federalism, in which powers are divided between the national and state governments. Some students incorrectly extend this American feature to other countries, and assume that all democracies must function under federalism. It may surprise some American students to learn that not only are there many forms of federalism, but some democracies do not use a federal arrangement at all.

First, let us define *federalism*. William Ricker has defined federalism as "a political organization in which the activities of government are divided between regional governments and a central government in such a way that each kind of government has some activities on which it makes final decisions."[38] In the United States, both the federal government and the fifty state governments have rights under the Constitution. When conflicts arise between a state and the federal government, or between two or more states, the Constitution charges the Supreme Court with the responsibility of settling those disputes. The system of federalism was invented by the framers of the Constitution as a way to both ensure that the national government would be strong enough to function effectively and allow the states autonomy in local affairs.

The strength of the American federal system lies in the fact that the relationship between the national and state governments is somewhat ill-defined. For example, the Tenth Amendment (part of the Bill of Rights) states that "the powers not delegated to the United States by the Constitution, nor prohibited by it to the States, are reserved to the States respectively, or to the people." In contrast, Article VI asserts that the Constitution and all federal laws made under it "shall be the supreme law of the land," regardless of any "laws of any state to the contrary." While Article VI gives the balance of power to the federal government, the Tenth Amendment shifts that balance toward the states. The framers, fearful of a repeat of the weak government under the Articles of Confederation, shored up the powers of the new national government. But the states would not ratify the Constitution unless there were some guarantees of their autonomy.

Throughout American history, the federal government has increased its power and authority as the country has grown larger, the economy has expanded, and the issues that the national government deals with have become more complex. Periodically, the states have made attempts to increase their power vis-à-vis the federal government, with increasing success as the twentieth century drew to a close. The unique feature of American federalism is that it recognizes a sort of dual citizenship: individuals are citizens of the state in which they reside, as well as of the nation as a whole. While the distinction may not seem obvious, it is nonetheless important. One of the major problems under the Articles of Confederation was that the federal government was a loose confederation of states. Individuals were citizens of the state in which they resided; states were members of the confederation. Under the Constitution, it is not the states that have formed the government, but the people themselves. This lends the federal government more legitimacy in a democracy, which relies on popular consent. While states were granted rights under the Constitution, in practice, the federal government has had the upper hand. In recent decades, states have reasserted their rights to make autonomous decisions, and the federal government has devolved some of the powers it has taken on, giving them back to the states. Welfare is just one example of a government program that had been increasingly centralized after World War II, but was decentralized in the 1990s, giving more power back to the states. Federal-state conflicts continue in the twenty-first century: one problem with the Affordable Care Act is that some "Red" (Republican-dominated) states have been reluctant to implement its provisions, and resent federal intrusion into what they believe is state policy.

Although invented in the United States, federalism today exists in many variations throughout the world. Spain, for example, adopted a quasi-federal structure in 1978, in which the central government shares powers with each of seventeen autonomous communities. Article 2 of the 1978 Spanish Constitution states that "the Constitution is based on the indissoluble unity of the Spanish nation, the common and indivisible motherland of all Spaniards, and recognizes and guarantees the right to autonomy of the nationalities and regions of which it is composed and the common links which bind them together." The 1978 Spanish Constitution recognizes both the important unifying role of the central government and the need for some local control. Or, as Kerstin Hamann has aptly observed, "even if Spain is not a 'pure' federal state according to some definitions, it has been and still is undergoing a process of federalization—that is, moving from a unitary state to a federal state."[39] Spain adopted this quasi-federal system after the 1975 death of the dictator General Francisco Franco, who had favored a unitary system, for two main reasons: first, it was a reaction against some thirty-five years of overcentralization under Franco, and second, it was a response to many regional demands that the new democracy devise an arrangement that would find an appropriate fit between an effective national government and regional autonomy.[40]

In contrast, other contemporary democracies function under a unitary framework—defined as one in which the central government exercises authority over the regional or local governments. Even though there may be elected city or regional governments under a unitary system, ultimate power rests with the central government. For example, in Great Britain, which uses a unitary system, Parliament may grant more power to, or may take power away from, local officials.[41] That is, the central government retains ultimate sovereignty over all of the regions, and faces few competing sources of power.

In the late twentieth century, central governments that use a unitary system transferred some of their powers to local authorities in many countries. Known as devolution or regionalization, this process is similar to the one that has occurred in the United States. The national government decentralizes its own power by giving authority back to the subnational units. That is, devolution involves the transfer, or the devolving, of some central powers back to the regions. This process came about due to demands by inhabitants for more say on political decisions that affect their towns and communities. In Great Britain, regional assemblies have been instituted in response to demands by an overwhelming majority of the citizens in Wales and Scotland. The future implications of the trend toward devolution for unitary systems are unclear, as Michael Curtis observes:

> For comparison the distinction between federal and unitary systems is useful, but modern trends in government have sometimes blurred the distinction. In many federal systems, such as the United States, the central institutions have grown stronger, while in some unitary states, such as Britain and France, some decentralization and devolution of power has occurred to countries, regions and local authorities.[42]

In general, legislatures functioning under a federal system have more limited powers than those under unitary systems. Among the most convincing explanation for that phenomenon is that federal systems force national legislatures to contend with the legitimate authority and competing claims from the state, or local, governments. Central governments in a unitary framework face no such challenges for power and authority.[43]

Finally, a confederal system can be defined as a union of separate states that retain their autonomy but cooperate in certain common areas. From 1781 to 1787, the United States functioned under a confederal system. Under the Articles of Confederation, each individual state retained its own power and autonomy; the states were connected to each other by a weak national government. The American confederation was not an effective system. The national government did not have the power to tax, which meant that it did not have the power to raise funds to pay debts left over from the War of Independence, or to properly provide a national defense. The system enabled local interests to dominate, even at the expense of the national good. As we shall see in chapter 2, the American Constitutional Convention in 1787 was originally called to find solutions to the problems inherent in the confederal system. There are no nations currently operating under a confederal system, and the closest modern-day example of a confederal system may be the United Nations. Under the United Nations Charter, certain legal guarantees have generally allowed member states to protect their sovereignty from the world government (this is especially true for those nations that sit on the powerful United Nations Security Council).

Table 1.2 demonstrates the wide variety of federal and unitary systems currently used by contemporary democracies.

Misperception 3: There Must Be a National Bicameral Legislature

American government in Washington, D.C., is characterized by the three branches of government (i.e., the executive, legislative, and judicial). The leg-

TABLE 1.2
A Sample of Contemporary Democracies
Using Federal or Unitary Arrangements

Country	Federal or Unitary
Brazil	Federal
Canada	Federal
France	Unitary
Germany	Federal
Japan	Unitary
India	Federal
Israel	Unitary
Italy	Semi-federal
Portugal	Unitary
Spain	Semi-federal
United Kingdom	Unitary
United States	Federal

Source: U.S. Central Intelligence Agency, *The World Factbook*. www.cia.gov/library/publications/the-world-factbook/geos/xx.html. Accessed 13 May 2013.

islature is further divided into two houses: the House of Representatives and the Senate. Given this structure, some Americans have come to the mistaken conclusion that any democracy must have a national bicameral legislature as well. The truth is, however, that although some democratic countries do have two legislative chambers like the United States, other countries only have one legislative chamber, or a unicameral legislature. There is no simple formula to account for why some countries have a single chamber, and others have two: the decision characteristically reflects a country's size, as well as its political, historical, and cultural choices and experiences.

Whether unicameral or bicameral, the legislature in any democratic country is primarily charged with a law-making function—we can define this as the process of preparing, debating, and passing laws. Its members consider and debate bills, which are proposals for legislative action.[44] The discussion among legislators over bills is called *legislative debate*, which takes place on the floor of the legislature. Throughout the legislative debate, the political party in the minority plays the important function of criticizing the actions of the majority, and offering the public an alternative vision and alternative policies.

Legislatures are governed by various types of rules, some of which, including those governing the British Parliament, are designed to give the majority party more control, and others, such as the rules in the United States, enable the minority to slow down the initiatives of the majority. As we shall demonstrate in chapter 2, the parliament actually has a minimal role in formulating proposals of law in the United Kingdom, because the prime minister's cabinet sends legislation already in advanced form for floor consideration. This procedure holds true for many Westminster-style parliamentary democracies. The American Congress, on the other hand, is a legislature that actually formulates policy, subject to executive approval.

In bicameral legislatures, the two chambers have historically been referred to as the upper and lower chambers, or houses. Gregory Mahler has noted that the terms developed in the United Kingdom. Originally, the House of Lords represented the upper segment of the population and was considered a more prestigious body, whereas the House of Commons represented the lower strata of society. In the period since the democratic revolutions of the seventeenth and eighteenth centuries, however, the lower chamber has become the dominant chamber in the United Kingdom and elsewhere. Today the lower house in a legislature is representative of the entire population, whereas the upper house may represent one of several possible constituencies in a country—either the former aristocratic element in a society, such as the House of Lords in the United Kingdom, or the geographical interests of a region or a state, such as the Senate in the United States and the Bundesrat in Germany.[45]

The two chambers do not always have roughly equal power. In Germany, for example, the lower chamber (the Bundestag) represents the national population as expressed in electoral results, whereas the upper chamber (the Bundesrat) represents the interests of the states, or *Laander*. While both chambers are of roughly equal power when it comes to state issues, the lower chamber in Germany is more able to dominate the upper one on other matters. In the United Kingdom, the lower chamber has more power than the upper as well.

Some contemporary democracies function with a unicameral legislature—a legislature with only one chamber. In general, small countries are more likely to function with a unicameral legislature than are large countries. That is, there may be little need for an upper chamber to represent the territorial interests of states or regions in a country with a small territory, when those interests can be adequately represented in a single chamber.

Finally, Jean Blondel has found that whereas the vast majority of federal regimes in the world function with bicameral legislatures, there is no clear pattern with unitary regimes. Some unitary regimes, including France and Britain, function with a bicameral legislature. Others, such as Portugal, have a unicameral legislature.[46] Table 1.3 indicates some of the legislative institutional variation in democratic countries.[47]

TABLE 1.3
A Sample of Contemporary Democracies Using Different Legislative Arrangements

Country	One House or Two	If Two Houses, Which Has More Power?
Brazil	Two	Roughly equal powers between the two houses
Canada	Two	Lower house dominates
France	Two	Lower house dominates
Germany	Two	Lower house dominates
Japan	Two	Lower house dominates
India	Two	Lower house dominates
Israel	One	Unicameral Knesset
Italy	Two	Roughly equal powers between the two houses
Portugal	One	Unicameral Assembly of the Republic
Spain	Two	Lower house dominates
United Kingdom	Two	Lower house dominates
United States	Two	Roughly equal powers between the two houses

Source: U.S. Central Intelligence Agency, *The World Factbook*. www.cia.gov/library/publications/the-world-factbook/geos/xx.html. Accessed 13 May 2013.

Misperception 4: The Chief Executive Must Be Both the Head of State and the Head of Government

Given that the American president is both the head of government and the head of state, it may seem to Americans that in democratic settings, it will always be the case that one executive performs both of these roles. However, this is not true of all contemporary democracies. For instance, these two executive roles are divided in England, where the prime minister is the head of government and the monarch is the head of state.

By way of definition, the *head of government* is charged with effective national administration, whereas the *head of state* is asked to carry out symbolic functions, such as representing the country at the Olympics, or appearing in public during national holidays. These are two distinct executive roles, but may be performed by the same person in some countries. In other countries, two different people perform these two roles.

In general, the head of government—variously termed the *prime minister, premier,* or *chancellor*—is directly elected to office by the people or by the majority party in the legislature. On the other hand, the head of state—known as *king, emperor,* or *president*—may be elected or appointed to office, or may assume office by tradition. In addition, it is important to keep in mind that although some democratic systems have elected presidents, this does not necessarily mean that that country operates under a presidential regime. In dual-executive countries, for example, elected presidents perform the head-of-state

IMAGE 1.4
Leaders from around the world gather at the L'Aquila G8 Summit on 9 July 2009.
From left to right: Canadian Prime Minister Stephen Harper, U.S. President Barack
Obama, French President Nicolas Sarkozy, Italian Prime Minister Silvio Berlusconi,
and Russian Premier Dmitry Medvedev. © Giuseppe Lami/Demotix/Demotix/
Demotix/Corbis.

role, while their respective prime ministers carry out the head-of-government
function. As table 1.4 shows, the role of head of state is played by a variety of
political actors, depending on the country.

Misperception 5: There Can Only Be One Winner in an Election and Only One Representative per Electoral District

Those who think that there can only be one winner in an election and only
one representative per electoral district are incorrectly correlating the system
used for the election of representatives to the United States Congress with
the very nature of democratic elections. In fact, that system is not the only,
or even the most representative, system available to democracies. For clarity,
let us examine two of the major electoral systems used in contemporary democracies: the single-member district plurality system and the multimember
district proportional representation system.

The American electoral system, also known as the single-member district
plurality voting system, is rather straightforward and easy to understand.
Under the rules of this system, elections take place within specific electoral

TABLE 1.4
Executive Variation in Sample of Contemporary Democratic Countries

Country	Head of Government	Head of State
Brazil	President	President
Canada	Prime Minister	Governor-General
France	Prime Minister and President	President
Germany	Chancellor	President
India	Prime Minister	President
Ireland	Prime Minister	President
Israel	Prime Minister	President
Italy	Prime Minister	President
Japan	Prime Minister	Monarch
Portugal	Prime Minister and President	President
Russia	President	President
Spain	Prime Minister	Monarch
Sweden	Prime Minister	Monarch
United Kingdom	Prime Minister	Monarch
United States	President	President

Source: U.S. Central Intelligence Agency, *The World Factbook*. www.cia.gov/library/publications/the-world
-factbook/geos/xx.html. Accessed 13 May 2013.

districts with approximately the same population size. There is only one winner per district: the one candidate who has received the greatest number (a plurality) of votes. In England this system is referred to as *first-past-the-post*. That term evokes the imagery of a horse race, in that the first candidate who passes the finish line wins the race. The margin of victory makes no difference to the outcome. If there are only two candidates, and one receives 50.1 percent of the vote, and the other receives 49.9 percent of the vote, the candidate with the larger share wins the seat. If there are three candidates, who receive 35, 33, and 32 percent of the vote, respectively, the one with 35 percent wins, even though he or she has not received a majority (more than 50 percent) of the votes cast. In that case, the person has received a plurality, the greatest amount of votes among the candidates.

This electoral system rewards those large political parties that are able to run a comprehensive and unified campaign, and gives incentives to smaller interests to join with a larger organization. Therefore, the countries that use this system tend to have only two or possibly three major political parties. This system tends to produce legislative majorities and foster close relations between the representative and his or her district. This system is used by both presidential and parliamentary countries, including the United States, the United Kingdom, and Canada.

Critics of the single-member district plurality voting system have argued that it can actually distort the will of the people, because it is possible that the winning candidate will have received less than half of the total votes. Remember that in 1992, Bill Clinton won the presidency with only 43 percent of the vote, to George Bush's 37.4 percent and Ross Perot's 18.9 percent. Since this electoral system allows candidates to win even if a majority of the people has voted against them, some have argued for the adoption of a proportional representation system.[48]

The multimember district proportional representation voting system is the key alternative to the single-member plurality system available to contemporary democracies. Simply put, the proportional system allocates legislative seats in proportion to the votes received by each party, providing for a more accurate measurement of the will of the electorate than other electoral systems. Frank Wilson observes that "the idea [of proportional representation] is to make the legislature reflect as accurately as possible the division of political views in the electorate."[49]

A Hypothetical Case of an Election under
Proportional Representation Rules

The following example of a hypothetical election operating in a fictional country that uses straightforward proportional electoral rules will demonstrate the idea behind the proportional representation electoral system.

Let us assume that there are four political parties contending for one hundred legislative seats. Unlike the single-member plurality arrangement, this proportional electoral system divides the legislative seats into large, multimember electoral districts. Each of the political parties (Parties A, B, C, and D) puts forth to the public a rank-ordered list of candidates. These lists are also referred to as closed lists, because the various political parties, and not the voters, decide the names and the order of the candidates appearing on the list. In general, the top-ranking names on each of the candidate lists represent those party members with the most seniority or are distinguished citizens, intended to attract electoral support. Each party runs one candidate for each of the available seats in each of the districts.

Once in the voting booth, the people must vote for one of these party lists—not for a particular candidate. The voters, of course, are aware of the contenders running for office, as each party is required to publish their candidate lists prior to the election. The voters cannot pick and choose among the candidates from the various lists. They must vote for a party list. In our hypothetical case, the following results were rendered from these elections:

Party A	40 percent of the vote
Party B	30 percent of the vote
Party C	20 percent of the vote
Party D	10 percent of the vote

If the hundred legislative seats in our hypothetical parliament were allocated in direct proportion to these percentages, they would be allocated to the four parties as follows: the first forty names on Party A's candidate list would be awarded forty legislative seats, the first thirty names on Party B's list would be allocated thirty seats, the first twenty names on Party C's list would be allocated twenty seats, and the first ten names on Party D's list would be allocated ten seats. As such, the legislative makeup would be as follows:

Party A	40 seats
Party B	30 seats
Party C	20 seats
Party D	10 seats

This hypothetical demonstrates the basic mechanics of the proportional electoral system: representatives are elected from multimember electoral districts in proportion to their party's share of the vote.

Proportional representation systems favor the formation of coalition governments among the various political parties. When there are four or five parties with representatives in parliament, governing can become very complex. This is especially true if no one party enjoys an absolute majority of seats. The coalition among political parties is a solution to this problem—it can be defined as an agreement among two or more parties to work together on a legislative program. Usually the terms of a coalition bargain involve the parties splitting the important cabinet ministries among them. Ordinarily, the leader of the party with the larger share of the vote becomes prime minister, the leader of the coalition party with the next largest share of the votes becomes deputy prime minister, and the other ministries are allocated in a like manner.

The advantages of a coalition government are clear: it can create a strong parliamentary majority that can govern effectively. Referring back to the hypothetical case, if a coalition were formed between Party A and Party B, their seventy combined seats could form a powerful and effective ruling majority. Alternatively, if Parties B, C, and D wanted to block party A, they could form a majority with their combined sixty seats. The possibilities for coalition are seemingly endless. Certainly, if no coalition at all were formed, our fictional nation could face a period of governmental turmoil.

A Hypothetical Case of an Election under Plurality Rules

In contrast, imagine a hundred-member legislature under a single-member district plurality system such as the one in the United States. Imagine that there are one hundred districts, and for purposes of simplicity, that all districts vote in the same proportion as the entire nation did under the proportional system. Remember that each election is for an individual candidate, not for the party itself. Let us also assume that the electoral results in each of the hundred single-member districts are the same as the results under our proportional representation example:

Candidate representing Party A	40 percent
Candidate representing Party B	30 percent
Candidate representing Party C	20 percent
Candidate representing Party D	10 percent

Under these electoral rules, Party A would win every seat in the legislature, because in each district, the candidate representing that party won a plurality of the vote. Conversely, there would be no representatives from the other three parties. As such, the composition of the legislature would be as follows:

Party A	100 seats
Party B	0 seats
Party C	0 seats
Party D	0 seats

The single-member plurality electoral system awards seats on the basis of which political party wins the election. Under this system, whether the winning party secured an absolute majority or only managed a plurality of the votes does not matter for the allocation of seats. A proportional representation system, on the other hand, allocates seats to political parties on the basis of the percentage won by each party. Obviously, and as our two hypothetical cases demonstrate, the legislative makeup may vary greatly depending on which electoral system a country uses.

Two Key Forms of Proportional Representation Electoral Systems

In reality, there are several forms of proportional representation electoral systems. Let us examine two of the more commonly used ones: the d'Hondt system and the single-transferable vote system.

Invented by Victor d'Hondt of Belgium, the d'Hondt system, also referred to as the highest-average system, is one of the most used versions of proportional representation. Under the rules of this system, each political party presents a closed list of candidates to the voters. Once in the voting booth, voters are required to vote for one of these party lists, and not for a particular candidate. As was the case in our hypothetical, the d'Hondt system does not allow people to pick and choose among the candidates from the various lists; rather, they must vote for a party list.

Once all the votes are counted, the d'Hondt system weighs the amount of votes each party received on the basis of a formula to determine the highest average of votes cast per party. The precise calculations used to determine the allocation of legislative seats from the vote totals vary somewhat from country to country. Suffice it to say that, in general, the party with the highest average of votes cast places the greatest number of candidates from their list in the legislature, and conversely, the party with the lowest average places the fewest. Under this system it is safe to assume that those candidates at the top of each of the party's lists will be elected, and those at the bottom of the lists will not receive a seat, unless the winning party completely dominates the elections. In general, the d'Hondt method of allocating seats in a legislature tends to favor larger parties, and the countries that use it usually do not have more than three or four major parties. Variations of this system are used in many countries, including Austria, Belgium, Finland, Portugal, and Spain.

The single transferable vote system is a form of proportional representation that does not use party lists. Developed in the nineteenth century by the Englishman Thomas Hare, it is also appropriately referred to as the Hare system. According to the rules of this version of proportional representation, political parties present candidates in multimember districts. In the ballot booth, voters rank their preferred candidates, not party, in order of preference on the ballot (first preference, second preference, third preference). Once the elections are tabulated, those candidates who have received the necessary quota of first-preference votes win a seat. The actual quota is based on the size of the district. Surplus votes beyond this quota are transferred to the candidates with second-preference votes, and each of those who then are able to garnish enough support are also awarded a seat. This process continues until all seats are allocated in a constituency. This system is used in several countries, including Ireland.[50]

Critics have argued that the multimember districts used by the various forms of proportional representation are too large and impersonal. This leads to the related problem that the voters are never able to develop a relationship with their representative, and no single representative has the electoral incentive to learn about the needs of his or her district. The internal politics of drawing up closed candidate lists can also be very negative for the various political parties. In addition, whereas with a presidential system, people know who will be president immediately after the electoral results are announced, the prime minister may not be known until the various political parties negotiate the terms of their coalition government under parliamentary rules.[51] Supporters of proportional representation elections hold, however, that even if this system has flaws, it remains the most representative electoral system currently available to democratic regimes.

There are a number of other innovative types of electoral systems currently in use as well. France, for instance, uses a two-ballot system based on single-member districts. If no candidate wins over 50 percent of the vote on the first ballot, a second ballot is held the following week. A simple plurality is sufficient for a candidate to win in the second ballot. Germany has come up with its own rather complicated version as well: half of its national representatives are elected by plurality, and the other by proportional representation.[52] Table 1.5 offers a sample of this great variety in electoral systems.

Misperception 6: The American Constitutional System Would Work Anywhere

Some might think that if only a country would adopt the institutions, rules, and procedures set out in the American Constitution, it could have a successful presidential-style democracy as well. The truth, however, is that even if a particular institutional arrangement can result in a long-lasting democratic regime in one country, there is no guarantee that it will have similar results elsewhere. In that regard, adaptations of the American Con-

TABLE 1.5
A Sample of Contemporary Democracies Using Various Electoral Systems

Country	Type	District Type
Austria	PR- list system	Multimember
Belgium	PR-list system	Multimember
Canada	Plurality	Single-member
Finland	PR-list system	Multimember
France	Mixed PR/Plurality	Single-member
Germany	Mixed PR/Plurality	Mixed single-member/multimember
Ireland	PR-stv system	Multimember
Italy	Mixed PR/Plurality	Mixed single-member/multimember
Portugal	PR-list system	Multimember
Spain	PR-list system	Multimember
United Kingdom	Plurality	Single-member
United States	Plurality	Single-member

Source: U.S. Central Intelligence Agency, *The World Factbook*. www.cia.gov/library/publications/the-world
-factbook/geos/xx.html. Accessed 13 May 2013.

stitution to other countries have not worked out very well. The experience of Latin America is illustrative.

Many Latin America countries, upon winning their independence from Spain, patterned their political structures on the American presidential system and incorporated the separation of powers doctrine into their own constitutional frameworks. Table 1.6 indicates the wide adoption of presidential arrangements in Latin American countries, which has prompted some political scientists to dub Latin America the "continent of presidentialism."[53] And yet, for a variety of reasons, all of these countries have suffered through periods of political turmoil, coups d'état, and regime breakdown.

Why has presidentialism had such a tumultuous history in Latin America and worked so peacefully in the United States? Many valuable explanations have been offered to account for this discrepancy, including the role of a political culture hostile to liberal democracy, or the undue influence and power of the military establishment in Latin American politics.[54] While we certainly recognize the insights of these explanations, we will focus—in line with this book's general argument—on the institutional explanation as to why presidentialism has not worked very well in Latin America.

Political scientists favoring an institutional explanation have pointed to the problematic relationship between the executive and legislative branches under presidential rules. This relationship, they argue, has negatively impacted most Latin American democracies. Whereas critics of American government point to divided government, gridlock, and the lack of account-

TABLE 1.6
A Sample of Different Regime-Types in Latin American Democracies

Country	Current Regime Type	Date of Independence	Mother Country
Argentina	Presidential	9 July 1816	Spain
Bolivia	Presidential	6 August 1825	Spain
Brazil	Presidential	7 September 1822	Portugal
Canada	Parliamentary	1 January 1867	England
Chile	Presidential	18 September 1810	Spain
Colombia	Presidential	20 July 1810	Spain
Ecuador	Presidential	24 May 1822	Spain
El Salvador	Presidential	15 September 1821	Spain
Haiti	Presidential	1 January 1804	France
Honduras	Presidential	15 September 1821	Spain
Mexico	Presidential	16 September 1810	Spain
Nicaragua	Presidential	28 September 1821	Spain
Peru	Presidential	28 July 1821	Spain
United States	Presidential	4 July 1776	England
Venezuela	Presidential	5 July 1821	Spain

Source: U.S. Central Intelligence Agency, *The World Factbook*. www.cia.gov/library/publications/the-world-factbook/geos/xx.html. Accessed 13 May 2013.

ability as troublesome features of presidentialism, these very factors have contributed to the collapse of many Latin America presidential regimes over the past fifty years. Indeed, in some cases the executive branch has even refused to accept the legitimacy of the legislature's participation in governing the country. Similar problems with the presidential institutional arrangement have occurred in almost every Latin American country; some scholars have argued that a move to a parliamentary form of government might improve the institutional relationship between the executive and legislative branches.[55]

Whether because of an antidemocratic political culture, the power of the military establishment, or the problematic institutional structure of a presidential regime (or a combination of these three factors), the adoption of the American Constitution in Latin America has not resulted in a happy and long-lasting experience with democracy. One cannot simply export the American Constitution to another country and wait for democracy to set roots and grow. Politics, unfortunately perhaps, is much more complicated than that.

The above discussion builds on Blyth's argument in a few ways. First, it demonstrates that although the framers established the political institutions in the eighteenth century, their key ideas continue to influence the way people think about political institutions two centuries later. Second, and related to that first point, the discussion shows how difficult it can be to introduce innovative public policies into a cognitively locked political environment. Finally, it shows how, following Blyth, "ideas are essential components of explanations of institutional change."[56]

Conclusion

Among the world's democracies, the United States has perhaps been the most self-conscious about preventing majority tyranny. The framers' solution to the dilemma of the majority rule versus minority rights was to hazard executive-legislative deadlock rather than risk majority tyranny, leaving us with an institutional structure thoroughly antagonistic to majority rule. If it is true that this institutional design is currently responsible for a perception among citizens that their political system is not responsive to them, perhaps a move to a parliamentary system is the solution to what ails contemporary America.

The American Constitution has established only one of many possible institutional structures available to contemporary democracies. There are a variety of ways available for devotees of democracy to organize a legislature, to design the executive branch, to structure the government, and to hold elections. Separated or fused executive and legislative chambers, unicameral or bicameral legislative bodies, single-member district or multimember district, federal or unitary systems, and even more variations, are all possible.

Woodrow Wilson suggested almost one hundred years ago that if the United States functioned under a British-style parliamentary system, change could conceivably take place very quickly, enabling governmental leaders to rapidly adopt new laws, and adapt the government to the changing times. Was President Wilson correct? Is the British parliamentary system the answer to the foundational tension between majority rule and minority rights in the United States? What would American government look like under Westminster parliamentary rules? Is American government really unresponsive? If yes, what are we to do? Let us consider these questions in the following chapters.

Structure of the Book

This book introduces some of the key themes of comparative public policy, as it illustrates how the American constitutional system of checks and balances functions in comparative perspective. Chapter 1 examines the founding ideational and institutional tension of American democracy, as well as its associated cognitive locks. Chapter 2 illustrates the concept of path dependence; it will contrast and compare the historical development and institutional structure of executive and legislative branches in the United States with the Westminster system in the United Kingdom. Both chapters 3 and 4 highlight several distinctive features of the American institutional framework, including the separation of powers, the system of checks and balances, and the role of political parties and elections. They examine the ways that American policy makers might "frame" issues, and how they present proposals in order to improve the chances for policy adoption. These two chapters also examine the concepts of issue framing, agenda setting, and agenda control. Chapter 3 does so in its legislative history of the Republican Contract with America, which dominated the first hundred days of the 104th Congress; chapter 4 does the same in its legislative history of the battle over heath care during the 111th Congress. Chapter 5 revisits the notion of path dependence, and considers what politics in the United States might look like if it had—like most of England's other former colonies—adopted a version of the British parliamentary model at the founding in 1789. Chapter 6 revisits how ideational and institutional constraints limit policy formation and adoption in the United States, and suggests some ideas to streamline the process in the American presidential system. This book does not argue for American government to adopt a British-style parliamentary system. Rather, it seeks to challenge the reader to consider in what ways ideas and institutional frameworks influence how a country forms public policies.

Notes

1. Jeremy Peters, "House Votes Again to Repeal Health Law," *New York Times*, 17 May 2013.

2. Michelle Bachmann, press release, "House Passes Bachmann's Bill to Repeal Obamacare," bachmann.house.gov/press-release/house-passes-bachmanns-bill-repeal -obamacare.

3. David A. Fahrenthold, "Once Again, the House Votes to Repeal Obamacare," *Washington Post*, 17 May 2013.

4. *Politico.com*, "Obama Begins Fresh Healthcare Push," 10 May 2013.

5. See Kaiser Family Foundation, "Kaiser Health Tracking Poll, April 2013," kff. org/health-reform/poll-finding/kaiser-health-tracking-poll-april-2013/.

6. Speaker John Andrew Boehner (R-OH) is the sixty-first Speaker of the United States House of Representatives. He was first elected to the House in 1991. Governor Mitt Romney served as the seventieth governor of Massachusetts from 2003 to 2007. He was the Republican Party's nominee for president of the United States in the 2012 election. President Obama won 332 electoral votes and 50.6 percent of the popular vote in the 2012 election; Romney won 206 electoral votes and 47.8 percent of the popular vote.

7. See Lawrence R. Jacobs and Theda Skocpol, *Healthcare Reform and American Politics: What Everyone Needs to Know* (New York: Oxford University Press, 2012), especially pp. 6–16; David Burnham, *Above the Law: Secret Deals, Political Fixes, and Other Misadventures of the U.S. Department of Justice* (New York: Scribner, 1996); Martin L. Gross, *A Call for Revolution: How Government Is Strangling America—and How to Stop It* (New York: Ballantine, 1993); Amitai Etzioni, *Capital Corruption: The New Attack on American Democracy*, 2nd ed. (New Brunswick, NJ: Transaction Books, 1988); Joseph S. Nye Jr., Philip D. Zelikow, and David C. King, eds., *Why People Don't Trust Government* (Cambridge, MA: Harvard University Press, 1997); Drew Pearson, *The Case against Congress: A Compelling Indictment of Corruption on Capitol Hill* (New York: Pocket Books, 1969); Kevin P. Phillips, *Arrogant Capital: Washington, Wall Street, and the Frustration of American Politics* (Boston: Little, Brown and Company, 1994).

8. There are several important contributions examining the institutional dimension of comparative public policy, including Paul Pierson, "Increasing Returns, Path Dependence and the Study of Politics," *American Political Science Review* 96, no. 4 (June 2000): 697–712; Vivien A. Schmidt, "Discursive Institutionalism: The Explanatory Power of Ideas and Discourse," *Annual Review of Political Science* 11 (2008): 303–26; Elinor Ostrom, "Coping with Tragedies of the Commons," *Annual Review of Political Science* 2 (1999): 493–535; James Mahoney and Kathleen Thelen, eds., *Explaining Institutional Change: Ambiguity, Agency, and Power* (Cambridge: Cambridge University Press, 2010); Kathleen Thelen, "Historical Institutionalism in Comparative Politics," *Annual Review of Political Science* 2 (1999): 369–404; Jonas Pontusson, "From Comparative Public Policy to Political Economy: Putting Political Institutions in their Place and Taking Interests Seriously," *Comparative Political Studies* 28, no. 1 (April 1995): 117–47; Paul Pierson, "When Effect Becomes Cause: Policy Feedback and Political Change,"

World Politics 45, no. 4 (July 1993): 595–628; Simon Reich, "The Four Faces of Institutionalism: Public Policy and a Pluralistic Perspective," *Governance* 13, no. 4 (October 2000): 501–22; Fritz W. Scharpf, "Institutions in Comparative Policy Research," *Comparative Political Studies* 33, nos. 6–7 (September 2000): 762–90.

9. R. Kent Weaver and Bert A. Rockman, *Do Institutions Matter? Government Capabilities in the United States and Abroad* (Washington, DC: Brookings Institution, 1993), especially pages 10–11.

10. The sitting president has faced a hostile majority in at least one of the legislative chambers for forty-eight of the sixty-eight years from 1946 through 2014. Also see Michael A. Bailey, "Comparable Preference Estimates across Time and Institutions for the Court, Congress, and Presidency," *American Journal of Political Science* 51, no. 3 (2007): 433–48; David W. Brady, "The Causes and Consequences of Divided Government: Toward a New Theory of American Politics?" *American Political Science Review* 87, no. 1 (1993): 183–94; Leon D. Epstein, "Changing Perceptions of the British System," *Political Science Quarterly* 109, no. 3 (Special Issue 1994): 494; Morris P. Fiorina, *Divided Government* (Boston: Allyn & Bacon, 1996).

11. See Timothy J. Penny and Steven E. Schier, *Payment Due: A Nation in Debt, A Generation in Trouble* (Boulder: Westview, 1996), and G. Calvin Mackenzie and Saranna Thornton, *Bucking the Deficit: Economic Policymaking in America* (Boulder: Westview, 1996). For a description of the budgetary process during the Reagan years, see Allen Schick, *The Capacity to Budget* (Washington, DC: The Urban Institute Press, 1990).

12. Leon Epstein has pointed out that every year that the federal deficit exceeded three percent of the gross national product was a year in which the government was divided. See Leon D. Epstein, "Changing Perceptions of the British System," *Political Science Quarterly* 109, no. 3 (1951), 495.

13. Seymour Martin Lipset, *American Exceptionalism: A Double-Edged Sword* (New York: W. W. Norton, 1996). Also see Seymour Martin Lipset and Gary Wolfe Marks, *It Didn't Happen Here: Why Socialism Failed in the United States* (New York: W. W. Norton, 2001); Charles Lockhart, *The Roots of American Exceptionalism: Institutions, Culture and Policies* (New York: Palgrave Macmillan, 2003); Charles W. Dunn, *American Exceptionalism: The Origins, History, and Future of the Nation's Greatest Strength* (Plymouth, UK: Rowman & Littlefield, 2013).

14. Bill Frenzel, "The System Is Self-Correcting," in *Back to Gridlock? Governance in the Clinton Years*, ed. James L. Sundquist (Washington, DC: Brookings Institution, 1995), 105–8. Also see David R. Jones, *Political Parties and Policy Gridlock in American Government* (Lewiston, NY: Edwin Mellen Press, 2001); David W. Brady and Craig Volden, *Revolving Gridlock: Politics and Policy from Jimmy Carter to George W. Bush*, 2nd ed. (Boulder, CO: Westview, 2005); Thomas E. Mann and Norman J. Ornstein, *It's Even Worse Than It Looks: How the American Constitutional System Collided with the New Politics of Extremism* (New York: Basic Books, 2012).

15. David R. Mayhew, *Divided We Govern: Party Control, Lawmaking, and Investigations, 1946–2002*, 2nd ed. (New Haven, CT: Yale University Press, 2005). Also see David R. Mayhew, "Divided Party Control: Does It Make a Difference?" in *PS: Political Science and Politics* 24, no. 4 (December 1991): 637.

16. A government can be said to be accountable when the electorate is given the opportunity to clearly and intelligently evaluate the achievements of a sitting government on the basis of its legislative record: Did the economy improve? Were social problems ameliorated? Or, simply, did the government do what it promised it would do? All of these factors, and perhaps more, may go into a citizen's calculations before he or she decides to vote for that particular political party again.

17. See James L. Sundquist, *Constitutional Reform and Effective Government*, rev. ed. (Washington, DC: The Brookings Institution, 1992).

18. *Washington Times*, "What's the Big Idea: Sequestration: A Tale of a Dysfunctional Family," 23 May 2013; *USA TODAY*, "Political Gridlock Personified; Fliers Get Stuck as Delays Stack Up Airports: Let the Blame Game Begin," 24 April 2013.

19. Weaver and Rockman, *Do Institutions Matter?*, 2–3. C. Douglas Dillon's quote originally appeared in "The Challenge of Modern Government," in *Reforming American Government: The Bicentennial Papers of the Committee on the Constitutional System*, ed. Donald L. Robinson (Boulder, CO: Westview, 1985), 26. Weaver and Rockman have argued that "institutions alone do not deter responses to the problems, but they can make it harder to find solutions. . . . America's institutions do not make it easy to lead." Weaver and Rockman, *Do Institutions Matter?*, 481.

20. Theodore Lowi, "Presidential and Parliamentary Democracies: Which Work Best?" *Political Science Quarterly* 104, no. 3 (Special Issue 1994): 414. Lowi is dissatisfied with the use of the term *gridlock*, "which may imply that there is a single, definable obstruction, which, once removed, would permit the flow to resume." Quote is from page 415.

21. Theodore J. Lowi, "Presidential Democracy in America: Toward the Homogenized Regime," *Political Science Quarterly* 109, no. 3 (1994): 401.

22. Walter Bagehot, *The English Constitution* (London: Fontana, 1993), 70. (Originally published by Chapman and Hall in 1867.)

23. Woodrow Wilson, "Cabinet Government in the United States," *International Review* 7 (August 1879): 146–63.

24. Woodrow Wilson, *The Politics of Woodrow Wilson. Selections from His Speeches and Writings*, 1st ed. (New York: Harper and Brothers, 1956), 44, 41–48.

25. Ibid.

26. Mark Blyth, "Ideas, Uncertainly and Evolution," in *Ideas and Politics in Social Science Research*, ed. Daniel Beland and Robert Henry Cox (New York: Oxford University Press, 2011), 98–99.

27. Mark Blyth, "The Transformation of the Swedish Model," *World Politics* 54, no. 1 (October 2001): 1–26. Blyth builds his argument on previous work, including Peter A. Hall, *Governing the Economy: The Politics of State Intervention in Britain and France* (Oxford: Oxford University Press, 1986) and Paul Pierson, "Increasing Returns, Path Dependence, and the Study of Politics," *American Political Science Review* 94, no. 2 (2000): 697–712. Also see Carolyn Forestiere and Christopher Allen, "The Formation of Cognitive Locks in Single Party Dominant Regimes," *International Political Science Review* 32, no. 4 (September 2011): 380–95.

28. Joseph Schumpeter, *Capitalism, Socialism and Democracy*, 2nd ed. (New York: Harper and Row, 1947). The 2011 reprint of the 1947 second edition by Martino Press features an introduction by Tom Bottomore.

29. Philippe C. Schmitter and Terry Lynn Karl, "What Democracy Is . . . and Is Not," *Journal of Democracy* 2, no. 1 (Summer 1991): 75–89. Quote is from page 76.

30. Giovanni Sartori, *Comparative Constitutional Engineering: An Inquiry into Structures, Incentives and Outcomes* (New York: New York University Press, 1994), 83–94.

31. Of course, an important exception to this is the process of *impeachment* spelled out in the U.S. Constitution. The framers decided on the impeachment process as a way to remove a president from office on the basis of criminal charges, not for political reasons. The president may be removed from office if he is impeached (formally charged with a crime) by the House of Representatives (Article I, Section 2). Impeachment by itself does not guarantee removal from office. The Senate must vote to convict the president, and the vote requires a two-thirds majority (Article I, Section 3). Grounds for impeachment are treason, bribery, and "other high crimes and misdemeanors" (Article II, Section 4). Two presidents, Andrew Johnson and Bill Clinton, have been impeached; in both cases, the Senate failed to return a conviction, and so each man remained in office. Nixon resigned before he could be impeached.

32. While it is certainly true that presidential systems can be responsive, and that parliamentary systems can be stable, looking at the dominant traits and tensions among them allows for an approximate comparative typology. As Juan Linz astutely observed, "all presidential and parliamentary systems have a common core that allows their differentiation and some systemic comparisons." Juan Linz and Arturo Valenzuela, *The Failure of Presidential Democracy: Comparative Perspectives* (Baltimore: Johns Hopkins University Press, 1994), 5.

33. Ibid., 5–22.

34. Arend Lijphart, *Democracies: Patterns of Majoritarian and Consensus Government in Twenty-one Countries* (New Haven, CT: Yale University Press, 1984), 216.

35. Ibid. The consensual parliamentary system is another important form of parliamentary democracy. Arend Lijphart notes that this model, whose name comes from the word *consensus* (to get along), is designed so that all of the members of parliament can discover broad-based agreement on legislation. Whereas the rules of the Westminster system tend to pit winners against losers, this arrangement encourages the majority party to seek input on legislative bills from opposition parties. Often, rigorous legislative debate takes place on the floor of the parliament, and the opposition leadership, as well as lower-ranking government members, have opportunities to suggest amendments. As such, the open and flexible nature of the consensual parliamentary model encourages increased participation from all sides. Belgium, for example, has used this system to guarantee that its two major nationality groups will cooperate in governmental policy making, no matter which party wins the elections.

36. See Sartori, *Comparative Constitutional Engineering*, 101.

37. See *Constituição da República Portuguesa: As Três Versões Após 25 de Abril 1989/1982/1976* (Lisbon: Porto Editora, 1990), 228–31. The seventh revision of the

Portuguese Constitution took place in 2005, and can be found at: app.parlamento.pt/ site_antigo/ingles/cons_leg/Constitution_VII_revisao_definitive.pdf. David Corkill, "The Political System and the Consolidation of Democracy in Portugal," *Parliamentary Affairs* (October 1993): 517–32; Paul C. Manuel, *The Challenges of Democratic Consolidation in Portugal, 1976–1991: Political, Economic and Military Issues* (Westport, CT: Praeger, 1996).

38. William H. Riker, "Federalism," in *Handbook of Political Science: Governmental Institutions and Processes*, vol. 5, ed. Fred I. Greenstein and Nelson W. Polsby (Reading, MA: Addison-Wesley, 1975), 101.

39. Kerstin Hamann, "The Creation of Regional Identities and Voting Behavior in Spain," paper presented to the Iberian Study Group, Center of European Studies, Harvard University, 17 February 1998, 5. Also see Kerstin Hamann, "Federalist Institutions, Voting Behavior, and Party Systems in Spain," in "Federalism and Compounded Representation in Western Europe," special issue, *Publius* 29, no. 1 (Winter 1999): 111–37.

40. Peter J. Donaghy and Michael T. Newton, *Spain: A Guide to Political and Economic Institutions* (Cambridge: Cambridge University Press, 1987), 100–101.

41. It is important to note that the national legislatures in both Great Britain and France, while dominant, do face some local challenges. New "country" parliaments are being developed in Great Britain; regional assemblies in France exercise some delegated powers.

42. Michael Curtis, *Introduction to Comparative Government*, 5th ed. (New York: Longman, 2006), 30. In 2013, there were three devolved governmental structures in the United Kingdom, seventeen autonomous communities in Spain, six autonomous regions in France, and five in Italy.

43. Frank L. Wilson, *Concepts and Issues in Comparative Politics*, 2nd ed. (Upper Saddle River, NJ: Pearson, 2001), 161.

44. Legislatures are known by a host of different designations. Terms include *Congress* in the United States, the *Parliament* in Great Britain, the *Knesset* in Israel, the *Diet* in Japan, the *Daíl* in Ireland, the *Vouli* in Greece, and the *National Assembly* in Portugal, among many others.

45. See Gregory S. Mahler, *Comparative Government: An Institutional and Cross-National Approach*, 5th ed. (Englewood Cliffs, NJ: Pearson, 2007), 75.

46. Jean Blondel, *Comparative Legislatures* (Englewood Cliffs, NJ: Prentice Hall, 1973), 144–53.

47. For more information, see Gabriel A. Almond, G. Bingham, J. Powell Jr., Russell J. Dalton, and Kaare Strom, *Comparative Politics Today: A World View, Update Edition*, 9th ed. (New York: Longman, 2009); Mahler, *Comparative Government*.

48. See useful discussion by Philip Laundy, *Parliaments in the Modern World* (Hafts, Canada: Dartmouth Publishing Company, 1990), 15–16. Also, Philip Laundy, *Parliament and the People: The Reality and the Public Perception* (Surrey, UK: Ashgate, 1997), 3–9.

49. Wilson, *Concepts and Issues in Comparative Politics*, 66.

50. Laundy, *Parliaments in the Modern World*, 15–16.

51. Wilson, *Concepts and Issues in Comparative Politics*, 66–67.

52. See William Safran, *The French Polity*, 7th ed. (Englewood Cliffs, NJ: Prentice Hall, 2008), and David Conradt and Eric Langenbacher, *The German Polity*, 10th ed. (Lanham, MD: Rowman and Littlefield, 2013).

53. Linz and Valenzuela, *The Failure of Presidential Democracy*. Also see Scott Mainwaring and Arturo Valenzuela, eds., *Politics, Society, and Democracy: Latin America. Essays in Honor of Juan J. Linz* (Boulder, CO: Westview, 1999), 13–14; Joan Marcet and José Ramon Montero, eds., *Roads to Democracy: A Tribute to Juan J. Linz* (Barcelona: Institut de Ciencies Politiques i Sociais, 2007).

54. See discussion of these various approaches in Ronald Chilcote, *Theories of Comparative Politics: The Search for a Paradigm Reconsidered*, 2nd ed. (Boulder, CO: Westview, 1994). A classic work in this field is James A. Bill and Robert L. Hardgrave Jr., *Comparative Politics: The Quest for Theory* (Wasington, DC: University Press of America, 1981). Also see Mark Irving Lichbach and Alan S. Zukerman, *Comparative Politics: Rationality, Culture, and Structure*, Cambridge Studies in Comparative Politics (Cambridge: Cambridge University Press, 2009); Howard J. Wiarda and Harvey F. Kline, *Latin American Politics and Development*, 7th ed. (Boulder, CO: Westview, 2010); Alain Rouquié, *The Military and the State in Latin America*, trans. Paul Sigmund (Berkeley: University of California Press, 1987); and Alfred Stepan, *Rethinking Military Politics* (Baltimore: Johns Hopkins University Press, 1988).

55. See Juan Linz, "Presidential or Parliamentary Democracy: Does It Make a Difference?" in Linz and Valenzuela, *The Failure of Presidential Democracy*, 3–74. Also see important discussion by Matthew Soberg Shugart, "Presidentialism, Parliamentarism, and the Provision of Collective Goods in Less-Developed Countries," *Constitutional Political Economy* 10 (1999): 53–88; and Arend Lijphart, *Thinking about Democracy: Power Sharing and Majority Rule in Theory and Practice* (London: Routledge, 2007), especially pages 139–58; Arend Lijphart, *Patterns of Democracy*, 2nd ed. (New Haven, CT: Yale University Press, 2012).

56. Blyth, "The Swedish Model," 26.

2

The Path of Political Development in Great Britain and the United States

A Brief Comparative History

The United States came within a hair's breadth of adopting a kind of parliamentary system.

—Robert Dahl

I have argued that path dependence occurs when a contingent historical event triggers a subsequent sequence that follows a relatively deterministic pattern.

—James Mahoney

The extent to which political decision making is path dependent (Pierson 2000, 2004) is largely determined by the design of institutions.

—Mark A. Kleiman and Steven M. Teles

TODAY, PRESIDENTIAL AND parliamentary systems are the two principle forms of democratic organization. Although there are many variations of these two systems among the democratic countries in the world, Great Britain is commonly considered to be the archetype of a parliamentary system, while the most famous example of a presidential system is the United States. How did these two great democracies adopt their present institutional forms? Why does the United States function under a complex constitutional arrangement of checks and balances, while Great Britain does not? Which factors are responsible for this discrepancy? How does it affect the practice of democracy in each country today?

The concept of path-dependence in the field of comparative public policy may be of some help in accounting for the variation in political institutions between these two countries. The path-dependence literature posits that past decisions might limit the range of subsequent policy options available to policy makers. For instance, political scientist Terry Lynn Karl suggests that the notion of path dependence may be understood as follows: "the impact of decisions made in the past persists into the present and decide the alternatives for the future." She further notes that "[past] decisions become embodied in socioeconomic structures, political institutions, and rules that subsequently mold the preferences and behaviors of individuals, thereby enhancing (or reducing) the probability of certain outcomes."[1]

Although certainly promising as a way to account for how the past may impact the present, path dependence has not yet been developed into a rigorous social science theory capable of offering a well-defined theoretical understanding of how historical variables interrelate. Paul Pierson warns against the use of path-dependence arguments in accounting for a full range of outcomes.[2] He suggests that, at best, it is able to link disparate variables into a coherent whole, and offer explanations about how political ideas and institutions were created, and how they might influence the future direction of an institution or a policy.[3] Likewise, James Mahoney, as quoted in the introduction of this chapter, seeks to overcome any conceptual fuzziness associated with path dependence in his careful operationalization of the concept, in a way that is particularly useful for this chapter:

> I have argued that path dependence occurs when a contingent historical event triggers a subsequent sequence that follows a relatively deterministic pattern. In the case of a self-reinforcing sequence, the contingent period corresponds with the initial adoption of a particular institutional arrangement, while the deterministic pattern corresponds with the stable reproduction of this institution over time.[4]

Building on Mahoney's insights, this chapter will compare and contrast how the impact of past decisions has influenced the creation of a self-reinforcing sequence of subsequent decisions in the United States and the United Kingdom. The chapter examines how and why the United States and the United Kingdom are on distinctive institutional paths, and how each nation's political history has influenced the development of its present form of democracy.[5]

Why American Government Operates under Checks and Balances, and British Government Does Not

The United States and Great Britain are on distinctive historical paths. They have faced very different obstacles and challenges in the history of their political development. In his seminal work, *Political Order in Changing Societies*, Samuel Huntington argues that disparate patterns of political development in the two countries resulted in very different institutional structures.[6] That is, unlike the case in Great Britain, the framers of the American republic did not have to dislodge a domestic monarchy, aristocracy, or clergy from a privileged place in society in order to implement their new constitutional order. Therefore, the Constitution was afforded the luxury of setting its own roots and developing over time into the preeminent governmental authority. In contrast, the end of the feudal order was a tortuous and divisive process in Great Britain, as democratic forces seized power from the entrenched establishment of the monarchy, the church, and the landed aristocracy. Over the centuries-long process of British political development, Parliament managed to establish itself as that country's preeminent political authority. Currently, Great Britain's parliamentary legislation has become sovereign, taking on the status that we in the United States accord the Constitution.[7]

One effect of these divergent paths has been the development of very different meanings of the term "the Constitution" in the United States and in Great Britain. The word itself comes from the verb "to constitute," which means to compose or create. A constitution creates a government. American government was created by a written document. The framers basically started from scratch and wrote down what the government could do, what it could not do, and how political power would be divided. The very flexibility of the document, which contains general principles and provisions for amendment, meant that constitutional government in the United States was given a chance to flourish as well as change. The Constitution is a relatively short document that gives the outline of government; it is left up to future generations to fill in that outline. However, the general principles in the Constitution are expected to be immutable. In the United States, the Constitution is the "supreme law of the land," superseding laws written by Congress or the states and actions taken by the president. Obviously, eighteenth-century America did not have as long a history of government as did nations in Europe at that time, so the framers had the benefit of making a fresh start and of learning from the past mistakes of other nations.

The United Kingdom and the United States are clearly on different institutional paths. To illustrate these distinctive paths, which have resulted in significant differences between the formation of government in the United States and Great Britain, let us take a brief look at the history of each country's political system, starting with England.

The Evolution of the British Parliament

Political development in the United Kingdom is singular. Unlike the experiences of other European countries, it evolved relatively peacefully over several centuries.[8] That is not to imply that the United Kingdom did not confront long periods of violence and political instability—it did—but rather, in the long sweep of British history, it successfully confronted the challenges of political modernization slowly and sequentially.[9] For the sake of brevity, we will focus our inquiry on some of the key stages in the evolution of the British parliament:

- the adoption of the Magna Carta and the origins of Parliament in the thirteenth century,
- the expansion of parliamentary power in the sixteenth and seventeenth centuries,
- the emergence of the working class as a potent parliamentary political force in the nineteenth and twentieth centuries, and
- the ascension of the House of Commons as England's most powerful governing body.

The Origins of Parliament

The origins of the British parliament may be traced to the battle over the *Magna Carta* between a nascent governing council and the monarch in 1215. At that time, absolute political power and legitimacy in Great Britain were in the hands of the monarch, according to the terms of the political and religious doctrine known as *the divine right of kings*. That doctrine, employed by monarchs throughout Europe, held that the king's power and authority flowed to him directly and absolutely from God. Further, as God's custodian on earth, the monarch should be given the same solemn respect and unquestioning obedience a person would offer to God. This doctrine granted monarchs a great deal of political legitimacy and authority—if the people in a country believed that God had chosen a particular person to rule over a nation, who

IMAGE 2.1
The Houses of Parliament on the River Thames in London—the birthplace of parliamentary democracy. The tower on the left is the House of Lords, and the clock tower is, of course, Big Ben. © Paul Hardy/Corbis.

would be in a position to contest God's will? The doctrine of the divine right of kings helped to maintain political stability and a hierarchical social order in continental Europe and, to a lesser extent, in Great Britain, for centuries. Indeed, the emperor in Japan effectively used this claim to political legitimacy until the end of World War II.

No monarch, however, could tend to all aspects of governance on his own. Even in the thirteenth century, the demands on a political leader were great. So a practice developed in Great Britain by which the monarch would consult with a so-called Great Council, comprising the earls, barons, and church hierarchy, prior to the introduction of new rules or new taxes. These consultations were not an invitation to the Great Council to struggle with the monarch over policy issues, but rather served to help the monarch to implement decisions he himself had already made. While the advisors could offer opinions, it was up to the monarch to decide if any suggestions proposed by the Great Council were to be incorporated into law.[10] The Great Council served as an advisory board to the monarch, but it held very little power of its own.

This system of governance was challenged by Great Britain's leading barons in 1215, when they submitted the Magna Carta, or "Great Charter," to King John I (Lockland) for his approval. Predicated on the principle that

Great Britain should be ruled by law, the Magna Carta placed express boundaries on the arbitrary power of the king. Among the provisions outlined in the Magna Carta were guarantees that the established feudal rights of the privileged class of landowners existed beyond the control of the monarch; protections for freemen, merchants, and clerks from arbitrary arrest; and the right to trial and judgment in accordance with the due process of law for all free men. Most importantly, the Magna Carta limited the powers of the monarch, especially in matters concerning justice and finance.

Not unexpectedly, the reaction by King John I was negative. He repudiated the Magna Carta, insisting that he had the right to rule absolutely. After an arduous period in which armies loyal to the monarch took up arms against those loyal to the barons, the monarch was defeated and was forced to accept the Magna Carta. Finally adopted in 1225, it remains part of British law today.[11]

The question of why the barons composed, submitted, and fought over the Magna Carta is an interesting one. Perhaps the best explanation involves the experience they gained by helping the monarch govern as members of the Great Council. This experience led many barons to believe that the country should be governed by a set of laws, not just by the whims of a monarch. It is easy to imagine how difficult it would be for barons and church officials, powerful men in their own right, to be prohibited from incorporating their ideas into the king's proposals. These individuals came to together with a singular purpose: to propose a document that would be accepted as the law of the land.[12]

To be sure, the adoption of the Magna Carta placed Great Britain on a very different political trajectory from the rest of Europe, which remained under the doctrine of the divine right of kings for centuries to come. The Magna Carta established the framework for what would become the British parliament.

The Expansion of Parliamentary Power

The resolution of the battle over the Magna Carta changed British political history, but it did not resolve the relationship between the monarch and what eventually became the parliament. Many questions still remained. What ramifications would it have for the rule of the monarch? What powers did the parliament actually have? Who, finally, would actually govern Great Britain? These, and many similar questions, were at the crux of a power struggle between the monarch and the parliament over the next several centuries.

We start in the sixteenth century with a series of events surrounding Henry VIII's quest for power. Henry VIII needed a male heir to the throne, but his twenty-five-year marriage to Catherine of Aragon resulted in only one child who survived infancy: a girl (Mary, who later became the first queen of England). Frustrated, Henry demanded that the marriage be declared null and void, in the hope that a new wife might bear him a son. The pope, however, refused to act on Henry's request for an annulment. Because Britain was then a Catholic country, the British king was subject to decisions made by the pope on religious issues. Furious, Henry sought to find a way around the pope's decision. But the pope, for both moral reasons (divorce was against Catholic canon law) and political reasons (he did not want to offend the powerful Catholic nation of Spain), was unrelenting: as a Catholic king of a Catholic country, Henry had to stay married to the Spanish Catherine, unless the pope annulled the marriage. Despite both Henry's and Catherine's pleas for quick action on Henry's annulment request, the pope refused to issue a decision. So Henry decided to find another way.

Beginning around 1529, he mobilized anticlerical elements in Parliament. Parliamentary leader Thomas Cromwell supported King Henry VIII's break with Rome and well understood the potential political gains for Parliament. In 1534, Henry, after consulting with scholars (who of course had incentive to agree with him), announced that his twenty-five-year marriage to Catherine had never been valid, and then proceeded to marry Anne Boleyn, who had been waiting in the wings for six years. The pope finally acted the next year, declaring the marriage between Anne and Henry null and void, and demanding that the king return to Catherine or face excommunication. After gaining the support of key parliamentarians, with Cromwell's assistance, King Henry VIII announced his decision to break relations with the Roman Catholic Church. In its stead he created the Church of England, placing himself in charge.[13]

After the king made the break official, Cromwell pushed through a number of religious reform measures in Parliament. These included the dissolution of all monasteries, and the transfer of the property wealth of the Roman Catholic Church to Parliament. In the end, the king ended his marriage with Catherine, and the Roman Catholic Church lost its privileged position in England. Further, under Thomas Cromwell's leadership, Parliament filled the void left by the dissolution of the Roman Catholic Church, thereby dramatically expanding its power and authority. Matters previously left to the Church were now under the purview of Parliament. In sum, this series of events reinforced the development of parliamentary power in Great Britain, continuing a political trajectory originally started some three hundred years earlier with the adoption of the Magna Carta.

Let us fast-forward to the first half of the seventeenth century. At this time, the rulers of Great Britain, the Stuart monarchs, wanted to return Roman Catholicism to Great Britain, against the wishes of Parliament. The Stuarts hoped to follow the example of the absolute monarchs in continental Europe, particularly in France. At that time, political modernization was occurring in

France under the concept of the divine right of kings, which served to justify modern centralization under the traditional authority symbols of God and the Church. Power was centralized in the monarch, and the bureaucracy developed specialized departments to carry out his edicts. There was no provision for popular political participation: the only act required of citizens was to pay homage to the king in the form of taxes. By asserting its absolute powers as the nation's unifying force, the monarchy was able to centralize national institutions, and rapidly create modern armies and navies. Samuel Huntington refers to this process as the Continental European model of political modernization, well illustrated by the cases of France, Spain, and Portugal.[14] Indeed, the imperial power of Portugal and Spain in the fifteenth and sixteenth centuries, and the military and economic power of France in the seventeenth and eighteenth centuries, generated widespread aristocratic support for this absolutist model of political development on the European continent. Consequently, the Stuart monarchs felt that the return of monarchical absolutism was the best way for Great Britain to modernize and stay competitive with its neighbors. Yet since the adoption of the Magna Carta in the thirteenth century, and Henry VIII's break with the Roman Catholic Church in the sixteenth century, England had been on a different trajectory from the rest of Europe. The Stuarts wanted to change that.

As you might expect, Parliament reacted strongly against the plans of Stuart King James I, who was succeeded by Charles I in 1625. Parliament passed the *Petition of Right* in 1628, which set limits on the king's power. The idea behind this legislation was to prevent the monarch from inviting the Roman Catholic Church back, and thus, to preserve Parliament's independence and authority. This parliamentary challenge to royal authority did not sit well with Charles I. As tensions heated up, both the king and the parliament appealed to their respective followers, and each ordered the outfitting of armies. With all peaceful resolutions exhausted, the armies loyal to Charles I engaged the armies loyal to Parliament in 1642, leading to a bloody civil war. This conflict eventually ended with the victory of the parliamentary forces, who quickly consolidated their power. They ordered the beheading of King Charles I, which took place in 1649, abolished the monarchy, and declared England to be a Commonwealth. A Council of State was appointed to rule in the place of the monarch, led by Oliver Cromwell.[15]

These events bring us to the last half of the seventeenth century. One might think that having won the civil war, Parliament would be enjoying its newfound authority. The reality in 1660, however, was that Parliament's experiment in government *sans roi* was a disaster. Cromwell turned out to be a despotic ruler, and his death in 1660 left Parliament with few options. Incredibly, Parliament decided to restore the Stuart monarchy. Charles II, son of Charles I, became king in 1660; he, in turn, was succeeded by James II in 1685. This new generation of Stuart kings wanted the return of Roman Catholicism to England, and continued to fight with Parliament. After almost thirty more years of monarch-parliamentary conflict, the sides took up arms against one another once again. This time, however, a civil war was avoided, as Leonard Freedman points out:

> There was one more impasse between king and Parliament. Again an army took the field against the incumbent monarch, James II, whom Parliament accused of scheming to bring back Catholicism. This time the insurgents were an invading force led by William of Orange, who had been invited by Parliamentary leaders to take over the throne. But this time there was no civil war. James, with his army defecting, remembered what happened to Charles I, and fled into exile without a struggle. Thenceforth the British spoke of the "Glorious Revolution" of 1688, so named because it was successful, popular and bloodless.[16]

The 1688 Glorious Revolution resolved the religious question and constructed the monarchy on a new basis: William of Orange and his wife Mary owed their very position as the new British monarchs to Parliament. This new relationship was codified in the Bill of Rights approved by Parliament, which provided that Parliament had authority over the monarch to raise taxes and pass laws. This bill specified that the monarch did not have the power to either promulgate or rescind a law. Later, the Act of Settlement of 1701 further placed the monarchy under the power of Parliament, and established new succession rules to the Crown.[17] In total, these provisions clearly established the preeminent position of Parliament in British politics and society—a remarkable development, especially when considering that the French Revolution would not happen until 1789.

A Democratizing Parliament

Although parliamentary domination and autonomy eroded the authority and power of the monarch in the seventeenth and eighteenth centuries, it remained an undemocratic body in the eighteenth century. At this time Parliament's upper house, the House of Lords (which evolved from the King's Great Council), dominated Parliament and was composed of the nobility, landowners, and the Church of England. The lower body, known as the House of Commons, was also not representative of the general population. Its representation was tilted to favor the less-populated rural areas, and was dominated by rural landowners. They maintained their position by the use of *rotten boroughs*—a corrupt system of representation that enabled a small group of rural electors to dominate parliamentary districts.[18]

Simultaneously, a larger economic and social event was gradually gaining steam that would dramatically change the nature and internal operation of Parliament: the Industrial Revolution. Once it took root, the industrial revolution radically changed British society and caused much social and political instability.[19] There were social dislocations as many peasants flocked to the cities for work from the countryside, creating great pockets of poverty in the cities. As vividly depicted in the novels of Charles Dickens, including *Oliver Twist* and *A Christmas Carol*, conditions in the eighteenth and nineteenth centuries for working-class people in London, Manchester, and elsewhere in England were abysmal. And yet, as mentioned above, the aristocrats and rural landlords controlling Parliament were preventing this developing urban working class from participating in the political life of the country.

At this time two major parliamentary political groups, the Tories and Whigs—considered to be the forerunner of modern political parties—argued over reform measures to remedy these new social problems caused by industrialization. The Tories, who were mostly conservative and rural aristocrats, dominated Parliament in the early part of the eighteenth century, and resisted dramatic change. The Whigs, a grouping of the new entrepreneurial elite, believed in free trade, and argued that the Tory conservative leadership was depriving the country of business opportunities. They took particular aim at the rotten-borough system, which, they claimed, was manipulated by the Tories to maintain a parliamentary majority.[20] The Whigs took advantage of elite concerns that the societal unrest among the working class could develop into a violent class revolution, and gained power in the 1830 parliamentary elections. Once in power, the Whigs initiated a process of reforms aimed at restoring social order and improving the business climate. In particular, the 1832 Reform Act eliminated the rotten-borough system, expanded the electorate, and added electoral districts in urban areas. More reforms followed throughout the nineteenth and twentieth centuries, including the 1867 Reform Act, which enfranchised the urban working class. In their totality, the various reform acts not only expanded the franchise, but led to the democratization of the internal workings of Parliament as well. Indeed, the parliamentary acts of 1911 and 1949 completed the democratization process by restricting the power and authority of the undemocratic House of Lords, and by placing ultimate governing authority squarely with the democratic House of Commons.[21]

The Long Sweep of British History

The cumulative effect of British political development has been the construction of a democratic and parliamentary government under a symbolic monarch. Of note, two significant landmarks were realized over the centuries-long evolution of parliamentary power. First, centralized authority came

---

TEXT BOX 2.1
Important Events in the Path of British Democracy

I.   The Origins of Parliament
     1215–25:   The Great Council of Barons wins passage of the Magna Carta.
II. The Expansion of Parliamentary Power
     1534:   Parliament passes Act of Settlement during the reign of Henry VIII.
     1642:   Civil war between Parliament and Stuart kings.
     1649:   Parliament wins civil war. Charles I beheaded; Parliament installs Oliver Cromwell as England's new leader.
     1660:   Cromwell, who proves to be a despotic ruler, dies. Parliament restores Charles II to the British throne.
     1688:   The Glorious Revolution brings William and Mary to the British throne. Parliament passes the Act of Settlement, which established new succession rules for the British Crown.
III. A Democratizing Parliament
     1832:   Parliament passes reform act that enfranchises the middle class.
     1867:   Parliament passes reform act that enfranchises the urban working class.
     1911:   Parliament passes reform act that limits power of the House of Lords.
     1949:   Parliament passes reform act that provides for the domination of the House of Commons over the House of Lords.

---

to be located in the lawmaking machine, the parliament.[22] Second, rejecting the notion of a fixed and fundamental set of laws, the country adopted the idea of a flexible and sovereign legislative body. As James Q. Wilson has pointed out, "in Great Britain . . . the Parliament can do almost anything that it believes the voters will accept."[23] This approach to government holds that it is preferable to accord the legislative body the authority to enact laws in response to the societal needs of the time, rather than have it be limited by a set of checks and balances detailed in a written constitution.

Key Institutional Features of British Democracy

The British Constitution

The British Constitution is referred to as an "unwritten constitution," because the rules and procedures that orient British political life were not devised and set down on paper at one particular moment in time. Rather, the term "British Constitution" encompasses a series of documents and precedent-setting laws. Technically, then, the British Constitution is written, in that it consists of existing documents. It is unwritten in the sense that governmental principles are not drawn together into one concise document written for the specific purpose of forming a government. In clear distinction from the American Constitution, it is perhaps better to think of the so-called British Constitution as a constitutional framework, which has evolved over the past several hundred years and loosely directs political life in Britain. It is not a single written document, nor does it specify the component parts of government and the powers of each branch. This "unwritten" constitution derives from five distinct sources:

- statute law,
- common law,
- conventions,
- authoritative works, and
- external agreements.[24]

Statute law, the first basis of the British constitutional framework, is made up of certain parliamentary acts that have defined the institutional relationship between and within the monarchy and Parliament. As we have just seen, the 1215 Magna Carta, the 1689 Bill of Rights, and the 1911 and 1949 parliamentary acts helped to define those institutional relationships, and are examples of statute law.

Common law, a second source of the British constitutional framework, takes one of two forms: executive prerogative powers and the judicial interpretation of statute law. The first of these, executive prerogative power, technically belongs to the Crown, although, in practice, it is utilized by the prime minister and government. As we shall see later in this chapter, the British monarch no longer has any real power, and all executive decisions are now made by the prime minister. These include the right to appoint ministers, make treaties, and declare war. The second form of common law, judicial interpretation of statute law, establishes that once a court has held that a statute law is part of common law, a precedent is created that is to be followed by other courts.

Convention is the third basis of the British constitutional framework. Convention typically embodies the terms of resolution of a generalized social and political crisis of the past, and as such, carries authority. For example, although there are no specific rules governing the parliamentary motion of confidence, a sitting government must resign if it loses, *by convention*. This happens in spite of the fact that no lawful, authoritative document sets forth these rules, and there are no criminal penalties if they are disobeyed.[25] Philip Norton points out that political actors follow conventions because they fear that the British constitutional system is unworkable without them:

> [Conventions] derive their strength from the realization that not to abide by them would make for an unworkable Constitution. They are, so to speak, the oil in the formal machinery of the Constitution. They help fill the gap between the constitutional formality and the political reality.[26]

Significant and authoritative *scholarly works* represent the British Constitution's fourth source of power. These works have been authored by British scholars throughout history, and have influenced policy makers' understanding of how the organs of government should be organized, how they should function, and how they should relate to each other. These scholarly works include the writings of A. V. Dicey and Walter Bagehot, among others.[27] A. V. Dicey, for example, is credited with emphasizing the supremacy of Parliament in British politics, including the idea that the government is accountable to Parliament. In addition, and as we saw in chapter 1, Walter Bagehot's 1867 work titled *The English Constitution* strongly argues for the need for fused executive and legislative powers to avoid the problems intrinsic to a divided power arrangement.[28]

Lastly, a number of recent *international agreements* have had bearing on the British constitutional framework. These agreements include the European Convention of Human Rights in 1951, the European Communities Act of 1972, and the European Communities (Amendment) Act of 1986. These external agreements provide that European Community laws might take precedence over British law, and their long-term implications for Parliament indicate that there may be a shift of power to some sort European Parliament. The full implications, of course, are not yet known.[29]

Taken as a whole, these five distinct sources have contributed to the development and evolution of the British constitutional framework today.

The Westminster Parliamentary System

Technically, the British parliament is composed of the monarch, the House of Lords, and the House of Commons, and all three continue to have a role to play in the law-making function of the parliament. In fact, the House of Commons—the only democratically elected institution of the three—controls all legislative initiatives.

As we learned in chapter 1, there are two executives in the British parliamentary system, the head of government and the head of state. The British head of government is the prime minister, and the British head of state is the monarch (king or queen). By convention, the monarch performs a symbolic legislative function. If you look at a popular magazine or newspaper in Britain, you will immediately see the difference: the British prime minister is often pictured at his official residence of 10 Downing Street speaking about legislation, whereas members of the royal family, including Queen Elizabeth, Prince Charles, and Prince William, perform symbolic functions. You will see them representing Great Britain at various events, such as the Olympics, or at an opening of an art gallery or the symphony season. At the opening of each session of Parliament, the monarch reads the government's proposals for the upcoming legislative session. The leaders of the majority party in Parliament prepare this text, and the monarch must read whatever is put before him or her. After every parliamentary election, the monarch sends for the leader from a new majority. The monarch also must sign any statute passed by Parliament. Ironically, even if Parliament were to pass a law that abolished the monarchy, the queen would be required to sign it. Thus the monarch remains involved in British politics, but is no longer is an active player.[30]

The 29 April 2011, marriage of Prince William to Catherine Middleton may serve as an illustration of the monarchy as a symbol of British culture and government. The public, at home and abroad, watched their wedding, televised from Westminster Abbey, and anxiously awaited the birth of an heir (though at the time of their marriage, British law was changed to allow a daughter to inherit the throne). The marriage of Prince William and Catherine, Duke and Duchess of Cambridge, and the birth of their son, George Alexander Louis, on 22 July 2013, instilled a sense of pride in Great Britain and put a young, fresh face on the monarchy, and thus the country in general. This symbolism was a boost that Britain needed, given the difficulties the monarchy faced after the 1997 death of Diana, Princess of Wales. Although Princess Diana's status had been diminished by her divorce from Prince Charles, Britain and the rest of the world clearly viewed her as an embodiment of British society and culture: the public accorded her status as a symbol of Britain. When the public perceived funeral preparations made by Queen Elizabeth and Prince Charles to be a slight to Diana, the monarchy was shaken. The monarchy's power as head of state derives from its symbolic nature. If the symbol is tarnished, as it appeared to be when Charles and Elizabeth seemed less distraught over the princess's death than the rest of the world, its power is diminished. If the symbol shines brightly, as it did as William and Catherine embarked on marriage and family, its power is strengthened.

Like the monarch, the upper house in the legislature, known as the House of Lords, is not a democratic body: *none* of its members has been elected to serve. As was the case in the eighteenth century, the House of Lords continues to be composed of the elite segments of British society. Today there are several ways to get into the House of Lords: the monarch may appoint you, if you have attained a prominent position in British society; you may have a birthright, if you are born into a noble family; or you may serve if you are part of the hierarchy of the Church of England. The House of Lords has very restricted powers, but may play a constructive role as a debating society on the important issues of the day. It is possible for the government to appoint new members to the House of Lords as life peers. In 1999, the House of Lords Act provided for elections to take place to determine the ninety-two hereditary peers who would remain there. There are ordinarily no elections for the House of Lords, save for when vacancies occur in the hereditary peerage.[31] Unlike the House of Commons, the number of seats is not fixed in the House of Lords; there are usually somewhere between 750 and 800 members at any one time.[32]

The majority party in the lower legislative body, the House of Commons, controls British politics. That party selects the head of government, known as the prime minister, to be the executive and to direct the legislative branch. To help govern, the prime minister designates a cabinet from among the ranks of the majority party in the legislature. The British cabinet differs from the American cabinet in two main ways. First, British law allows cabinet members to continue to serve out their term as representatives as well. In the United States, cabinet secretaries can be selected from outside of Congress, and members of Congress who serve on the cabinet are required to resign from their elected position. Second, in Britain, the term "government" refers to the prime minister and his or her cabinet, which has the exclusive responsibility for administration of the country, and not to the parliament.

The Westminster system allows the prime minister to dominate the parliament, as long as he or she can maintain a legislative majority. Unlike a U.S. president, who faces reelection after four years and cannot serve more than two terms, the British prime minister has no fixed term and no term limits on his or her office. In addition, the prime minister can expect to have all of his or her legislation passed without any revisions from the loyal opposition.

At present, there are 650 members in the democratic House of Commons. Each Member of Parliament, known as an MP, is elected to represent a single-member constituency under a first-past-the-post electoral system (explained in chapter 1). Parliamentary elections must be held no later than five years after the previous election. For many years, the government could decide when to schedule the next parliamentary elections, which offered it an enormous advantage over the opposition—at any point within five years of the previous election, the government could call for new elections. That decision was frequently made based on their poll numbers. That is, when the poll numbers were favorable, the incumbent government could call for new elections with the reasonable expectation of winning, thereby extending their term of office. The Conservative Party effectively used this strategy to maintain a legislative majority for almost eighteen years; first under the skillful leadership of Margaret Thatcher from 1979 until 1991, and then under John Major from 1991 until 1997. In 1997 the Labour Party, led by Tony Blair, finally regained power. Blair was in office until 2007, and then followed by fellow Labour Party member Gordon Brown, from 2007 to 2010. The ability to call for early elections by the sitting government was ended after the "split-decision" election of 6 May 2010, when no party claimed an overall majority, and so the Liberal Democrats joined a coalition government with the Conservatives. As part of their coalition-formation negotiations, the leaders of the Conservative Party and Liberal Democrats, David Cameron and Nick Clegg respectively, agreed that members elected by popular vote would complete their five-year terms unless the House was dissolved earlier.[33] Nick Clegg insisted on this reform as part of the deal to form the coalition government. It remains to be seen whether this notable change of tradition will be reversed by a future government.

The government and the opposition sit facing each other in the House of Commons. Members of the leadership of the majority party, the government, sit on the front benches across from the leadership of the minority party. The minority party is also called *the loyal opposition*, which is a term from British history. It signifies that even if a political party may disagree with the policies of the majority party, it remains loyal to the Crown and to the country.

Viewed from the public sitting area in the House of Commons, the government sits on the left-hand side, and the opposition sits on the right-hand side. The leadership of the government and opposition sit across from each other on the front benches. As such, those in a leadership capacity are known as frontbenchers. Further, the opposition leadership is referred to as the shadow cabinet, because they sit across from the government's ministers, in a sense shadowing their counterparts.

Both government and opposition junior-ranking members of Parliament sit on the benches behind their respective leaders, and, as such, have come to be known as backbenchers. Independent MPs represent a specific region or issue area, and are not officially allied with either the government or the opposition. They are known as crossbenchers.

The speaker, chosen from the ranks of the parliament, performs an arbiter role. The speaker does not have to be a member of the majority party. For example, Baroness Betty Boothroyd, the speaker from 1992 to 2000, was a Labour MP elected to the position when the Conservative Party held a majority in the House. She was the first female in that role. The speaker sits in the so-called speaker's chair, located at the far end of the building.[34]

The job of the government is to present, pass, and implement a legislative package; the opposition tries to block its legislative initiatives. Unlike in the American system of checks and balances, the parliamentary opposition in Great Britain has little chance to amend or challenge legislation prepared by the government; for the most part, members of the opposition are limited to criticizing the legislation in the hope that they might prevail in the next elections. If, however, a government proves to be incompetent and has lost sufficient legislative support from among the ranks of the majority party, it may be possible for the opposition to successfully request that the government face a vote of confidence. If the government loses such a motion, it will have to resign, and new elections will almost certainly be held.

One of the most entertaining British political events in the House of Commons is question time. This is when government ministers, including the prime minister, are subjected to questions from the opposition leadership, opposition backbenchers, and government backbenchers. Whereas the questions asked by government backbenchers tend to be tame and respectful of the government, opposition questions from both the leadership and the backbenchers have been known to be rather abusive.[35]

Finally, it is important to note that although there are no constitutional checks and balances on the actions of Parliament, there are some general limitations on parliamentary action. The rights of free speech and assembly, for example, are important elements of British convention, and tend to frame the legislative activities of the parliament. In addition, mindful that the public will hold the government accountable for its actions in the next elections, prime ministers have been, on the whole, careful to respect and safeguard democratic liberties.[36] One can safely state today that after some eight hundred years of evolution, Great Britain is presently a fully democratic nation operating under a parliamentary institutional structure without a formal set of checks and balances.

The Creation of the American Presidential System

Originally a British colony, the United States became an independent nation in the last half of the eighteenth century. As we have shown, by the time the United States was established, Britain had already gone through a great deal of change in its governmental system. The government in place in Britain in 1787 was the result of *evolution*; the Americans were creating a new system as the result of a *revolution*. Therefore, the Americans could both dispense with elements of the British system they found oppressive, and hold on to elements that they felt furthered their notions of the proper role of government. As Gitelson, Dudley, and Dubnick note:

> With few exceptions, the leaders of the American Revolution respected the British constitutional system. Indeed, many of them saw the Revolution as a fight to secure the rights they had assumed to be theirs as Englishmen. Therefore, when the time came to devise their own system of government, the framers relied heavily on the British constitutional system.[37]

In that it was based on British constitutional principles, then, the American Constitution was another step in the evolution of British government. Of course it was also a clear rejection of at least some of those principles. And on its own, the American Constitution has evolved over time, sometimes going in a very different direction from the British Constitution. Nevertheless, there was a distinct point in time at which American government was consciously created, using democratic principles without the baggage of feudal and monarchical history. The framers of the American Constitution created a system of checks and balances as a reaction to their experience as colonists. They were more concerned with limiting government than with creating a responsive government.

In a sense, the writing of the American Constitution established a second trajectory for the development of British constitutional principles. While the parliament was consolidating power in itself, the framers centralized power in the Constitution and explicitly rejected monarchical absolutism. In this regard, James Q. Wilson has noted that "The American revolt against British rule, culminating in 1775 in the War of Independence, led many colonists to conclude that political power should never again be entrusted to rulers whose authority was based on tradition and other unwritten understandings. The central idea behind a written constitution as to limit and define political authority."[38]

The following sections of the chapter will focus on the development of the American political system: its philosophical influences, its roots in the colonists' experiences as subjects of the British Crown, and its evolution over time. In particular, the chapter will address the following four issues:

- The origins of American democracy, especially the Articles of Confederation, the Declaration of Independence, the Constitutional Convention, and the Virginia Plan (perhaps the world's first plan for a modern parliamentary system).
- The concerns of the framers of the Constitution, including their fears of excessive executive power and tyranny of the majority, and their attempts to avoid both.

- The key institutional features of the new government, especially the system of checks and balances.
- The subsequent development and expansion of democracy in the United States.

The Origins of American Democracy

The United States began as thirteen colonies subject to the British Crown. Each of the colonies had some amount of self-governance, and each was in many ways independent of the others. Although Britain had ultimate political authority over the colonies, for many years that control did not have an effect on the everyday lives of colonists. In the late 1700s, however, that began to change. Britain passed a series of legislative initiatives that the colonists found oppressive: the Sugar Act in 1764, the Stamp Act in 1765, Townsend Duties in 1767, and the Tea Act in 1773. Each of these acts was an attempt by Britain to gain revenues by taxing the American colonists. British lawmakers saw these acts as reasonable: the nation had a sizable debt, due in large part to its assistance to the colonies in the French and Indian War. The colonists saw it differently, and "no taxation without representation" became a rallying cry. Radical revolutionaries led by Samuel Adams organized the Boston Tea Party as a protest against the Tea Act. The revolutionaries had two purposes: to galvanize opposition against Britain, and to make British lawmakers so angry that they would pass punitive measures, further encouraging rebellion.[39]

The Declaration of Independence from Great Britain

In 1774, the first Continental Congress was called to consider action against the British government. It did not go beyond a call for a boycott of British goods. By 1776, however, the seeds of independence had been sown, and the Second Continental Congress, convened in that year, asked Thomas Jefferson to write what became the Declaration of Independence. The declaration gave voice to the frustrations of the colonists. It claimed that the king's actions were unfair, that he had violated the colonists' rights, and that such unjust actions were sufficient to warrant the rejection of one form of government and the creation of another. The declaration also set out the Enlightenment ideals of consent of the governed and natural rights, including life, liberty, and "the pursuit of happiness." The Declaration of Independence contained fighting words. Its purpose was not only to let the king know, in no uncertain terms, the extent of colonial anger about his actions, it also was to draw foreign attention to the colonists' plight, in the hopes of raising funds and armies for the inevitable conflict. Finally, and perhaps most importantly, the document was written in the hopes of mobilizing public opinion in the colonies in favor of rebellion. Thus, it contained a list of grievances against the king, in addition to its statement of principles.

The Declaration of Independence is a powerful document that sets out America's philosophy of government: individual rights, equality, and consent of the governed. What the declaration did not do was to actually specify the form that the government should take. Another document was necessary to constitute a government, and the Articles of Confederation, adopted in 1771, served as the earliest constitution of our fledgling government. Ratified even as the War of Independence was being waged, the Articles of Confederation specified the form of national government under which the newly independent colonies would operate. Unfortunately, as we shall see, that form proved unworkable, and a second, more long-lasting form of government was finally established with the ratification of the Constitution in 1789.

The Articles of Confederation

As we saw in chapter 1, the United States under the Articles of Confederation functioned under what is known as a confederal system. In this system, each individual state retains its own power and autonomy; the states are loosely associated under a weak national government. Individuals are citizens of the state in which they reside, and the federal government has no real authority over individual citizens. The states, not their citizens, make up the confederation. The confederation, called a "league of friendship," was similar to the United Nations today, in which each individual nation retains its sovereign status. As a form of government for a single nation, however, the confederation proved to be unworkable.

The biggest problem was that the national government was too weak to function effectively. Thomas Patterson aptly notes that "the consequences of an overly weak authority were clear: public disorder, economic chaos, and inadequate defense."[40] The confederation had no separate executive branch (although there was a plural executive, controlled by Congress and with limited power), there was no judicial branch, and Congress was unicameral. Each state had only one delegate, and those delegates were chosen not by popular election but by the state legislatures. Further, the confederation had no power to levy taxes or regulate commerce. Since the new federal government did not have the power to tax, it did not have the power to pay war debts or to properly provide a national defense. Without the power to regulate commerce, it also had no real means of coordinating activities among the states. By 1787 it became clear that this system could not last. Patterson usefully points out that the system was about to collapse:

> By 1784, the nation was unraveling. Congress was so weak that its members often did not bother to attend its sessions. Finally, in late 1786, a revolt in western Massachusetts prompted leading Americans to conclude that the country's government had to be changed. A ragtag army of two thousand farmers, armed with pitchforks, marched on county courthouses to prevent foreclosures on their land and cattle. Many of the farmers were veterans of the Revolutionary War; their leader, Daniel Shays, had been a captain in the Revolutionary army. They had been given assurances during the Revolution that their land, which lay fallow because they were away at war, would not be confiscated for reasons of unpaid debts and taxes. They had also been told that they would get the back pay owed to them for their military service (Congress had run out of money during the Revolution). Instead, no back pay was received, and heavy new taxes were placed on farms. Many farmers faced loss of their property and even jail because they could not pay their creditors.[41]

The American Constitutional Convention, which eventually devised the balance of powers system and federalism, was originally convened to find solutions to the problems inherent in the confederal system.

The Constitutional Convention

Having found the Articles of Confederation to be unsuccessful, the new nation felt it had to return to the drawing board. In 1787, delegates from twelve of the thirteen states (Rhode Island chose not to send a representative) gathered in Philadelphia to discuss amending and revising the articles. As there were no other viable functioning democratic models in the world to emulate, their deliberations were both inventive and original. There was general agreement that the articles had created a central government that did not have enough power, but beyond that, there was little agreement as to what should be done to strengthen it, or even how strong it should be.

Indeed, delegates to the Constitutional Convention strongly disagreed over many questions. For example, Alexander Hamilton favored a hereditary executive. Delegates quarreled over the form of representation in the new national legislative body as well. The framers debated every aspect of the form and shape of their new democratic government. Even the first ten amendments to the Constitution, known as the Bill of Rights, which have been so important to American political life and development over the past two hundred years, were adopted because many of the delegates were concerned that the new national government might threaten individual liberty or states' rights.

The Virginia Plan: The First Design of a Parliamentary System?

You may already be familiar with some of the great controversies of the Constitutional Convention: whether representation should be based on population or given equally to states, whether slavery should be allowed, and how to account for slaves in determining population. What you may not know is that the framers of the Constitution very nearly decided to establish a parliamentary rather than a presidential system. Although the concept of a parliamentary government as we know it today was still evolving, England had, by the late 1700s, established one very important characteristic of its parliamentary system: that the executive would be selected from the legislature.[42] Following the British example (as well as the example of most of the original thirteen states, which then required that the governor be chosen by the state legislature), the delegates to the Constitutional Convention originally voted to have Congress select the "national executive."

While the delegates to the convention were still considering ways to amend the Articles of Confederation, the Virginia delegation quickly took control by submitting a proposal that would scrap the articles altogether. The Virginia plan created a strong national government and established a bicameral legislature, with representation based on population. In addition, the Virginia plan proposed that "a National Executive be instituted; *to be chosen by the National Legislature*" (emphasis added). Several elements of the Virginia plan created controversy; most remember the plan for its reliance on population in determining representation. The Great Compromise (also known as the Connecticut Compromise) took the bicameral legislature from the Virginia plan, and gave the lower house popular representation. The compromise allowed for equal representation for each state in the upper house, as suggested by the New Jersey plan (although the New Jersey plan had proposed a unicameral, or one-house, legislature).

But representation was not the only problem that delegates had with the Virginia plan. There was much discussion about whether the single executive proposed by the Virginia delegation was appropriate, and once that was decided, what was the best method of selection of the executive. Although the presidency is in many ways the defining feature of American democracy, it is important to remember that this office represented completely unknown territory to the framers. The only real example they had of a national executive was a monarch—and they had fought a war to end the tyranny that monarchy imposed. In 1787, no other country had a president, or even a prime minister in the modern sense (at the time in Britain, the prime minister was an agent of the king). The authors of the Constitution were charting new territory in the creation of the national executive:

In 1787, the problem was far more baffling than it would be today, because the democratic executive was all but unknown. A popularly elected President was a novelty; the chief alternative solution, a prime minister chosen by the Parliament, had not yet emerged in its modern democratic form even in Britain.[43]

The problem in creating the national executive revolved around how much power the office should hold. If Congress selected the president, then the office would be relatively weak, subject to the whims and desires of the legislature. On the other hand, a single national executive, independent of Congress, might concentrate power too narrowly, thus creating the possibility of tyranny in the executive branch. Tyranny in the hands of one individual was to be avoided at all costs, given the experience of the colonists with the British monarchy. One way to limit the concentration of power in the presidency had already been tried and found wanting: having a plural executive. The Articles of Confederation had created an executive committee, which ultimately proved to be unwieldy. A single executive would create more energy in the office and eliminate the possibility of stalemate, which might occur if the members of a plural executive could not come to agreement on an issue. The delegates knew they wanted a single executive, but they didn't know how to guarantee its autonomy from Congress. The framers were not sure what to do. As a matter of fact, they voted in favor of the executive being chosen by the legislature a total of three times.

Delegates ended up with two choices: either the legislature would choose the executive, as proposed under the Virginia plan, or selection would be made by an electoral college, as suggested by the New Jersey plan. After a great deal of discussion, the convention sent the matter to committee for consideration. The committee decided that an electoral college would choose the executive, and resolved another related issue, term of office, by deciding that the president would be elected for a four-year term, and would be eligible for reelection. The committee's decision was sent back to the full convention, which eventually voted in favor of the revised plan. Thus was the presidency born, a new and untried institution, which ultimately proved to be one of the great successes of the Constitutional Convention.[44] And thus died the possibility of sending American political development in a parliamentary direction.

The Fear of Tyranny at the Founding

One of the greatest fears of the framers at the Constitutional Convention was that pure democracy might degenerate into a form of tyranny. The form of tyranny that they feared was not only the despotism of a single individual, but also the tyranny of the majority, or the potential for mob rule. To guard against the danger of tyranny of the majority (as we shall discuss later in this chapter), the framers fashioned a representative democracy that provided for individual liberty by limiting the power and authority of the majority (and which, not coincidentally, favored the interests of the propertied minority). The ideas offered by two notable political philosophers influenced their thinking on this matter: the concepts of individual rights and the consent of the governed from the Englishman John Locke, and the notion of separation of powers from the Frenchman Baron de Montesquieu. Let us briefly examine these influential ideas of Locke and Montesquieu.

In his work titled *The Two Treatises of Civil Government*, published in 1689 and 1690, John Locke advanced the then-controversial argument that all individuals possess natural rights given to them by God. The existing government in Britain relied on the doctrine of the "divine right of kings," which declared that kings derive their right to rule directly from God. In contrast, Locke suggested that every person has a right to "life, liberty and property." Further, Locke stated that these rights were not granted by governments, but were "natural": granted to individuals by their very nature as human beings. Natural rights are God-given rights and, as such, can neither be acquired nor given away. The rights suggested by Locke are rightly understood as negative rights: rights that cannot be legitimately taken away by a government. Since God (not government) has granted these rights to each individual, no government can ever have the authority to take them away.[45]

Locke envisioned a political order without the absolute rule by a king, arguing that the rights of life, liberty, and property were natural to mankind, and existed in the original state of nature. Unlike the British political theorist Thomas Hobbes, who described life in the state of nature as "nasty, brutish and short," with individuals locked in a perpetual conflict over scarce resources, Locke envisioned a more peaceable state of nature. In Locke's view, individuals had the right of liberty as long as they did not violate the rights of others. The problem, however, was that the God-given rights of individuals could become imperiled by other individuals in an unchecked state of nature. Consequently, Locke suggests that government emerged from the state of nature by the terms of an agreement among people to provide for the protection of their rights.

The decision by individuals to leave the state of nature and form a government brings us to one of Locke's most important concepts: the social contract. He understood social contract theory to mean that individuals only agree to leave the state of nature as part of the terms of a social contract; consequently, the *people* are rightly understood as the source of government. This concept is an important departure from the "divine right of kings," in that it holds that the government does not have a divine right to rule. In Locke's view, government is a human creation, because humans *precede* government: that is, although there can be people without a government, there can never be a government without people. Government, then, rules by the consent of the people, or of the governed.

The framers also borrowed liberally from the ideas of another political philosopher, the French Baron de Montesquieu. In his 1748 work titled *On the Spirit of the Laws*, Montesquieu gave the framers an intellectual justification for the necessity of separated and equal branches of government. Montesquieu persuasively argued that fused legislative and executive powers would naturally lead to tyranny: "When legislative power is united with executive power in a single person in a single body of the magistracy, there is no liberty, because one can fear that the same monarch or senate that makes tyrannical laws will execute them tyrannically."[46]

Montesquieu held that the best way to prevent tyranny, whether of the one or the many, was to divide political power into three separate branches, defined as the executive, the legislative, and the judicial. He envisioned that in such a three-branch arrangement, the legislature would have the authority to enact the law, the executive would be granted the power to both execute and enforce the law, and the judicial branch would be required to punish any and all violations against it. Once these powers were clearly separated, Montesquieu argued that liberty could be safeguarded, for even if a person were to advance his selfish interests in one of the branches, the other two branches would be able to limit his ascent to absolute power.[47]

Perhaps James Madison best articulated the vision of the framers in the Federalist 47, stating that the very definition of tyranny was to consolidate all powers into one central authority. James Madison, in particular, agreed with Montesquieu, and viewed the separation of powers as a necessary precaution against the ambitions of those holding power. He held that it was of primary importance to create a system of checks and balances among the three branches of government, which would effectively balance power against power and thus prevent tyranny. He argued for shared as well as divided powers, noting that "the accumulation of all powers, legislative, executive, and judiciary, in the same hands, whether of one, a few, or many, and whether hereditary, self-appointed, or elective, may justly be pronounced the very definition of tyranny."[48]

Political philosopher Harvey Mansfield has observed that Montesquieu's insights not only influenced Madison, but also pulled a majority of the framers in the direction of divided executive, legislative, and judicial powers. Mansfield notes that Montesquieu influenced the framers' conclusion that the separation of powers was a needed precaution against the "encroaching" and ambitious nature of politicians.[49]

These views were evident in the Declaration of Independence in 1776. The declaration was a statement predicated on the Locke's principles of individual rights and the consent of the governed, and Montesquieu's principles of separated powers. The very first two sentences of the 1776 preamble of the Declaration of Independence reveal this influence:

> We hold these truths to be self-evident: that all men are created equal, that they are endowed by their creator with certain unalienable rights, that among these are life, liberty and the pursuit of happiness. That to secure these rights, governments are instituted among men, deriving their just powers from the consent of the governed.

The ideas presented in these two sentences clearly echo the thoughts of John Locke. In particular, Thomas Jefferson refers explicitly to Locke's concept of negative rights, and designates them as "unalienable."[50] Further, he uses Locke's phrase *consent of the governed* to legitimize the new government, and uses the term *equality* in Locke's restricted sense that each individual has an equal right to the God-given gifts of life, liberty, and the pursuit of happiness. These concepts informed the central philosophy behind the design of the new American republic at the Constitutional Convention in Philadelphia in 1787, and are at the root of the contemporary dilemma of majority rule versus minority rights in the United States.

Key Institutional Features of American Democracy

The American Constitution

Enacted in 1789, the new American Constitution established separate executive, legislative, and judicial branches. The Constitution provides for, in the words of Seymour Martin Lipset, "a weak and internally conflicted political system,"[51] by according each branch the necessary power to prevent the other branches from absorbing more power. Or as James Sundquist argues:

> The men who made up the Federal Convention of 1787 wavered during the course of their deliberations on most of the specific features of the constitutional structure that evolved, but they never vacillated on its central principle. That was the doctrine that the powers of the government must be separated into independent branches—legislative, executive, and judicial. Nearly all the delegates arrived in Philadelphia clearly committed to that objective. . . . The British government was cited as the model, but not today's British government. It was the government that existed—or was understood to exist—at that time, which was a government of separated powers.[52]

As such, and paradoxically, the same Constitution that assigns the president of the United States the duty to be the commander-in-chief of what has become the world's most powerful nation simultaneously limits his ability to get Congress to pass his legislative package.

The American Constitution is the oldest written constitution still in use, and its intricate design and complex system of checks and balances represent a uniquely American contribution to the art of democratic governance. It sought to divide, restrict, limit, check, and balance national governmental powers, and is predicated on five central and interrelated principles:

- The Constitution subordinates the elected political leadership to itself, as the fundamental law of the nation.
- It divides and balances powers among the legislative, executive, and judicial branches: *legislative power* is assigned to Congress under Article I; *executive power* is delegated to the president under Article II; and *judicial power*, or the power to interpret laws, is entrusted to the Supreme Court under Article III.
- It restricts the power, authority, and activities of national government vis-à-vis individuals through the Bill of Rights.
- It limits the power of the national government by granting state governments their own legal and political power and authority by the terms of Article IV and the Tenth Amendment.
- The framers also made provisions for the Constitution to be amended.

In these interlocking ways, the Constitution has patterned the structure and behavior of American government. Over the past two hundred years, as political and social conflicts have been settled, the resolutions of the various political and social disputes have been codified by amendments to the Constitution, and have themselves become part of the fundamental law. Once part of the Constitution, these very settlements have then demarcated the contours of subsequent change.[53]

Further, the framers feared that the House of Representatives might be more likely than the other branches of power to wrest power away from the Senate, the executive, and the judiciary. To limit this possible tendency, the framers decided to have the three branches chosen by different means:

> It seems to have been widely assumed at the convention that the House of Representatives would be the driving force in the system; that the people's representatives would be turbulent and insistent; that they would represent majorities and would be indifferent to the rights of minorities; that the people would be the winds driving the ship of state and their representatives would be the sails, swelling with every gust.[54]

As we shall see in the next chapters, the framers were most prescient in their views of the House of Representatives; Congressional action during health-care reform and consideration of the Contract with America are apt illustrations of the House as the "driving force in the system," with "turbulent and insistent" members.

The framers were steadfast in their desire to put a brake on the wily House of Representatives. In order for legislation to be passed, they required that the Senate approve it also. And the framers expected the Senate to be a quite different chamber from the House. Again using Britain as an example, the framers in some measure modeled the Senate after the House of Lords. They expected senators to be from the landed aristocracy, propertied and learned men.[55] The method of election of senators would also be different from representatives; whereas members of the House were to be chosen by direct popular election every two years, senators would be elected in staggered six-year terms, and chosen by state legislatures. (This was changed in 1913 with the adoption of the Seventeenth Amendment, which provided for the direct election of senators.) And, of course, senators represent their entire state, while the constituencies of representatives are districts of similar population. In the case of states entitled to only one House seat, those representatives represent their entire state as well.

The framers were afraid of the concentration of power, whether in the hands of one, a few, or many. So they made certain that each branch would have some measure of control over the other branches, by giving each one some of the powers of the others. Thus, the president can veto congressional legislation; Congress can override presidential vetoes; Congress must approve presidential appointments; the president appoints justices to the Supreme Court (with congressional approval); and the Supreme Court can hear cases arising under the Constitution (this eventually evolved into the power of judicial review—deciding whether an action of the president or Congress is constitutional). In this way, each branch has the power to check another branch, and power is diffused rather than concentrated.

The framers' invention of the Electoral College is noteworthy. The framers, although fearful of an executive too dependent on Congress, did not propose popular election of the president. Instead, they decided to have each state "appoint, in such manner as the legislature thereof may direct, a number of electors, equal to the whole number of Senators and Representatives to which the state may be entitled to in Congress." Further, representatives and senators were not to be eligible to become electors (Article II, Section 1). By now, all states have established popular elections as the method of selecting electors (that is, members of the Electoral College), but under the Constitution, other methods of selection—for example, having the state legislature choose the

IMAGE 2.2
The United States Capitol Building in Washington, D.C. © Ron Chapple/Corbis.

electors—would also be acceptable. That was the case for the first fifty years or so for some states. Although Americans tend to think of the president as being popularly elected, in fact, when Americans go to the voting booth, they are casting their ballots not for a particular candidate, but for the electors who have promised to vote for that candidate. This of course became crystal clear in the 2000 election, when there was a discrepancy between the popular vote and the Electoral College vote.

Judicial Review

One further restriction on government was not specifically discussed in the Constitution: the idea of judicial review. The framers set up a separate judicial branch that would have the power to interpret the law. Judicial power allows judges to decide whether the law has been applied correctly in individual cases. Judicial review gives the court additional authority. In the United States, the Supreme Court can rule on whether or not Congressional legislation, acts of the president, or state laws adhere to the Constitution. There is evidence that the framers also expected the Supreme Court to exercise judicial review. The Court established judicial review in the 1802 case *Marbury v. Madison*, giving the judicial branch a powerful check on both the president and Congress. If the Court says that a law is unconstitutional, that law becomes invalid. The Court's decision can be changed only by an amendment to the Constitution or by its own reversal. This is one reason why Supreme Court appointments are often controversial. For example, electing Republican Mitt Romney in the 2012 election instead of Barack Obama might have meant the appointment of more conservative justices to the Supreme Court, which in turn would have had an impact on a variety of issues, from gun control to same-sex marriage.[56] In the 1980s, Republicans were hoping that Reagan would be able to appoint enough conservative justices to achieve a majority on the Supreme Court and overturn the *Roe v. Wade* decision, which had made abortion legal in all fifty states. *Roe v. Wade* is an important example of the use of judicial review, which, over time, has been applied more frequently to state laws than federal laws. *Roe v. Wade* invalidated *state* laws restricting abortion.[57]

Democratizing American Government

In the years since the ratification of the Constitution, American government has gradually become more representative of the population. Unlike the British case, where the electorate was expanded by acts of Parliament (as we saw with the 1832 and 1867 Reform Acts), the expansion of the electorate in the United States has tended to take the form of constitutional amendments.

The Constitution, which in its original form implicitly condoned slavery and did not extend rights to slaves, was significantly altered after the American Civil War (1861–1865). The addition of the Thirteenth, Fourteenth, and Fifteenth Amendments to the Constitution, the so-called Civil War amendments, ended slavery, granted citizenship to the former slaves, and granted the former slaves the right to vote. Similarly, the Twentieth Amendment was approved in 1921, granting women the right to vote after a long struggle for suffrage. In 1971, the Twenty-eighth Amendment gave eighteen-year-olds the right to vote, in response to youth protests that they were eligible for the draft at eighteen, and yet had to wait three more years for the right to vote. These changes have been made largely within the constitutional context that the framers left us. At the beginning, for example, representation for "We the

---

TEXT BOX 2.2
Important Events in the Path of American Democracy

I.   The Philosophical Influences of the Framers of American Democracy
     1512:   Baron de Montesquieu and the doctrine of separated powers.
     1660:   John Locke and the principle of limited government.
III. British Laws and Taxes that Led to the American Declaration of Independence
     1764:   Sugar Act (repealed by Parliament in 1766)
     1765:   Stamp Act (repealed by Parliament in 1766)
     1767:   Townshend Duties (taxes on a number of imported goods, including tea)
     1770:   Boston Massacre
     1773:   Boston Tea Party
     1776:   Declaration of Independence
     1776–81:   War of Independence
     1781–87:   Articles of Confederation
III. The Constitutional Convention
     1787 (May): Representatives convene in Philadelphia.
     1787 (July): Virginia Plan is presented and ultimately rejected.
     1789 (July): Delegates vote on the Constitution.
     1791:   Constitution ratified by the states.
IV. A Democratizing American Government
     1865–70:   Thirteenth, Fourteenth, and Fifteenth Amendments to the Constitution grant citizenship to former male slaves.
     1920:   Nineteenth Amendment grants women the right to vote.
     1964:   Civil right legislation helps African Americans overcome local restrictions on voting.
     1971:   Twenty-sixth Amendment grants eighteen-year-old Americans the right to vote.

People" was restricted to white men who were at least twenty-five years old. Over time, a series of difficult and contentious events have led to a generalized awakening of the principle of liberty and have resulted in the expansion of American citizenship. Today, the concept of "We the People" includes African Americans, women, and people over the age of eighteen.

Scholars point to the flexible nature of the Constitution as one of the key reasons why American democracy has survived for over two hundred years. The framers developed a document that not only gave structure to the government, but also created a structure for change. When Americans refer to constitutional rights and principles today, they have a somewhat different version in mind than the framers did. Yet the fundamental rights—life, liberty, self-governance—remain intact. American history shows a gradual expansion of those rights to include more varied segments of the population than the framers originally intended.

Conclusion

In line with Mahoney's cautious operationalization of path dependence, this chapter has examined how the impact of past decisions has influenced the creation of a self-reinforcing sequence of subsequent decisions in the United States and in the United Kingdom. It has briefly compared and contrasted the historical paths in Great Britain and in the United States to illustrate how each nation's political history influenced the evolution of its form of democracy, and to explain why the United States adopted a system of checks and balances and Great Britain did not.

It is important to remember that the evolution of political development in Great Britain led that country to reject the notion of a fixed and fundamental set of laws, and to instead adopt the idea of a flexible and sovereign legislative body. This British approach to government holds that it is preferable to accord the legislative body the authority to enact laws in response to the societal needs of the time, rather than be limited by a set of checks and balances detailed in a written constitution. In clear contrast, the American framers rejected the notion of legislative supremacy and sovereignty. Rather, they upheld the concept of checks and balances operating under constitutional law.

A core difference between the British and American systems can be found in their views of the purpose of government. Britain relies on a flexible legislative body to respond to societal needs; the United States advocates limiting government to guarantee individual freedoms and avoid tyranny. As the preceding review of their respective political histories suggests, their distinctive paths are predicated on different foundational ideas and institutional structures: Great Britain was most afraid of despotic tyranny and so concentrated power in the legislature; the United States was not only afraid of despotic tyranny, but also feared any concentration of powers—even in an elected legislature. So the framers of the American Constitution separated powers in a representative system as a method of limiting government; their decision continues to constrain the range of options available to American policy makers, two centuries on.

The intricate design and complex balancing of powers in the Constitution represent a uniquely American contribution to the art of democratic governance. The framers were fearful of tyranny, whether of the one, the few, or the many. To guard against the danger of tyranny, they created a system of separated powers to avoid concentrating powers in the hands of one or a few: they instituted a representative government in order to avoid tyranny of the majority, and limited government and created a system of checks and balances within government in order to avoid both tyranny of the majority and a concentration of power.[58] In the next two chapters, we examine how this path continues to limit policy adoption in the United States.

Notes

1. Terry Lynn Karl, *The Paradox of Plenty: Oil Booms and Petro-States* (Berkeley: University of California Press, 1997), 11. Some of the path-dependence literature offers the concept as a metaphor, to help account for differences among nations. See, for instance, B. Guy Peters, Jon Pierre, et al., "The Politics of Path Dependency: Political Conflict in Historical Institutionalism," *The Journal of Politics* 67, no. 4 (2005): 1275–300; Kathleen Thelen, *How Institutions Evolve: The Political Economy of Skills in Germany, Britain, the United States and Japan* (New York: Cambridge University Press, 2004), especially "The Political Economy of Skills in Comparative Historical Perspective" (1–38) and "Conclusions: Empirical and Theoretical" (278–96).

2. See Paul Pierson, *Politics in Time: History, Institutions, and Social Analysis* (Princeton, NJ: Princeton University Press, 2004), 17–54. He notes that "path-dependence arguments offer an important tool for understanding political dynamics" (52). Also see Paul Pierson, "Increasing Returns, Path Dependence, and the Study of Politics," *American Political Science Review* 94 (2000): 251–67; James Mahoney, "Path Dependence in Historical Sociology," *Theory and Society* 29, no. 4 (2000): 507–48; Kathleen Thelen, "Historical Institutionalism in Comparative Politics," *Annual Review of Political Science* 2 (1999): 369–404; Ellen M. Immergut and Karen M. Anderson, "Historical Institutionalism and West European Politics," *West European Politics* 31, nos. 1/2 (January–March 2008): 345–69.

3. Ian Greener argues in his article "The Potential of Path Dependence in Political Studies," "Path dependence has become, within a relatively short space of time, a widely used concept in social science" (62). Greener notes that there are several criticisms of path dependence; it "lacks a framework for delimiting what elements might comprise a path-dependent system, preventing case comparisons and the possible generation of additional theoretical insights from their use. A number of specific criticisms emerge from the literature that we must consider if we are to use path dependence as a coherent framework in political analysis" (64). Ian Greener, "The Potential of Path Dependence in Political Studies," *Politics* 25, no. 1 (February 2005): 62–72.

4. Mahoney, "Path Dependence," 535. There has also been an effort in the literature to operationalize path dependence in terms of increasing return for past decisions. See, for instance, Pierson, "Increasing Returns."

5. There is a variety of good comparative scholarship on path dependence. See, for instance, Desmond S. King, "The Establishment of Work-Welfare Programs in

the United States and Britain: Politics, Ideas, and Institutions," in *Structuring Politics: Historical Institutionalism in Comparative Perspective*, ed. Sven Steinmo, Kathleen Thelen, and Frank Longstreth, 217–50 (Cambridge: Cambridge University Press, 1992); Wolfgang Streeck and Kathleen Thelen, "Introduction: Institutional Change in Advanced Political Economies," in *Beyond Continuity: Institutional Change in Advanced Political Economies*, ed. Wolfgang Streeck and Kathleen Thelen (Oxford: Oxford University Press, 2005), 1–39; Thelen, "Historical Institutionalism"; Kathleen Thelen and Sven Steinmo, "Historical Institutionalism in Comparative Politics," in *Structuring Politics: Historical Institutionalism in Comparative Perspective*, ed. Sven Steinmo, Kathleen Thelen, and Frank Longstreth (Cambridge: Cambridge University Press, 1992), 1–32; George Tsebelis, "Decision Making in Political Systems: Veto Players in Presidentialism, Parliamentarism, Multicameralism, and Multipartyism," *British Journal of Political Science* 25 (1995): 289–325; G. Alexander, "Institutions, Path Dependence, and Democratic Consolidation," *Journal of Theoretical Politics* 13, no. 3 (2001): 249–70.

6. Samuel P. Huntington, *Political Order in Changing Societies* (New Haven, CT: Yale University Press, 1968; reissued 2006), 93–139.

7. Ibid.

8. For some background on British political history, see B. Kemp, *King and Commons, 1600–1832* (New York: Macmillan, 1957); David Robertson, *Class and the British Electorate* (New York: Basil Blackwell, 1985); Kenneth D. Wald, *Crosses on the Ballot: Patterns of British Voter Alignment since 1885* (Princeton, NJ: Princeton University Press, 1983); and Malcolm Pearce and Geoffrey Stewart, *British Political History, 1867–2001: Democracy and Decline*, 3rd ed. (London: Routledge, 2001).

9. See Huntington, *Political Order in Changing Societies*, 93–139.

10. See useful discussion in Michael L. Mannin, *British Government and Politics: Balancing Europeanization and Independence* (Plymouth, UK: Rowman & Littlefield, 2010), 11–36. Also see Colin Campbell, Harvey Feigenbaum, Ronald Linden, and Helmut Norpoth, eds., *Politics and Government in Europe Today* (Boston: Houghton Mifflin, 1995), 74–75.

11. See Gregory S. Mahler, *Principles of Comparative Politics* (New York: Pearson, 2012), especially chapter 9, "The British Political System." Also, Gregory S. Mahler, *Comparative Politics: An Institutional and Cross-National Approach*, 2nd ed. (Englewood Cliffs, NJ: Prentice Hall, 1995), 106–8.

12. See discussion by Philip Norton, *The British Polity*, 5th ed. (New York: Pearson, 2010), 44. He notes that "the Great Council itself was the precursor of the House of Lords."

13. Anne Boleyn never did provide Henry VIII with a male heir, though their daughter, Elizabeth, became a powerful queen after Henry's death, succeeding her Catholic sister, Mary, Catherine's daughter. For more details on this fascinating time in British history, see Alison Weir, *The Six Wives of Henry VIII* (New York: Grove Press, 1992).

14. See Huntington, *Political Order in Changing Societies*, 93–139.

15. See Mahler, *Comparative Politics*, 107.

16. Leonard Freedman, *Politics and Policy in Britain* (New York: Longman, 1996), 35.

17. Mahler, *Comparative Politics*, 183; Norton, *The British Polity*, 39.

18. Norton, *The British Polity*, 46.

19. See E. P. Thompson, *The Making of the English Working Class* (New York: Pantheon Books, 1964).

20. Norton, *The British Polity*, 46; Freedman, *Politics and Policy in Britain*, 35.

21. See Michael Curtis, *Introduction to Comparative Government*, 4th ed. (New York: Longman, 1997), 38–39.

22. See Herbert M. Levine, *Political Issues Debated: An Introduction to Politics*, 4th ed. (Englewood Cliffs, NJ: Simon and Schuster, 1993).

23. James Q. Wilson, *American Government*, 6th ed. (Lexington, MA: D. C. Heath, 2002), 6.

24. Norton, *The British Polity*, 65–66.

25. Ibid., 67. See also Gillian Peele, *Governing the UK*, 3rd ed. (Oxford: Blackwell, 1995), 1–47.

26. Norton, *The British Polity*, 67.

27. See A. V. Dicey, *Introduction to the Law of the Constitution*, 10th ed. (London: Macmillan, 1959); Walter Bagehot, *The English Constitution* (London: Fontana, 1993) (first published 1867); Ivor Jennings, *The British Constitution*, 5th ed. (Cambridge: Cambridge University Press, 1966); S. A. de Smith and Rodney Brazier, *Constitutional and Administrative Law*, 7th ed. (Harmondsworth, UK: Penguin, 1994); Geoffrey Marshall, *Constitutional Theory* (Oxford: Clarendon Press, 1971).

28. Peele, *Governing the UK*, 24–28.

29. Michael Curtis, *Introduction to Comparative Government*, 38–39.

30. Freedman, *Politics and Policy in Britain*, 120–21.

31. From www.cia.gov/library/publications/the-world-factbook/geos/uk.html.

32. As of 2012, there were approximately 670 life peers, 92 hereditary peers, and 26 clergy in the House of Lords, www.cia.gov/library/publications/the-world-factbook/geos/uk.html.

33. This was part of a compromise between the two parties to form a majority government in the House of Commons. The Liberal Democrats agreed to seat their 57 MPs with the Conservatives 307 MPs. Labour became the opposition, with 258 MPs. The next scheduled elections are to take place five years after the last. Also see Peele, *Governing the UK*, 145–78.

34. The British Speaker in the House of Commons should not be confused with the American Speaker in the House of Representatives. Both the American Speaker and the British prime minister are the leaders of the majority party in their respective legislative bodies.

35. If London is not in your immediate travel plans, C-SPAN regularly broadcasts taped sessions of question time. It is worth tuning in.

36. Freedman, *Politics and Policy in Britain*, 40–41.

37. Alan R. Gitelson, Robert L. Dudley, Melvin J. Dubnick, *American Government* (Boston: Wadsworth, Cengage Advantage Books, 2011), 32.

38. Wilson, *American Government*, 9.

39. See Theodore J. Lowi, Benjamin Ginsberg, and Kenneth A. Shepsle, *American Government*, 12th ed. (New York: W. W. Norton, 2012), especially the discussion in chapter 2. Also see John Kingdon, *America the Unusual* (New York: Worth Publishers, 1999).

40. Thomas E. Patterson, *We the People*, 4th ed. (New York: McGraw-Hill, 2004), 75.

41. Ibid., 41.

42. Although the framers considered an executive *chosen by* the Congress, as Matthew Shugart and John Carey note, the framers never envisioned making an executive *responsible to* the legislature. Matthew Soberg Shugart and John M. Carey, *Presidents and Assemblies: Constitutional Design and Electoral Dynamics* (Cambridge: Cambridge University Press, 1992), 5.

43. Robert A. Dahl, *Pluralist Democracy in the United States: Conflict and Consent* (Chicago: Rand McNally & Company, 1967).

44. Ibid., 80.

45. In contrast, a *positive right* is something the government must give to you, such as the right to a job, or to a minimum standard of living or to an education. Locke's views were especially controversial in seventeenth-century continental Europe, as kings continued to justify their rule as divinely sanctioned. It was possible to publish these ideas in England, however, as Parliament had won the Glorious Revolution in 1688 over the Stuart monarchy, who had sought to justify their rule on the basis of the divine right of kings doctrine.

46. Charles de Secondat, Baron de Montesquieu, *The Spirit of the Laws* (New York: Cambridge University Press, 1989), part 2, book 11, chapter 6.

47. Ibid.

48. James Madison, *Federalist #47*, www.constitution.org/fed/federa47.htm.

49. Harvey Claflin Mansfield, *America's Constitutional Soul* (Baltimore: Johns Hopkins University Press, 1991), 122–23. Also see Bradford P. Wilson and Peter W. Schramm, eds., *Separation of Powers and Good Government* (Lanham, MD: Rowman and Littlefield, 1994). Mansfield's quote is on page 10.

50. The only modification of Locke's original formulation of rights was the insertion of the expression "pursuit of happiness" in the place of "property."

51. Seymour Martin Lipset, *American Exceptionalism: A Double-Edged Sword* (New York: Norton, 1996), 39. Also see Graham K. Wilson, *Only in America? American Politics in Comparative Perspective* (Chatham, NJ: Chatham House, 1998).

52. James L. Sundquist, *Constitutional Reform and Effective Government* (Washington, DC: Brookings Institution, 1992). Also see Philip Norton, *The British Polity*, 3rd ed. (New York: Longman, 1994), 48, where he notes that the situation of apparent divided powers in England, in which the monarch served as the executive and the parliament as the legislature, influenced the framers in Philadelphia to devise a system of executive and legislative powers.

53. See the useful discussion in Lawrence S. Graham et al., *Politics and Government: A Brief Introduction to the Politics of the United States, Great Britain, France,*

Germany, Russia, Eastern Europe, Japan, Mexico, and the Third World (Chatham, NJ: Chatham House Publishers, 1994), 1–7.

54. Dahl, *Pluralist Democracy*, 111–12.

55. Sundquist, *Constitutional Reform and Effective Government*.

56. Geoffrey R. Stone, "The Supreme Court and the 2012 Election," *Huffington Post*, 13 August 2012. www.huffingtonpost.com/geoffrey-r-stone/the-supreme-court-and-the_b_1773347.html.

57. See Karen O'Connor, *No Neutral Ground* (Boulder, CO: Westview, 1996).

58. See David Samuels, "Separation of Powers," in *The Oxford Handbook of Comparative Politics*, ed. Carles Boix and Susan Stokes, 703–26 (New York: Oxford University Press, 2007); R. Kent Weaver and Leslie Pal, eds., *Government Taketh Away: Political Institutions and Loss Imposition in Canada and the United States* (Washington, DC: Georgetown University Press, 2003), 1–40; Donald L. Horowitz, "Electoral Systems: A Primer for Decision Makers," *Journal of Democracy* 14, no. 4 (October 2003): 113–27.

3

Agenda Setting and Agenda Control

Case One: A Legislative History of the 1994 Republican Contract with America

Gingrich seems to think of himself as a kind of Prime Minister, chosen by the House of Representatives, as a U.S. equivalent of the British Parliament. Since, under the Constitution, he cannot bring down the government, he appears ready to act a kind of "counter government."

—Eugene J. McCarthy

The 104th Congress came in like a lion and went out like a lamb.

—Cokie Roberts

THIS BOOK MAKES THE ARGUMENT that institutions matter. Path dependency implies that choices made long ago have an effect on today's decisions. In the United States, the framers decided to create a government that separates and blends powers, guaranteeing minority rights in a system of majority rule. The system is designed to limit expansive, far-reaching, or hasty policy decisions.

To illustrate these themes, we offer two in-depth case studies. The first case, the Contract with America of 1994, is an apt illustration of how the system usually works: an expansive legislative package was proposed, considered and largely failed. And this case is particularly intriguing, because Congress and its leadership acted like a parliament and prime minister. As we shall see, however, the separation of powers quickly stopped parliamentary-style comprehensive change.

The second case, the case of healthcare reform under President Obama, is an example of broad, comprehensive change that *did* happen. Despite all the checks in the system, a far-reaching healthcare policy was enacted. But the passage of the Affordable Care Act was far from easy, and the twists and turns on the way to its enactment illustrate how checks and balances (and legislative and parliamentary maneuvering) put roadblocks in the way of legislation. In other words, the exception proves the rule. As we consider these two cases, it is important to note that the first one examines an entire legislative program, and the second examines a single policy. In the United States, coalitions are built around one policy at a time. In parliamentary democracies, coalitions are built prior to legislative consideration, as part of forming the government. Coalitions in the United States, then, are more fragile and short-lived. It is difficult enough to hold on to a coalition long enough to pass a bill; as we shall see, it is next to impossible to build and maintain a coalition to support a broad legislative agenda consisting of several bills. In both cases, it is also important to note that it is easier to create a change in policy than it is to change the way things are done, something that both the Republicans in 1994, and President Obama in 2008 attempted to do. The remainder of this chapter examines in depth the process of enacting the 1994 Contract with America; in the following chapter, we turn to the 2010 Affordable Care Act.

The 1994 Contract with America

The 1994 midterm legislative elections marked a watershed event in American political history. Running on a ten-point legislative agenda known as the "Contract with America," the Republican Party gained control of both the House of Representatives and the Senate for the first time since 1954. When the 104th Congress convened in January of 1995, all eyes turned to the new Speaker of the House, Newt Gingrich, who had played a leading role in the design of the Contract. In a flurry of activity during the congressional session's first one hundred days, Gingrich's leadership resulted in the House of Representatives approving nine of the Contract's ten proposals. In spite of this rapid legislative work, however, most of the Contract's legislative initiatives had not been enacted into federal law as Congress adjourned for summer recess. Why not? What was going on in Washington? Why did the American political system appear to be so unresponsive?

This chapter—in keeping with the comparative public policy literature on political, cultural, and institutional constraints on policy making—will examine the role that the framers' institutional constraints on governmental activity played in the stalling of the 1994 Republican Contract with America. Following our discussion on the 1994 Republican Contract with America, we will find a similar institutional dynamic in the case of President Obama's experience with healthcare reform in the next chapter. Both cases illustrate the various ways that the constitutional system of checks and balances constrains policy makers, including the separation of powers and the legislative process.[1]

Introduction to the 104th Congress

27 September 1994: On a beautiful early fall day, more than 350 Republican congressional candidates lined the steps of the United States Capitol. The group included both current members of the House of Representatives (incumbents) and others trying to gain a seat in the House (challengers). There was more than a sense of optimism among the group; there was almost a sense of euphoria. These men and women had gathered in the warm fall sun to make a dramatic statement. They were trying to wrest control of the House from what they saw as its Democratic stranglehold, and they were doing so on a conservative party platform that essentially nationalized the election. The 367 Republicans who signed the Contract promised that they would debate and vote on a ten-point legislative agenda within the first hundred days of Congress. Further, they told their constituents, "If we break the Contract, throw us out." In an era when elections had been criticized for being too focused on local issues, the Republican candidates brought forth a national agenda. In a time when the public was fed up with gridlock in Congress, the Republicans promised swift action. And in a time when the country seemed to be moving toward the middle, the Republican Contract pulled the political debate to the far right.

The sense of euphoria that was just beneath the surface on that beautiful September day emerged in full force just six weeks later, when the Republicans swept the congressional elections. For the first time in forty years, the Republican Party won the majority of seats in the House. They also took control of the Senate, bringing back the "divided government" that had been a mainstay of American politics throughout the 1970s and 1980s. Only this time, it was the Democrats who had the presidency and the Republicans who controlled Congress. For the Democrats, the election results were staggering. "When the returns were in, dozens of Democratic incumbents were swept away, while not one Republican House member, senator or governor was defeated."[2] Not only that, some of the Democrats who lost were among the most powerful players in Congress, including Speaker Thomas Foley, who was the first sitting speaker in 130 years to be voted out by his constituents. Only two years earlier, the Democrats had been filled with a similar sense of euphoria as they finally gained control of the White House

IMAGE 3.1
House Republican leader Newt Gingrich opens a ceremony in front of Capitol Hill on
27 September 1994 to present the Contract with America to the American people. It
contains a ten-point reform program that a Republican majority would seek to enact
in the first hundred days of the 104th Congress. © Ira Schwarz/Reuters/Corbis.

for the first time in twelve years. Now, they faced a weakened and relatively
unpopular president and a Congress dominated by the opposing party.
In Washington, it seemed as if the world had been turned upside down.
Although the 2010 election had similar results, with Republicans gaining a
majority in the House in a midterm election with a democratic president,
the 1994 election was still more dramatic, given that the Democrats had
held a majority in the House since 1954.

Not surprisingly, the Republicans seized the moment with vigor. Having
run for reelection on a national platform that had received intense media
coverage, the House Republicans were quick to claim that they had a mandate for change. In fact, "the 'Contract' proved to have far more signifi-
cance after the election than before it, serving as the key organizing force
for the newly minted majority."[3] Elected politicians often claim to have a
"mandate" for their policies, but this time it was different. The Republicans
had an actual document with specific details; their mandate was almost
palpable. Conservative commentator Charles Krauthammer summed up
the Republican position in 1994: "Having intentionally nationalized the

campaign on this program, the Republicans have acquired the mandate to enact it."[4] The Republicans had an agenda, and they had control. Nothing could stop them from making their Contract into law. Right? Well, let's fast-forward for a moment to 1996, as the 104th Congress came to a close. The Republicans had had two years to enact the Contract; one might think that it would have become the law of the land. In fact, only three major provisions of the Contract had been signed into law: the line-item veto, welfare reform, and the elimination of unfunded federal mandates (requirements that the federal government imposed on states without reimbursement).[5]

Welcome to the World of Checks and Balances

What on earth happened? How could those jubilant fall days of 1994 have led to such limited legislative success? Welcome to the world of checks and balances. In fact, and as we saw in chapter 2, the framers of the Constitution specifically set out to create a system that would thwart legislative initiatives such as the Contract with America. Obviously, they couldn't have had the Contract in mind when they wrote the Constitution, but they were fearful of debate that was ruled by passion, and instead tried to institutionalize deliberation.

What happened to the Contract, first of all, was that the Senate (whose Republicans had *not* run on the Contract) refused to be rushed by the flurry of activity in the House. The framers of the Constitution required that, in order for a bill to become law, it must pass both chambers of Congress (the House and Senate) in identical form. Second, the president also balked at going along with everything that was coming out of the Republican Congress. And, since the Constitution gives him power to veto legislation, even if the House managed to get the Senate to agree to a particular bill, there was no guarantee that the president would sign it. The Constitution also gives Congress the power to override a presidential veto, but makes it more difficult than passage of legislation. For a bill to pass Congress, there must be a simple majority in both houses. To override a presidential veto, the bill must receive a two-thirds majority, which is much more difficult to obtain. Despite their majority in both houses, the Republicans did not constitute two-thirds of the members of either house, meaning that they would have to convince Democrats to vote to override the veto. Many Democrats in Congress were doing everything in their power to delay or postpone consideration of items on the Contract and were not about to vote for veto overrides. (Very optimistic Republicans had been hoping to gain a "veto-proof" majority of sixty-six seats in the Senate, which would give them a two-thirds majority and eliminate the necessity to get Democrats to vote for veto overrides.)

The Framers' Fears of the Tyranny of the Majority
and the 1994 Republican Contract with America

About now you might be protesting, "But this is gridlock! Surely the framers of the Constitution didn't intend to create gridlock!" While the framers didn't exactly go about trying to create gridlock, they realized that legislative inaction could be a reasonable price to pay for the elimination of what they thought was a greater evil: tyranny. "How can the Contract with America represent tyranny," you might be thinking, "when the electorate clearly voted for the Republicans?" In fact, as we discussed in chapter 2, the framers were as much afraid of tyranny of the majority as they were of tyranny of the few or of one person. Let us briefly review the framers' fear of tyranny in terms of the Republican Contract with America.

To start, James Madison, in *Federalist No. 10*, describes the evils of a "faction," which could lead to tyranny of the many: "By a faction I understand a number of citizens, whether amounting to a majority or minority of the whole, who are united and actuated by some common impulse of passion, or of interest, adverse to the rights of citizens or to the permanent and aggregate interests of the community."

In other words, a faction is a group united by a common interest, an interest that is in opposition to the public good. While Republicans and Democrats can have endless debates over whether or not the Contract was in fact "adverse to the rights of citizens," that is actually beside the point. In creating the general principles of government, the framers had to establish broad protections against large-scale political movements, and had no way to predict whether such movements would be good or bad. Madison explains in *Federalist No. 10* that a minority faction would be easy to control, while a majority faction would create more difficulties:

> If a faction consists of less than a majority, relief is supplied by the republican principle, which enables the majority to defeat its sinister views by regular vote: It may clog the administration, it may convulse the society; but it will be unable to execute and mask its violence under the forms of the Constitution. When a majority is included in a faction, the form of popular government on the other hand enables it to sacrifice to its ruling passion or interest, both the public good and the rights of other citizens.

A majority faction, according to Madison, has great potential for harm in a democratic system. If an idea that is contrary to the public good takes hold of the majority of citizens, then the public good could be sacrificed to the will of the majority. How, then, can we control a majority faction? The framers of the Constitution believed that only a "republican" form of government could do this. They weren't referring to what we know today as the Republican Party; instead the framers meant a representative form of government. Elected representation, according to Madison, could eliminate the threats of a faction, by allowing representatives "to refine and enlarge the public views, by passing them through the medium of a chosen body of citizens, whose wisdom may best discern the true interest of their country, and whose patriotism and love of justice, will be least likely to sacrifice it to temporary or partial considerations."[6]

Madison and the framers were also afraid of tyranny within government itself, as Madison's *Federalist No. 51* makes clear. "You must first enable the government to control the governed; and in the next place, oblige it to control itself. A dependence on the people is no doubt the primary control on the government; but experience has taught mankind the necessity of auxiliary precautions."

What are these auxiliary precautions? The very checks and balances we discussed a few paragraphs ago. In *Federalist No. 51*, Madison says that "the great security against a gradual concentration of the several powers in the same department, consists in giving to those who administer each department, the necessary constitutional means, and personal motives, to resist encroachments of the others." By "departments," Madison was referring to the institutions of government; thus, the president can "resist encroachments" from Congress by exercising the veto, the Senate can resist encroachments from the House by refusing to pass identical legislation, and both houses can resist encroachments from the president by overriding his vetoes.

The framers forced public opinion to be muted in two ways. First, Congress, as an elected body, would deliberate over issues that had sparked the passions of the people, and second, the system of checks and balances would create a further brake on initiatives led by one part of government. As such, they knowingly made it difficult for legislation to pass, and created a system that inevitably thwarted House Republicans' plans for the Contract with America. In fact, the architects of the Contract were well aware of the institutional obstacles they faced in passing the legislation. That is why their campaign promise was *not* passage of the items that were part of the Contract, but merely bringing them to a vote in the House, a much more achievable goal.

The history of the Contract with America is an apt illustration of our central dilemma: that the rule of the majority is often impeded by constitutional protections of minority rights. The remainder of this chapter will examine the history of the Contract, by:

- exploring the background against which the Contract was developed,
- examining the actual tenets of the Contract itself, and
- taking a look at what actually happened in Congress as the Contract was being debated.

Throughout, readers will note the frustrations of both the majority and minority parties. Chapter 5 will imagine what might have happened if the United States functioned under a parliamentary system. For now, let us turn to the congressional system in existence.

Background: Where Did the Contract Come From?

Imagine that you are a Republican representative in 1994. You have been part of the minority party for as long as you can remember. The last time the Republicans held the majority was in 1954, which was certainly before you were elected and possibly even before you were born. What has this minority status meant to you? Most likely it has meant immense frustration, as you have watched your legislative proposals die before even being considered and seen even your attempts at amending Democratic proposals thwarted by Democrats' limitations on amendments to bills on the floor. You have been excluded from the decision-making process, perhaps even cut out of important meetings by Democratic representatives. From your perspective, at least, a form of the tyranny of the majority has been alive and well in the Democratic-controlled Congress for the past forty years! Your fellow Republicans, who have experienced similar setbacks in their attempts at legislating, share your frustration.

Aside from having your party gain control of Congress, what would be at the top of your wish list? Probably two things: First, you would wish for a change in the way the House works. You would like to see an easing of the rules, so that your voice could be heard, your proposals considered. Second, you would probably have some pet legislative ideas that you would like to see enacted, probably some conservative policies that don't have a chance in a Democratic Congress. In fact, these were the two major goals of the architects of what eventually became the Republican Contract with America.

The first goal, changing the rules, was shared by some frustrated Democrats. Congressional Scholar Roger H. Davidson notes that:

> Agitation for changing the way Congress does its business came to a head in the 1990s. There were tensions between senior leaders and junior members, between appropriators and authorizers, between House and Senate members. Most troubling was the escalating combat in the House between an entrenched Democratic majority and a restless Republican minority.[7]

During the 103rd Congress, while Democrats still held the majority, Republicans submitted a proposal to change House rules. Proposed by Gerald Solomon (R-NY), the "Mandate for Change in the People's House" listed forty-three reforms to change the way the House did business: from floor and committee procedures to relations with the president. Although many rank-and-file Democrats supported at least some of the changes, the House leadership was obviously not pleased with the proposal, which ultimately failed. However, Democratic leaders had been persuaded to appoint a Joint Committee on the Organization of Congress, which considered the proposals and held hearings on congressional procedures. The hearings drew attention to the procedural problems in Congress, and strengthened the Republicans resolve.[8]

In early 1994, as the midterm elections were drawing near, Republicans began to work on a national campaign strategy. House Republicans got together for a conference in Salisbury, Maryland, on a snowy February weekend. The purpose of the conference was to develop and refine a legislative agenda for the 104th Congress. Members of the conference defined five major goals of what they called their "vision" of America:

1. Individual liberty
2. Economic opportunity
3. Limited government
4. Personal responsibility
5. Security at home and abroad[9]

The goals of this conference eventually evolved into the Contract with America. Representatives Newt Gingrich and Dick Armey, who stood to gain much by a Republican victory (they became speaker and majority leader, respectively), pushed to develop a platform on which all Republicans could run. The decisions about what to include as the major planks of the platform were largely based on public opinion poll results. The Republicans chose to highlight those conservative issues that resonated with voters, and avoid more controversial subjects, such as abortion and school prayer. Eleven working groups made up of Republicans in Congress put together the ten planks, which were all versions of bills that had already been proposed by Republicans, but had been frozen out by the Democratic majority.[10] Somewhere along the way, Kerry Knott, executive director of the House Republican Conference, identified the ten bills as a "contract." As the document was being drafted, a preface was added that included eight procedural reforms initially proposed in the "Mandate for Change in the People's House."

The Contract with America was not the first time Republicans had attempted to use a contract as an electoral tool. In fact, Ronald Reagan went to the Capitol in 1980 to sign a similar contract with Republican candidates for Congress as he campaigned for the presidency.[11] The main difference was that the election of 1980, which resulted in a Republican president and Republican Senate, sent a Democratic majority back to the House of Representatives. The 1980 contract, while it spelled out Republican goals for governing, could not become the legislative tool that the 1994 contract became. Democrats in the House were able to maintain more control of the legislative agenda because of their majority status in the 97th Congress. While Reagan was successful in defining legislative priorities, the Democratic House was able to block some of his initiatives. Republicans used the idea of a contract in subsequent elections, although the contracts did not get significant press attention until 1994, when it appeared that the party might be able to take control of Congress.

There is another important caveat to remember about the Contract with America: While it defined the activities of the 104th Congress, it did not necessarily define the election in the minds of voters. Even with as much fanfare as it received, the majority of Americans were unfamiliar with the Contract in November of 1994. And some Democrats believed that without the Contract, the Republicans could have won even more seats in the House. In some districts, the voters who were aware of the Contract were more familiar with the Democrats' negative interpretation of it.[12] On the other hand, the Contract mobilized Republican candidates; moreover, voters, whether or not they were aware of the Contract itself, were able to differentiate between Republican and Democratic views of government. Shortly after the election, the *Washington Post* noted that "surveys clearly show Americans intended to seize the reins of government from Democrats and hand them over to Republicans."[13] The Contract, which may not have directly impacted voters' decisions, did help to create a national identity for the Republican Party. "Few would suggest that the Contract itself was the most significant factor in the GOP's historic gains. But it appears to have benefited Republicans overall by providing a national agenda and offering challengers a specific program to promote if they did not already have one."[14]

The Contract with America is particularly useful as a case study, because it provided a national platform on which one party could run and gave rise to a clearly identified, nationally known party leader in the person of Newt Gingrich. Both of these factors made the American congressional election of 1994 look very similar to an election in a parliamentary system, in which party is paramount, voters are shown clear differences between and among parties, and legislative leadership comes directly from party leadership. As we shall see, while the election superficially resembled a parliamentary election, the legislative process itself remained firmly rooted in the American constitutional system.

The Contract with America

Before getting into a discussion of how the Contract fared in Congress, let us step back for a few moments and examine the document itself. The Contract with America contained a preface that stated its purpose and proposed some changes in the way Congress worked. It also presented ten major legislative planks, which included recommendations for change in several substantive policy areas. The document emphasized the possibility of a new Republican majority in the House with the upcoming 1994 election; this new majority would "transform the way Congress works," reduce the size of government, and "restore accountability to Congress." The preface promised that if Republicans won the majority in the House, they would bring eight procedural reforms to a vote on the first day of the 104th Congress.[15] Following is a list of those procedural reforms:

1. Require all laws that apply to the rest of the country apply to Congress as well. (For years, Congress had exempted itself and its employees from most workplace and antidiscrimination laws.)
2. Select an independent auditing firm to audit Congress for waste, fraud, and abuse.
3. Cut the number of House committees and cut committee staff by one-third.
4. Limit the terms of all committee chairs.
5. Ban casting of proxy votes. (Previously, the rules of the House had allowed an individual committee member to authorize another member of the committee to vote in his or her absence. "Proxy" votes are convenient for members of Congress, who often have to be in several places at the same time, but they also mean that committee meetings are sometimes sparsely attended.)
6. Require committee meetings to be open to the public.
7. Require a three-fifths majority vote to pass a tax increase. (In Congress, most bills are passed with a simple majority vote—half plus one. A three-fifths majority would make tax increases much harder to pass.)
8. Implement zero-base budgeting. (Zero-base budgeting is an accounting tool that essentially requires all budgets to start from zero funding, rather than from last year's "base" budget, which is the usual starting point for governmental budgets.)

While these were by no means the only procedural changes favored by Republicans, the eight reforms would have a dramatic impact on day-to-day activities in the House. By voting on them on the first day, Republicans intended to demonstrate their intention to change the way Congress works.

The substantive portion of the Contract is contained in its ten major planks, which Republicans promised to bring to a vote on the floor of the House within the first hundred days of the 104th Congress. Although listed as "acts," the ten planks do not translate into ten pieces of legislation. Several planks included items that became two or more bills. Following is a list of the ten issues presented in the Contract:

1. *The Fiscal Responsibility Act* had two parts, both of which entailed amendments to the Constitution: the balanced-budget amendment and the line-item veto.
2. *The Taking Back Our Streets Act*, also known as the anti-crime package, eventually was divided into several bills dealing with victim restitution, the exclusionary rule, prison construction, and law enforcement.
3. *The Personal Responsibility Act* dealt with welfare reform, both giving more discretion to the states and providing restrictions on eligibility.
4. *The Family Reinforcement Act* provided tax breaks for families and the elderly, child-support enforcement, and penalties for child pornography.
5. *The American Dream Restoration Act* repealed the marriage tax penalty (married couples pay more in taxes than they would if single and making two incomes), and established a tax credit for children.
6. *The National Security Restoration Act* prohibited foreign (U.N.) command of U.S. troops, prohibited using defense cuts to finance social programs, and proposed developing an anti–ballistic missile system.
7. *The Senior Fairness Act* would raise the Social Security earnings limit (under which seniors who earn over a certain amount of money lose a percentage of their Social Security benefit) and also repeal the 1993 tax increases on Social Security benefits.
8. *The Job Creation and Wage Enhancement Act* gave incentives to small businesses, cut the capital gains tax, and eliminated "unfunded mandates" (requiring states or businesses to engage in specified activities without reimbursing them).
9. *The Common Sense Legal Reforms Act* was designed to discourage litigation. It would limit punitive damages, institute "loser pays" rules, and limit product liability.
10. *The Citizen Legislatures Act* would limit the terms of both senators and representatives.

Clearly, there was some overlap among the ten planks; for example, tax breaks for the elderly are addressed in both the Family Reinforcement Act and the Senior Citizens Fairness Act. In addition, several planks contained two or more bills; for example, the Fiscal Responsibility Act consisted of both the balanced-budget amendment and the line-item veto, which were considered as two separate pieces of legislation. These anomalies later made scoring of the Contract difficult. If the House passed the line-item veto, but not the balanced-budget amendment (which actually happened), would plank number one be considered a win or a loss? Nonetheless, the fact that the Contract included such detailed legislative initiatives gave the newly elected Republicans a focal point in Congress. Plus, it provided a scorecard, a way to keep track of how well Congress was doing. Although the Contract only promised to bring these items to a vote in the House, Republicans, Democrats, and the media all eventually used the scorecard to judge the issues based on final passage into law.

Note that the Democrats did not have their own contract, at least not in terms of a specific, detailed agenda. Scoring for the Democrats would be simpler—they could be judged successful if they kept the Republicans from passing items on the Contract. Fortunately for the Democrats, our constitutional system makes it easier to keep the status quo than to implement sweeping changes. This also illustrates a difference between a parliamentary system and our congressional system. In a parliamentary system, the opposition party (similar to what we would call the minority) is a "party-in-waiting" that develops and promotes an alternative legislative agenda, and is ready to implement it at any given moment, should there be a vote of no confidence to topple the majority party. Clearly, the Democrats had an agenda they wished to pursue, should they regain the majority (which could only occur at regularly scheduled elections; e.g., every two years). However, their agenda was not set forth in a written document, and, knowing that they had to face at least two years of a Republican Congress, their purpose was to block the majority party's legislation, rather than to promote their own. Of course, their role was similar to the role the Republicans had played in the previous Congress. The minority party in our system is put in the position of creating obstacles to the majority party, regardless of which party is in power.

The First Hundred Days of the 104th Congress

Let us now turn to the Contract's fate in the legislative process. Having won the elections of 1994 in a sweep, the Republicans wasted no time in flexing their newfound muscles. "The voters gave Republicans their first Senate majority in eight years, their first majority of governors since 1960, and their first House majority since 1954—a breadth of power few if any active

Republican politicians can recall."[16] To see what happened to the Republican legislative agenda, let's take a snapshot picture of three different days during those much-discussed first hundred days: Day One, or 4 January, when the Republicans took over the reins of Congress for the first time in fifty years; Day Fifty, midway through the first hundred days; and Day One Hundred, the deadline that the Republicans had set for themselves. For each day, we will mark the progress of the Contract and note the obstacles that had been set in its way and its successes.

Day One: Let the Hundred Days Begin

On the first day of the 104th Congress, an ebullient Newt Gingrich takes over the Speakership, to the raucous cheers of House Republicans and observers in the gallery. After the swearing-in and speeches, the House gets down to business, starting by changing some of the procedural rules that the Republicans felt had bogged down the Democratic Congress. The day ended well after 2 a.m., setting the stage for the long workdays to come.

The first day of the 104th Congress began officially at noon on 4 January, when the House chaplain opened the session with a prayer. All of the newly elected and reelected representatives were gathered in the House chamber on the south side of the Capitol building. Many had family members with them: husbands, wives, parents, and, reflecting the relative youth of the "freshman" class of Congress, lots of babies and children. The Republicans—both freshmen and incumbents—were ecstatic at their newfound majority status; in stark contrast, Democrats' faces reflected the gloom they felt at having been displaced from the locus of power. At about quarter to one, the vote for Speaker began. As the clerk called the roll in alphabetical order, members announced their preferences: Republicans voted for Gingrich, and most Democrats voted for Richard Gephardt (D-MO), although some voted "present" in a form of protest over a candidate they felt represented Democratic failures. At 1:17 p.m., the roll call was completed, and, to no one's surprise, Newt Gingrich had been elected as Speaker of the House—the first Republican Speaker in forty years. Republicans in the House and in the visitors' gallery erupted in boisterous applause. The new Speaker received a standing ovation, which repeated itself when he had made his way through the crowded House and arrived at the Speaker's podium. In contrast, a grim minority leader, Richard Gephardt—who had been the Speaker under the Democratic majority—was now responsible for transferring power away from his party and to the opposition. As the applause died down, Gephardt managed to joke: "This is not a moment I've been waiting for." In a testament to the system's peaceful transitions of power, Gephardt then announced, "With resignation but with resolve, I hereby end forty years of

Democratic rule of this House." Handing the gavel to Gingrich, Gephardt said, "You are now my Speaker. Let the great debate begin."[17]

The great debate began almost immediately. After Gingrich completed a thirty-minute speech, he was sworn in by the "dean" of the House (Democrat John Dingell of Michigan, the House's longest-serving member at that time—a role he continued to play in 2013). Gingrich, as the official Speaker, then administered the oath of office to the rest of the representatives, and the House got down to work. The first order of business was consideration of the rule changes specified in the preface to the Contract. The Contract had specified that these changes would be passed on the first day of the 104th Congress, and Republican leaders, intent on keeping that promise, prohibited amendments to the rules package. In a striking reversal of roles, Democrats loudly protested the prohibition, saying that the Republicans were locking them out of the process. Of course, when Republicans were in the minority, they had said the same thing about consideration of Democratic bills. In fact, Republicans had vowed to allow a more open amending process when they took over Congress. But, as a news account reported, adhering to the Contract was more important to Republicans than opening up the amendment process, at least on the first day.

> The Democrats began January 4 by saying the Republicans were hypocrites for bringing the package up under a procedure that prevented amendments, a practice the GOP had promised to curtail after complaining about it for years in the minority. But the Contract with America had committed the GOP to enacting its institutional measures on the first day of the session, and its leaders said they did not want to be denied by dilatory tactics or prolonged debate on Democratic amendments.[18]

For their part, Democrats borrowed from Republican practices, and complained that they were being held back from creating broader reform. Rep. David Bonior (D-MI) proposed several amendments, including one that would impose limits on book royalties (clearly aimed at Gingrich, who had accepted an advance of several millions of dollars for a book deal).

> In the sometimes acrimonious back and forth over who is more committed to reform, opening day continued a contest that has been under way for several years, only the parties have switched roles since the election. Now it is the Democrats, whose leaders once quashed efforts to radically restructure the institution, who contend that the majority party is stifling reform in Congress; and it is the Republicans, just after taking power, who must defend their operations.[19]

Opening day was taken up by legislative activity on the rule-change measures: debating and voting on procedural motions and then debating and voting on actual legislation. At the end of the day, the Republican House had voted in several sweeping changes to the way it does business: it eliminated some committees, changed the jurisdiction of others, eliminated six hundred (mostly Democratic) staff positions, ended proxy voting, required open committee meetings, limited individual representatives from holding committee and subcommittee chairs for more than three consecutive terms or the Speakership for more than four, required a supermajority for tax increases, and required an audit of the House's financial records. At 2:24 a.m. on Thursday, 5 January, the House adjourned, after a grueling fourteen-and-a-half-hour workday.

At the end of the day, the House had kept the promise made in the preface to the Contract with America. In so doing, it had reversed a years-long trend toward decentralization of power. Since 1974, when another famous freshmen class arrived in Congress (the so-called Watergate Babies, who were elected on a reform agenda in protest of the Nixon administration), power had been devolving away from the Speaker and toward committees and subcommittees. The 104th Congress ended that trend, placing more power in the hands of the Speaker, and limiting the powers of committee and subcommittee chairs. Despite the somewhat acrimonious debate, the House Republicans won every vote on that first day, and for the most part, Democrats voted in favor of the Republican reforms.

One day down, ninety-nine to go.

Day Fifty: Exhaustion Sets In

Midway to the hundred-day mark, Republicans in the House have passed only four of the ten planks of the platform, in addition to the procedural reforms outlined in the preface. Lawmakers are exhausted: Representatives as well as their staffs complain of long days, lack of sleep, and the otherwise frenetic pace of the "Contract" Congress. Now not just satisfied with voting on the Contract, Republicans are beginning to focus on getting it signed into law.

As 22 February dawned—the midway point of the first hundred days—Republicans in the House were able to claim some major legislative accomplishments, but they had a lot of work still ahead of them. After the marathon first day, Republicans had also been successful in passing a bill to end Congress's exemption from workplace laws. The hectic pace of the first day continued, as Congress abandoned the traditional break between opening day and the State of the Union address, and shortened the President's Day recess from its usual ten days to five.[20] In January and February, the House took up some of the more popular provisions in the Contract: the balanced-budget amendment and line-item veto (which together made up the first plank of the Contract), the crime bill (which was split into six smaller bills), the national security bill, and the unfunded-mandates legislation. Republican unity during consideration of these bills was extraordinary: in 73 of the first 139 roll call votes, Republicans were unanimous. On only 13 votes did more than ten Republicans defect to the other side.[21] Such statistics drew comparisons to Congress in the 1980s, when congressional Republicans were called "Reagan Robots" for showing unwavering support during votes on administration proposals. Remarkably, House Republicans in the 104th Congress were even more unified than the so-called Reagan Robots. Their majority status was clearly giving energy to the Republicans. "Republicans' unity is an illustration of a phenomenon familiar to political scientists: New majorities tend to be cohesive because the euphoria of newly acquired power is a strong unifying force."[22]

For their part, Democrats were adjusting to their minority status, which had taken them by surprise and for which they were completely unprepared.[23] Generally, liberal Democrats chose to work against the Republicans by offering "amendments designed to draw sharp distinctions between the parties rather than to lure Republicans to cross party lines."[24] On many votes, however, Democrats chose to cross party lines to go along with the Contract legislation. Republicans defected from the leadership on only a handful of occasions, and only once did they actually kill a Contract provision: on 15 February, twenty-four Republicans decided to vote with Democrats to eliminate the anti–ballistic missile defense provision. In the end, Republican leaders decided that strict adherence to the specifics of the Contract was less important than passage of legislation, and so gave in on this occasion and others to demands for compromise from within the party's ranks.

Day Fifty was a time for reflection, albeit a brief one. The GOP conference held a rally in the Cannon House Building Caucus Room. Speaking to that rally, Rep. John Boehner (R-OH) said, "We are changing America for the better just as we promised we would."[25] Representatives and staffers waved American flags and cheered. Although Republicans were pleased with their successes in the first fifty days, they also knew that they had been considering some of the most popular bills in the Contract, the ones most likely to gain bipartisan support. The second fifty days would be filled with more acrimonious debate as the House considered more contentious issues, such as welfare reform and term limits. Tax-reduction legislation, although popular, held its own perils, because any reduction in revenues would have to be offset by a concomitant decrease in spending. Spending cuts are always infinitely more difficult to pass than tax cuts. In addition, the House was also beginning to feel the reins being drawn in on the revolution by the Senate, which is a more deliberative body, and, in any case, was not inclined to go along easily with every House measure. Bills were already being slowed down by Senate consideration. In the first few weeks of February, House Republicans were operating at a breakneck pace, while the Senate was taking its time. "In the time House leaders have allotted for the line-item veto, several crime bills, a national security measure and regulatory reform over the next three weeks, the Senate will be debating just one thing: a constitutional amendment to balance the budget."[26]

This breakneck pace was beginning to take its toll on both members and staff. As the first fifty days were drawing to a close, House committees struggled to meet deadlines for legislation set by House leadership. Committee consideration of health, environmental, and safety regulations, for example, went into the wee hours of the morning.[27] Democrats (and some Republicans) began to complain about the cost of such a frenetic pace. According to the *Washington Post*, "critics are also beginning to notice frayed edges: sloppy legislation, uninformed debate and unseemly willingness to take on gargantuan tasks with little or no forethought."[28] The long days were immensely physically tiring as well. Staff and representatives regularly worked fourteen- or fifteen-hour days, getting little sleep, and eating a lot of junk food. (Imagine if the intensity of exam week lasted for one hundred days, and you get an idea of how exhausted they were.) Bad health habits inevitably led to irritability, lack of concentration, and illness, as many staffers and members came down with severe colds. Even Newt Gingrich came down with the flu shortly after the halfway mark in the first hundred days was reached.

An exhausted House of Representatives looked forward to 13 April, if only for a chance for a vacation.

Day One Hundred: The Reality of Checks and Balances

In the week of 3 April, with all but one of the Contract's planks having been voted on by the House, the time is ripe for the Republicans to celebrate, and celebrate they do. Events at the Capitol include several circus elephants performing on the East Plaza, a parody of Newt Gingrich performed by comedian Chris Farley, a video of the original "signing of the Contract" during the 1994 election, and speeches by several leaders, including, of course, Newt Gingrich. In a final ecstatic note, on Friday, 7 April, the House votes on the last plank of the Contract: the tax-reduction bill, finishing up the Contract legislation on Day Ninety-four, before their actual deadline. Newt Gingrich wraps up the week by addressing the public on prime-time national television, something that no Speaker has ever done before.[29] Still exhausted but happy, Republicans vow NOT to come up with a contract for the next hundred days. Their happiness is muted, however, by the knowledge that only one of the Contract's planks has actually been signed into law.[30]

The morning of 5 April dawned bright and sunny, a spring replica of the beautiful fall day that—was it only six months earlier?—had marked the signing of Contract with America. Now, although it was still more than a week away from 13 April, the actual hundred-day mark, the Republicans were beginning to celebrate. Barnum and Bailey was marking its 125th anniversary, and Republicans had invited the circus to bring its elephants to the East Plaza of the capitol, where the animals performed in unison, prompting comparison to the unified front the Republicans (whose symbol is the elephant) had presented throughout the first three months. On 7 April (Day Ninety-Four), with a last gasp of energy, the Republicans passed a tax reform measure, the last piece of the Contract legislation. Shortly after, the celebration began in earnest with the Republican National Committee sponsoring a party on the steps of the Capitol, where they replayed the video of the signing of the Contract.

What was the cause of all this celebration? Aside from the fact that the grueling first hundred days were almost over (on the actual Day One Hundred, Congress would be in recess), Republicans were pleased to report that they had kept the promise they made in September: the House had voted on every single one of the Contract's ten planks. Where did this leave the Contract? Well, it wasn't exactly law. Only one item, restrictions on unfunded mandates, had been signed by the president.[31] And this item was only one part of plank eight, Capital Gains and Regulations (see above), so technically, not one full plank was actually completed. The Senate had approved several measures, including the line-item veto, limiting child pornography, and the paperwork reduction act. The Senate had also explicitly rejected one House bill: the balanced-budget amendment, which was only half of the first plank. (The other half was the line-item veto.) Since the bills that the Senate approved were only pieces of various planks, then, depending on how you were keeping score, you could say that not one plank was completed in the Senate, either. And finally, the House itself had explicitly rejected some parts of the Contract, including the ABM proposal mentioned earlier and congressional approval of peacekeeping missions, both parts of the National Security plank.

And what were the prospects for House legislation that had not yet been considered in the Senate? Bills certainly weren't going to be considered as quickly by the Senate, and some faced the prospect of defeat or significant revision. And even those bills that survived Senate action and conference committee action might eventually be vetoed by President Clinton.[32]

Like the welfare bill, the most important and controversial legislation that the House has approved this year faces varying degrees of trouble in the Senate. "Most of the [House Contract] will be addressed in one form or another, but a lot of it may be changed," Senate Majority Whip Trent Lott (R-MI) said. Even if approved by the Senate, at least some could run into a presidential veto.[33]

One might think, actually, that Democrats had more cause to celebrate than Republicans. Despite the rhetoric about a Republican revolution tearing down laws that had been in place since the New Deal, by the first one hundred days, there had been little real change in the nation's laws, other than those affecting Congress. Nevertheless, Republicans had significantly altered the national agenda, and Democrats were preparing for difficult fights in the Senate. As the first hundred days came to a close, "Republicans headed home . . . in a state of weary euphoria," while Democrats "looked at the same legislative output and saw disaster."[34]

And how was everyone going to mark the end of the hundred days? With a three-week recess.

Constitutional Limitations on Passage of the Contract

Whatever Happened to the Senate?

With so much attention being paid to the House of Representatives for the better part of six months, one might have begun to wonder about the importance of the Senate. Although the House was clearly the focus of activity and media coverage, in our system of checks and balances, the Senate plays a critical role as a check on its companion chamber.

To begin with, the Contract wasn't nearly as important in the Senate as it was in the House. The much-ballyhooed signing ceremony in September 1994 was attended by House Republicans only. Although Senators had been invited to sign the Contract, they chose instead to have their own, much smaller campaign event a week earlier, at which they introduced the Senate campaign platform. Remember "Seven more in 94"? Probably not. Republicans needed seven more seats to gain a majority in the Senate, and so they came up with a seven-point legislative agenda that was not nearly as far reaching as the House Contract. Nor did it include some of the Contract's important provisions, such as tax breaks, the line-item veto, and eliminating unfunded mandates. In addition, senators did not sign their agenda, nor did they make any promises regarding scheduling or votes. Finally, while the House Contract included specific legislative language, the Senate pledge dealt more in generalities.[35]

The Senate is a much different body from the House. Individual members are granted much more leeway, and one senator can actually block legislation from coming to a vote. (Legislation is brought to the Senate floor by "unanimous consent," which means that if one person doesn't want that legislation considered, he or she can stop it.) Senators consider themselves to be much more individualistic than House members, and most would not want to commit to something as restrictive as a contract. Part of the reason for this is that the Senate has a much different electoral outlook than the House. In the Senate, terms are for six years, and elections are staggered so that every two years only one-third of senators are up for reelection. In the House, obviously, every Representative is up for reelection every two years. So, even if Republicans running for election or reelection to the Senate had chosen to sign the Contract, they would make up a very small percentage of senators. Additionally, only one-third of senators would face reelection in 1996. On the other hand, every House Republican would have to face his or her constituents in 1996, thus giving individual representatives a motive to keep the promises made in the Contract. Republican Senators would not face the same electoral concerns.

The framers of the Constitution knew what they were doing in 1789. They wanted Congress to be accountable to the people, and so the House of Representatives would have to face frequent elections. But they also wanted to create a check on the passions of the public, the "tyranny of the majority" discussed earlier, and so they created a senate that could have the luxury of being more deliberative and more reflective, since its membership would not have to concern itself as frequently with the vagaries of elections. While the framers were not specifically thinking about the Contract, they clearly wanted to put obstacles in place that would limit the ability of Congress to make sweeping changes, and they gave the minority party much more power in the Senate. In keeping with the framers' view of the Senate's role, Senate rules have evolved over the years to prioritize careful discussion over quick action. Senators can hold up legislation by simply talking it to death—a legislative tool known as the filibuster. According to Senator Robert Byrd (D-WV), himself a practitioner of the filibuster, "The rules of the Senate are made for the convenience of those who wish to delay."[36] The Senate today is indeed a more deliberative body than the House. And it is also more conservative, not in the strict ideological sense but in the sense of being cautious. For example, while House Republicans were prepared to push for tax cuts from the beginning of the 104th Congress, Republican Senators were more hesitant to pass such legislation. Pete Domenici (R-NM), chairman of the Senate Budget Committee, urged Congress to put its energies into reducing the deficit before tackling large-scale tax cuts.[37]

When House Republicans finished their versions of Contract bills, they sent them to the Senate for consideration, and often, especially in the beginning of the first hundred days, the Senate held up those bills. Majority Leader

Bob Dole (R-KS), who himself was running for president, wanted to establish clear differences between the House and Senate. He scheduled consideration of legislation based on the preferences of Senate Republicans, not the Contract. As the first hundred days drew to a close, however, Dole and the Senate Republicans saw the electoral advantages of going along with the Contract. According to Eddie Mahe, a Republican political consultant, "It may have been Newt Gingrich and the House that has the 'Contract with America,' but in the minds of the overwhelming majority of Americans who know anything about it, it's not a House Republican Contract, it's a Republican Contract."[38] Senators were wary of being accused of putting up obstacles in the way of House Republican reforms. Nevertheless, Majority Leader Dole would not make any promises about passing Contract bills: "The next 100 days will belong to the Senate. We aren't setting any deadlines, and no one expects the Senate to be a rubber stamp for the House."[39]

No wonder House Republicans only promised to bring Contract bills to a vote on the House floor. They knew there were no guarantees of what would happen to legislation once it left the House. What's more, they couldn't even guarantee passage in their own chamber, even with a Republican majority.

The President: The Bills Stop Here

As you know, in order for a bill to become law, it must pass the House and Senate in identical form, and then be signed by president. Although President Clinton, shortly after the 1994 elections, had been placed in the position of defending his "relevance" in the face of the Republican majority in Congress, he still had a very powerful tool: the presidential veto. Since the Senate hadn't even considered most of the Contract legislation by the end of the first hundred days, the president had had very little opportunity to exercise the veto. As the first hundred days came to a close, Clinton began to indicate that he just might veto some of the Contract bills. Clinton stated, "In the first 100 days, the mission of the House Republicans was to suggest ways in which we should change our government and our society. In the second hundred days and beyond, our mission together must be to decide which of these House proposals should be adopted, which should be modified, and which should be stopped."[40]

Although he had the ability to stop legislation with a veto, President Clinton ended up not using that tool frequently. The only Contract bill that he did actually veto after the hundred days were up was welfare reform, which was eventually retooled and sent back to him, and which he ultimately signed. As noted earlier, the Republicans did not have a "veto-proof" (two-thirds) majority in either chamber, so you might imagine that President Clinton would have used this tool more frequently. In fact, the Clinton administration had

IMAGE 3.2
First Lady Hillary Rodham Clinton (C) offers a toast to Speaker of the House Newt Gingrich (R) at the U.S. Capitol following President Bill Clinton's inauguration in Washington, D.C., on 20 January 1997. © POOL/Reuters/Corbis.

been pummeled by the healthcare debacle in 1994 and subsequent election of Republicans, and Clinton, facing his own reelection in 1996, chose not to differentiate himself too clearly from the Republicans. Seeing the popularity of the Contract among the American public, the president—with an eye to the 1996 election—made a political choice to support many of its provisions, even when they were at odds with his political inclinations.

One reason why the House was able to push the Contract was because Republicans perceived the president to be in a weak position. They wanted to get legislation through as quickly as possible, knowing the president would be unlikely to wield his veto weapon too fiercely during an election year. Although the power was there, it went relatively unutilized.

Conclusion: How the Constitutional System of Checks and Balances Makes the American Congress Function Differently Than the British Parliament

Despite all of the hoopla over the Contract, and comparisons made here between the election of 1994 and a parliamentary election, the legislative history of the Contract actually illustrates how different the American presidential system is from the British parliamentary one. What happened during the first three months of the 104th Congress is that Republican leaders attempted to impose some characteristics of the British parliamentary system on the American congressional process: notably, a well-defined legislative agenda and party discipline. "The normal inertia of the institution gave way to a frenetic pace, with major legislation actually passing the House and occasionally the Senate. The Congress acted more like a parliament than a traditional Congress."[41] Although they were successful in actually imposing these characteristics on the House (albeit for a limited time), the system itself is set up in such a way that other, outside barriers limited policy success in ways that are unheard of in the British parliamentary system. To conclude this chapter, let us examine some of the characteristics of the American system that distinguish it from politics in Great Britain.

The Legislative Process Is More Open

One of the reasons why there are so many steps to the American legislative process is to ensure that a large number of voices can be heard. For example, as bills are being considered in both chambers of Congress, there are generally committee hearings, at which outsiders (interest groups, individual citizens, even members of the administration) are invited to participate and testify. After the hearings, committees hold "markup" sessions, when a bill is debated and amended by committee members—both majority and minority. Usually markup is itself open, with the press and public welcome to attend. Prior to committee consideration, subcommittees have often already completed a similar process to consider the same bill. Finally, the bill is considered on the floor, where individual senators and representatives may also make amendments. Again, members of both the majority and minority parties can propose floor amendments to legislation. The process is long, convoluted, and often difficult. No wonder the old saw says that you don't want to watch either sausages or laws being made!

In contrast, the process for creating legislation is much more streamlined in the British parliamentary system. The majority party, having run on a well-defined agenda, is truly given a mandate to implement it. Party leaders work together to develop legislative language—without the input of the minority party (or parties, as the case may be). The actual writing of legislative language occurs in what we might think of as the old-fashioned "smoke-filled back room." The government sends legislation to the floor in advanced form, and it is usually not open for amendments. Traditionally, votes are according to party line, with the party in power voting for the legislation, and minority parties voting against. If party leaders can't keep their rank-and-file members (known as backbenchers) in line for votes, then they know their government is headed for trouble. In addition, the executive branch is not separated from the parliament. Cabinet ministers, unlike in the American system, do not have to resign their legislative seats to take their executive posts. And, of course, the British prime minister has enormous power, serving as both the chief executive (like the American president) and the head of the legislative majority party (like the American Speaker of the House). Gillian Peele has noted that Conservative Prime Minister Margaret Thatcher took full advantage of her powers:

> By the end of the 1980s, Mrs. Thatcher's government had itself generated a major constitutional and political debate as her style of premiership incurred charges of authoritarianism. Moreover, the Conservative administration's policies underlined the absence of checks and balances in the British system and the enormous extent of the powers vested in an elected government, powers which, while they might be lawfully exercised, were difficult to reconcile with ideas of limited, consensual or balanced government.[42]

Such a streamlined process makes the creation of legislation much easier, but it also keeps minority parties or even backbenchers in the majority party from having much say. Even in the 104th Congress, which was so dominated by Republican leadership, Democrats as well as rank-and-file Republicans had opportunities to amend legislation, and interest groups and the public had some opportunity to comment on legislation as it was being made (although Democrats complained loudly that Republicans were trying to stifle alternative views during committee hearings and floor consideration). Where the Republican 104th Congress was similar to the British parliament was in the creation of the Contract itself. Republican leaders got together outside the traditional legislative process to propose the planks of the Contract. The legislative language of the Contract was written outside the public eye, without input from the opposing party, which, of course, would not be interested in working with the other side as it created its campaign document. Working only with party members and interest groups favorable to its positions, the Republican Party was able to create an unabashedly conservative document.

At first glance, it appears that the creation of such a detailed legislative platform was highly unusual for the American congressional system. It should be noted, however, that congressional parties had been doing similar sorts of manifesto electoral programs for some time. If the Republicans had lost the 1994 Congressional elections, the Contract would have been ignored as well. The unexpected Republican takeover of the House for the first time in forty years brought an incredible amount of publicity to the Contract, and the Contract became a focal point for the legislative activities of the 104th Congress.

> The parliamentary tenor of the House in its first hundred days meant that deliberation in the classic sense—carefully thinking through alternatives, debating them, and then moving to a broader public judgment—was virtually absent in the House, either in committees or on the floor. The emphasis was on processing legislation, not on debate and discussion.[43]

The Republican Contract differed from a British parliamentary legislative agenda in one noteworthy way: despite the fact that the Republicans had detailed legislative language ready to go as soon as they were elected (which could also happen in a parliamentary system), they still had to go through the steps of the legislative process discussed above. Had the Republicans been in Parliament, they could simply have brought the bills up for a largely predetermined vote. Although floor votes were largely predetermined in the 104th Congress, there was a long way to go between introduction of a bill and voting on the floor. Despite having a majority and a specific legislative agenda, Republican legislative success was not assured. Note the aversion of minority leader Richard Gephardt to the pace of the legislative agenda: "This hundred days is a self-imposed national emergency that made no sense. It's caused all of them to jerk stuff through the procedure much faster than it should be. There hasn't been enough committee consideration or floor consideration."[44]

Party Discipline Is Fleeting, at Best

One notable characteristic of the first hundred days of the 104th Congress was the unity with which the Republicans voted. According to a survey of legislative votes conducted by *Congressional Quarterly*, most of the freshmen Republicans voted with the party on Contract legislation 94 percent of the time or more. Fifty-three of the seventy-five freshmen had scores of 100 percent; 141 of the 230 House Republicans voted with the party 100 percent of the time. The lowest-scoring Republican was Connie Morella (R-MD), with a 73 percent voting record on Contract legislation.[45] These numbers are striking because they are so high for the American Congress. They are not high at all compared to a parliamentary system, in which party discipline is paramount. The governing party in a parliament expects 100 percent of its members to vote with it on legislation.

On the other hand, the Democrats in the 104th Congress show a sharp contrast to a minority party in the British parliament: Southern Democrats, for example, voted with the Contract 67 percent of the time. Two southern Democrats had 100 percent voting records, and five southern Democrats had

94 percent voting records with respect to the Republican Contract.[46] Minority party members in Parliament would not be voting for the majority party legislation. Instead, they would be trying to distinguish themselves from the majority by creating an alternative legislative agenda. Backbenchers of both parties in Parliament tend not to act unilaterally or cross party lines. As a kind of "government-in-waiting," the minority party wants to have a plan of action should the majority party lose control of the legislature.

Coalition building—not a hallmark of the 104th Congress—used to be a characteristic of the American congressional system. Knowing that legislation has to go through an arduous process to get passed, proponents of a particular bill often try to create a bandwagon, by courting members of the other party and interest groups to gain their support. Compromise and bargaining are usually two characteristics of coalition building. Coalitions in American politics have historically formed around an issue or cluster of issues. In contrast, a "coalition" in a parliamentary system usually refers to two or more parties that have joined together to create a majority when no one party received a large enough percentage of votes in the election to form its own government. A coalition in a parliamentary system, then, is formed to create a government after an election; coalitions tend to be formed in the American presidential system as each bill is being considered. As such, coalition building is typically an ongoing process in the American Congress.

Accountability Is Limited

One very positive attribute of the party discipline that exists in the British parliamentary system is the high level of accountability. Since one party is in charge of both the executive and the legislative branches, that party can and must take full responsibility for both the enactment of legislation and its implementation. And if the voters don't like what is going on in government, they know exactly whom to blame: the majority party. In the American system, with its openness and separation of powers, it is often difficult to identify who is responsible for action or inaction in government. If public opinion turns against some aspect of legislation passed by a Republican majority, for example, governmental actors will busy themselves with playing the "blame game." Republicans could say that it is the Democratic administration's fault for not implementing the laws properly. Congressional Democrats could argue that it is the Republicans' fault—after all, they (the Democrats) did everything they could to stop the Republican legislation from passing. Congressional Republicans might counter that Democrats in Congress weakened the bill through the amendment process. And the president could contend that it is not his fault—he is just trying the best he can to implement the flawed legislation Congress sent him. The British prime minister has no such "pass the buck" option in Parliament. He or she is responsible for the creation and implementation of legislation, and the voters will hold him or her accountable.

In the American system, on the other hand, no one can ever really be held accountable for legislation, and so it is much easier for members of both parties to distance themselves from unpopular policies when running for reelection. Since the reelection motive is so strong, it is extremely difficult to establish responsibility, much to the chagrin of the voting public.

"Policy Windows" Are Only Open for a Short Time

In his book *Agendas, Alternatives, and Public Policies*, John Kingdon describes the process by which an issue reaches the top of a government's decision-making agenda in the U.S. Congress. According to Kingdon, a "policy window" opens up when politics, policy, and problems come together to create the right time for a particular piece of legislation to pass. That is, when a problem in society exists, and there is a proposal to solve that problem, and the political mood is right, legislation will be enacted. Otherwise, the legislation doesn't really have a chance. That is why large numbers of bills are proposed in Congress, but only a very limited number ever make it to a floor vote, much less become enacted. Members of Congress are aware of the fleeting nature of these policy windows, and rush to enact legislation when they feel a window has opened up. The 104th Congress clearly saw an open policy window during the first hundred days of the legislative session, and rushed to pass all of the Republican bills in the House. The idea for the hundred days came from the early days of the New Deal (which the Republican Contract was basically trying to undo). Because of the magnitude of the Great Depression, President Roosevelt rushed to pass legislation when he first got into office, and Congress pretty much went along with him (the roles were reversed during the 104th Congress; that is, Congress pushed legislation and the president went along with it). Roosevelt was able to push a great number of bills through during his first hundred days because of the palpable crisis the country was experiencing. The Republicans wanted to imitate that sense of urgency and immediacy during their first hundred days as the majority party, although the nation certainly was not facing a crisis as immediate as the Great Depression had been. The idea of the first hundred days, however, did create a window of opportunity—a policy window—during which the Republicans could control the legislative process.

The concept of a policy window (discussed further in chapter 4) and the idea of rushing to pass legislation are antithetical to the way a parliamentary system works. In a parliamentary system, the policy window opens up as soon as a party wins the majority, and remains open until the next election. The majority party has enough power and enough votes to pass any bill they would like, and so there's usually no sense in hurrying legislation through. The party in power may as well take as much time as it likes to develop legislation. There are some exceptions to this, of course. If there is an immediate crisis, such as a war or a depression, then the party will probably be in a rush to pass bills. In Britain after her 1979 victory and through the early 1980s, Prime Minister Thatcher rushed through legislation to take apart the welfare state that she had campaigned against. This was not so much because of a national crisis, but rather because she wanted to powerfully demonstrate the new direction in which she would take the country. In this regard, Gillian Peele notes:

> The experience of [British] government after 1979 underlined how . . . few barriers there were to restrain a radical government determined to press forward its programme even against opposition from local authorities, the courts and the House of Commons. It also underlined how ambiguous was the idea that government ought to consult affected interests, a requirement which constitutional writers such as Ivor Jennings had once emphasized strongly. Indeed, it was part of the Conservative government's strategy to ensure that organized interests should not be allowed to shape public policy.[47]

In contrast to the typical approach to legislation in parliamentary systems, House Republicans felt that quick passage of the Contract was necessary, not only as a powerful symbolic move, but also because they knew the policy window might not stay open for long.

Thus, the complicated American legislative process results in more openness, allows for minority voices to be heard, encourages compromise and bargaining, and favors deliberative processes. The British parliamentary system is less open, but allows the majority party to get its work done in an unencumbered fashion. The 104th Congress illustrates the strengths and weaknesses of our system, and is both an anomaly (in that the Republicans had a clearly defined legislative agenda and kept party unity, and the House acted quickly on legislation) and characteristic of the way Congress works (in that the outcome of Contract legislation was not foreordained, particularly when one takes into account the Senate, the president, and the judiciary, and in that Republicans had to work within a policy window).

Notes

1. The literature on comparative public policy examines the full range of constraints on policy makers, including political culture; globalization; and institutional,

economic, and political factors. See Ellen M. Immergut, "Institutional Constraints on Policy," in *The Oxford Handbook of Public Policy*, ed. Michael Moran, Martin Rein, and Robert E. Goodin, 557–71 (New York: Oxford University Press, 2006); Tom Conley, "Globalisation as Constraint and Opportunity: Reconceptualising Policy Capacity in Australia," *Global Society: Journal of Interdisciplinary International Relations* 16, no. 4 (October 2002): 377–99; James C. Clingermayer and Richard C. Feiock, *Institutional Constraints and Policy Choice: An Exploration of Local Governance* (Albany: SUNY Press, 2001).

2. Juliana Gruenwald, "Shallow Tactics or Deep Issues: Fathoming the GOP Contract," *Congressional Quarterly Weekly Reports*, 19 November 1994.

3. Norman J. Ornstein and Amy L. Schenkenberg, "The 1995 Congress: The First Hundred Days and Beyond," *Political Science Quarterly* 110, no. 2 (1995): 194.

4. Charles Krauthammer, "Republican Mandate," *Washington Post*, 11 November 1994.

5. For background on how a strong narrative like the 1994 Contract might lead to policy formation, see Deborah A. Stone, "Causal Stories and the Formation of Policy Agendas," *Political Science Quarterly* 104, no. 2 (Summer 1989): 281–300; Dennis Chong and James N. Druckman, "Framing Public Opinion in Competitive Democracies," *American Political Science Review* 101, no. 4 (November 2007): 637–55.

6. James Madison, *Federalist #10*, www.constitution.org/fed/federa10.htm.

7. Roger H. Davidson, "The 104th Congress and Beyond," in *The 104th Congress: A Congressional Quarterly Reader*, ed. Roger H. Davidson and Walter J. Oleszek (Washington, DC: CQ Press, 1995), 3.

8. Ibid.

9. Ed Gillespie and Bob Schellhas, eds., *Contract with America: The Bold Plan by Rep. Newt Gingrich, Rep. Dick Armey and the House Republicans to Change the Nation* (New York: Times Books, 1994).

10. Donna Cassata, "Republicans Bask in Success of Rousing Performance," *Congressional Quarterly Weekly Reports*, 8 April 1995, 988.

11. Linda Killian, *The Freshman: What Happened to the Republican Revolution?* (Boulder, CO: Westview Press, 1998), 5.

12. Gruenwald, "Shallow Tactics or Deep Issues."

13. Richard Morin, "Voters Repeat Their Simple Message about Government: Less Is Better," *Washington Post*, 13 November 1994.

14. Gruenwald, "Shallow Tactics or Deep Issues."

15. Note that members of the House of Representatives are elected for two-year terms. Elections are held in even years; members of Congress are sworn in the following January. A "Congress" consists of two one-year "sessions," which have been numbered in consecutive order starting with the first Congress in 1790. So 1995 was the first session of the 104th Congress; 1996, the second session; and the election of 1996 led to the swearing in of the 105th Congress in 1997.

16. David S. Broder, "Vote May Signal GOP Return as Dominant Party," *Washington Post*, 10 November 1994.

17. Janet Hook, "Republicans Step Up to Power in Historic 40-Year Shift," *Congressional Quarterly Weekly Reports*, 7 January1995, 92.

18. David S. Cloud, "GOP, to Its Own Great Delight, Enacts House Rules Changes," *Congressional Quarterly Weekly Reports*, 7 January 1995, 14.

19. Ibid., 13.

20. "GOP Plan for a Marathon January," *Congressional Quarterly Weekly Reports*, 31 December 1994, 3592. Note that congressional "recesses" are not exactly vacations. Members of Congress go home to meet with constituents and do other work in their districts, while Washington staff take the time to catch up on constituent mail and work out details of legislation. The 112th Congress started the practice of calling recesses "district work periods."

21. Janet Hook, "Republicans Vote in Lock Step, But Unity May Not Last Long," *Congressional Quarterly Weekly Reports*, 18 February 1995, 495.

22. Ibid., 496.

23. Ornstein and Schenkenberg, "The 1995 Congress," 202.

24. Hook, "Republicans Vote in Lock Step," 497.

25. David S. Cloud, "House GOP Shows a United Front in Crossing 'Contract' Divide," *Congressional Quarterly Weekly Reports*, 22 February 1995, 527.

26. "GOP Agenda Hits Snag in Senate," *Congressional Quarterly Weekly Reports*, 4 February 1995, 333.

27. David S. Cloud, "House Speeds Pace on 'Contract,'" *Congressional Quarterly Weekly Reports*, 11 February 1995, 437.

28. Guy Gugliotta, "Breakneck Pace Frazzles House," *Washington Post*, 7 March 1995.

29. Ornstein and Schenkenberg, "The 1995 Congress," 183.

30. Cassata, "Republicans Bask in Success," 986.

31. The president also signed legislation requiring Congress to comply with workplace laws, but this was actually part of the prologue and not one of the ten planks.

32. When a bill passes the House and Senate in different forms, the two versions are sent to a "conference" committee made up of members of both houses to work out the differences. The conference committee revision is then sent back to each chamber, where it must be voted on before being sent to the president.

33. Kenneth J. Cooper and Helen Dewar, "100 Days Down, but Senate to Go for Most 'Contract' Items," *Washington Post*, 9 April 1995.

34. Robin Toner, "GOP Blitz of First 100 Days Now Brings Pivotal Second 100," *New York Times*, 9 April 1995.

35. Steve Langdon, "'Contract' Dwarfs Senate GOP Pledge," *Congressional Quarterly Weekly Reports*, 25 February 1995, 578.

36. Jonathan D. Salant, "Senate Altering Its Course in Favor of Contract," *Congressional Quarterly Weekly Reports*, 29 April 1995, 1152.

37. Cloud, "House Speeds Pace on Contract," 437.

38. Salant, "Senate Altering Its Course."

39. Jeffrey L. Katz, "GOP Faces Unknown Terrain without 'Contract' Map," *Congressional Quarterly Weekly Reports*, 8 April 1995, 981.

40. Jonathan D. Salant, "Gingrich Sounds Familiar Themes," *Congressional Quarterly Weekly Reports*, 8 April 1995, 981.

41. Ornstein and Schenkenberg, "The 1995 Congress," 206.

42. Gillian Peele, *Governing the UK*, 3rd ed. (Oxford: Blackwell, 1995), 21–22.

43. Ornstein and Schenkenberg, "The 1995 Congress," 206.

44. Cassata, "Republicans Bask in Success," 990.

45. Ibid.

46. Ibid.

47. Peele, *Governing the UK*, 23. Peele notes that this experience under Thatcher led to reforms in 1997 under Prime Minister Tony Blair, designed to democratize the machinery of government. See Gillian Peele, *Governing the UK: British Politics in the 21st Century*, 4th ed. (London: Wiley-Blackwell, 2004), 56–87.

4

Agenda Setting and Agenda Control

Case Two: The 2008–2010 Battle over Healthcare

We have a two-party system, not a one-party scheme, and the fundamental differences between Democrats and Republicans create clear choices for the electorate. Obama should succeed or fail based on enactment of the Democratic platform. Voters will be the judge of Democrats' handiwork in 2010 and 2012. Leave "national unity" governments to parliamentary nations, and let the American two-party system work.

—Larry J. Sabato

Well, the government is us. These officials are elected by you. They are elected by you. I am elected by you. I am constrained, as they are constrained, by a system that our Founders put in place. It's a government of and by and for the people.

—President Barack Obama

G OING FORWARD FIFTEEN YEARS from the 1994–1996 Contract with America Congress, we find another apt illustration of the constraints the American system places on policy making. In this case, checks and balances did not actually stop legislation from passing, but instead placed great (though not insurmountable) obstacles before the passage of legislation. This chapter will explain the tortuous path of healthcare reform in the first term of Obama's presidency, demonstrating that the same institutional barriers we saw in 1994 were alive and well in 2010. In contrast to the Contract with America (an expansive legislative program consisting of several bills), the Affordable Care Act (ACA), though a major overhaul of a significant portion of the economy, was a single piece of legislation. Also in contrast to the Contract, the Affordable Care Act was finally enacted into law. Like the Contract, however, the ACA faced formidable challenges to its passage within both houses of Congress, as well as from constitutional actors outside of the legislature (including the Supreme Court and the states, which would implement the law). The remainder of the chapter explains the policy-making process for healthcare reform, before returning to a comparison between the ACA and the Contract with America.

Background

One of President Obama's main campaign themes in 2008 was fixing the broken healthcare system. His bruising battle for the Democratic nomination against Hillary Clinton (who was in charge of the failed healthcare push in the Clinton administration) signaled a more open process for reforming healthcare. And his insistent promise to "change the way Washington works," coupled with his theme of hope, boded well (at least in the minds of his many and ardent supporters) for a bipartisan, publicly acceptable compromise that would fix healthcare once and for all. The election of 2008 also gave Obama large majorities in both houses of Congress. These Democrats started to work to institutionalize, in a sense, the promises of hope and change through specific legislative accomplishments—most notably, healthcare. In the end, Congress passed the legislation, the president signed it, and the Supreme Court deemed it to be constitutional. It was, however, a very bumpy road, and there were many more challenges before the law could be fully implemented. In one sense, healthcare reform defied the odds, and illustrates that a majority faction *can* get something done under the American constitutional system of checks and balances. In that regard, despite all the favor the system gives to the minority, in this case, the majority won. But the fact remains that sweeping change was passed without a single Republican vote. And although the system is set up to make it difficult to pass broad changes, it is not impossible to do so.

Healthcare reform has been an issue on the American agenda at least since the Progressive Era. Unlike major European democracies, the United States did not nationalize healthcare in the twentieth century. This itself could be an example of path dependency: U.S. history demonstrates the preference that its citizens have for limited government and lower taxes. For much of our history, nationalized healthcare was referred to jeeringly as "socialized medicine"—as evidence of the big government that the more socialistic European countries were inclined to accept.

Agenda Setting and Agenda Control

The policy-making process in the United States can be long and convoluted, involving three different levels of government (state, local, and federal), three different branches of federal government, two major political parties, and numerous outside actors. Although the process itself is circuitous, rather than linear, public-policy literature describes several distinct stages: setting the agenda (also referred to more specifically as "problem definition"), policy formulation (creating policy options), legitimation (choosing an option), implementation (when the policy is put into place), and evaluation (determining how well the policy is working, often leading back to agenda setting).[1] The policy process generally refers to policy making at the federal level; it can be applied to state and local governments as well. And state and local governments are involved at several stages in the federal process, especially implementation, since it is at the state and local levels that the policy rubber hits the road, so to speak. This chapter addresses the healthcare policy process for agenda setting, formulation, and legitimation. Implementation of the law began when it was turned over to the Department of Health and Human Services, and had its own set of challenges, which are beyond the scope of this chapter.

According to John Kingdon,[2] in order for a policy to reach the top of the government's agenda and ultimately pass into law, what he calls a "policy window" must open, which requires the convergence of three streams: problem, policy, and politics. A public policy problem must be identified (and there is no point in creating a policy unless there is a problem to be addressed), solutions to that problem (policies) are identified and fleshed out, and then, if the political environment is favorable, one of those policies will be chosen and legitimized, usually through the legislative process. A policy window may be open for only a short time, and usually requires a "policy entrepreneur" to shepherd legitimation of the policy. And just because a policy window is opened, it is not necessarily the case that a policy will pass. For example, one could argue that a policy window for healthcare reform was open in 1993–1994, when Bill Clinton started his presidency. Despite the open window, no policy was passed. Most scholars and armchair politicos attribute the failure to the inexperience of Hillary Clinton (in charge of the reform). The closed nature of the process she shepherded and the complexity of the bill also contributed to its failure, as did the inability of the Clinton White House to engage Congress. Once a policy window closes, it may not open for a long time. It took almost twenty years for another policy window to open in healthcare reform. But open it did in 2008, with the election of Barack Obama as president. To prevail, the president needed to carefully define the agenda in order to maintain control.

The Problem Stream

The problem stream for healthcare was full to overflowing by the time of the 2008 election. Various problems related to healthcare included the following: rising costs, large numbers of uninsured (including children), the high cost of malpractice insurance, the fact that health insurance is tied to a job (a problem that was increasing as the economy soured and joblessness rose), issues with end-of-life care, and a host of others. But healthcare as a problem was and is tied to an even larger problem: the state of the economy. As both the debt and deficits rise,[3] Americans are rightly concerned about government spending. And healthcare costs contribute to the problem, because healthcare makes up around 17 percent of the gross domestic product (GDP), and 23 percent of total government spending.[4] Healthcare spending, however, is rising faster than GDP. If healthcare spending continues to increase at 2012 rates, by the year 2035, we will be spending 35 percent of GDP on healthcare.[5] So not only is healthcare a problem in itself, but the economic problems of the United States cannot be addressed until healthcare costs are reined in.

Healthcare was a problem, and had been for some time. A problem needs a solution.

The Policy Stream

There are numerous proposals to fix healthcare, ranging from tort reform to reduce costs associated with malpractice, to replacing our current privately run system with a government one, to figuring out ways to ration care, and numerous options in between. Generally, one can assume that Republicans will want to limit government intrusions, so they are more likely to support tort reform and keeping the system private. Democrats, viewing the government as a vehicle to provide for the public good, are more likely to support a publicly funded program, known in healthcare parlance as a "single-payer" solution. That is, rather than having individuals buy insurance from a variety of private companies, insurance would be provided by the government, which would therefore be the single paying entity for health costs. A discussion of the differing views of the role of government will be addressed later in the chapter. For now, suffice it to say that the election of a Democratic president put government-run health insurance on the table. As the debate progressed, various other policy issues emerged, including a model that would allow insurance companies to continue providing healthcare while also creating an *option* to receive healthcare from the government. Whether states could "opt in" to that coverage (i.e., the default would be private insurance) or "opt out" (the default being public insurance) was just one of the arcane sticking points related to healthcare's passage.

TABLE 4.1
Healthcare Committees and Their Jurisdictions

Committee	Jurisdiction	Chair
House		
Education and Labor	Access to affordable healthcare for working Americans	George Miller (D-CA)
Energy and Commerce	Covers healthcare as a commercial activity	Henry Waxman (D-CA)
Ways and Means	Deals with tax and payment issues; also Social Security, Medicare, and Medicaid	Charles Rangel (D-NY)
Senate		
Health, Education, Labor, and Pensions	Access to affordable healthcare for working Americans	Ted Kennedy (D-MA) Christopher Dodd (D-CT), acting chair
Finance	Deals with tax and payment issues	Max Baucus (D-MT)

We will discuss policy entrepreneurs presently, but here we would like to briefly address the question of whose healthcare policy it was, exactly. A policy usually has an author. Part of President Obama's strategy (also discussed later) was, learning from Hillary Clinton's mistakes, to let Congress take the lead and avoid any appearance of "shoving healthcare down the throats" of Congress. The president, therefore, did not release a specific healthcare plan, preferring instead to react to the plans coming out of Congress. So, in one sense, the president did not have a healthcare plan, at least not a specific, written one. On the other hand, one could easily infer from his campaign speeches what he preferred. In addition, there was not one, single congressional plan. As it happened, each committee in Congress with jurisdiction (Ways and Means, Energy and Commerce in the House; Finance, and Health, Education, Labor and Pensions in the Senate) came up with its own plan.

Finally, although this chapter will generally discuss broad policy outlines, there were a number of specific details that became sticking points, in addition to the opt-in vs. opt-out debate, including abortion.

In terms of Kingdon's model, there were many options floating around in the "primeval policy soup."

The Political Stream

The political stream, according to Kingdon, consists of changes in the national mood and political events, especially elections. What was most important in the political stream for healthcare was the election of 2008, which, in the minds of even the most casual observer of American politics, opened the door (or, in keeping with our metaphor, window), for health-care legislation to be passed.

Barack Obama ran his campaign on the themes of hope and change. He invigorated the voting public, especially young people. In the Democratic primary, he defeated the establishment candidate, Hillary Clinton, who at the beginning of the election cycle had an aura of invincibility and in-evitability. As a community organizer, he had experience in mobilizing the public behind a cause. One of his main campaign themes was fixing the broken healthcare system.[6] As noted above, the election of 2008 also gave Obama large majorities in both houses of Congress. Many Democrats who rode in on his coattails came from swing districts in which independents, who could easily swing from one party to the other, were the deciding fac-tor in the vote. Rahm Emanuel, who became Obama's chief of staff, was in-strumental in bringing these moderate, "blue dog" Democrats into the fold when the Democrats regained control of the House in 2006.[7] These swing districts changed the balance of power again in 2010, which, as we will see, also had an effect on healthcare reform.

Policy Entrepreneurs

Kingdon's model makes note of the necessity of a policy entrepreneur, someone who is a proponent of a particular policy and can shepherd it through passage, including making the necessary compromises for political feasibility. One thinks of a policy entrepreneur as a president (like Roosevelt and the New Deal, Johnson and the Great Society) or a member of Congress who comes up with a policy and then tirelessly works with both his or her friends and adversaries to make it happen. Healthcare did not have a typical policy entrepreneur, although it did have at least two quasi-entrepreneurs.

Barack Obama was not a policy entrepreneur in the typical sense. Yes, he proposed reforming healthcare. Yes, the policy window opened because of his election, and yes, it is the singular accomplishment of his presidency. However, he was not an active entrepreneur. He did not propose a specific policy. He did not, at first, badger Congress about getting his pet issues into the bill. He stayed above the fray, perhaps as part of his effort to change the way Washington works, perhaps as a way to keep his hands from get-ting dirty through the sausage-making process of Congress.[8] Obama waded into the process later, having a summit or two at the White House or Blair House, strategizing about final passage, calling fence sitters, and even speaking to a joint session of Congress as the vote neared. He did not send

Congress a healthcare plan, or even outline at the beginning of the process what his priorities or bottom line were. As a policy entrepreneur, he was more reactive than active.

The second policy entrepreneur was unusual in that his absence had almost as much impact on the process as his presence. That entrepreneur was, of course, Senator Edward (Ted) Kennedy (D-MA), who died in the summer of 2009 after a yearlong battle with brain cancer. Kennedy had been a champion of healthcare over his forty-seven-year career in the Senate, long pushing for a government-run system. Kennedy had also been instrumental in getting Obama elected. When he supported Obama over Hillary Clinton, he not only hurt and angered the Clintons, but he gave his imprimatur to a young upstart, giving Obama more legitimacy in his quest for the presidency. One would have expected Kennedy to be the primary moving force behind healthcare, but his own health began to deteriorate in the summer before the election, with his speech at the Democratic National Convention being, for Democrats, a bittersweet handing over of the torch to the next generation, as most people understood this was likely his last public speaking event.

Kennedy had chaired the Health, Education, Labor and Pensions (HELP) committee, but his illness required him to take a leave of absence, and Senator Christopher Dodd (D-CT) took his place. Kennedy died before healthcare was passed, making him a symbol to Democrats of the need to pass legislation. He was lionized in death as in life, and Democrats viewed healthcare as his legacy, giving them further incentive to pass a bill. His death also provided an ironic twist to the healthcare debate, when Democratic stronghold Massachusetts unbelievably elected a Republican, Scott Brown,[9] to replace him in January 2010, taking away the one vote needed to ensure passage of the legislation (see below for further discussion).

So in the minds of congressional policy makers, these two policy entrepreneurs were certainly hovering over the process (literally or figuratively), and, in that sense, making their mark. But neither one acted as chief architect, cheerleader, and strategist the way one normally expects a policy entrepreneur would act. Neither one was the driving force in creating the details of the policy or in developing the strategies for its passage, although the influence of each man was necessary for the enactment of healthcare, and the bill can certainly be seen as part of both their legacies.

There is one more person who could be considered a policy entrepreneur, and that is Nancy Pelosi, Speaker of the House in the 111th Congress. While she was (and is) a master at counting and courting votes, using parliamentary rules to her advantage, and generally keeping her caucus in line, she is not a policy entrepreneur for healthcare in the typical sense. She was more involved in the process than the policy, and her policy negotiations were in the form of

IMAGE 4.1
U.S. President Barack Obama escorts Senator Ted Kennedy (D-MA) into the East Room
of the White House before participating in remarks at the White House Forum on
Health Reform in Washington on 5 March 2009. © LARRY DOWNING/Reuters/Corbis.

making the deals necessary to ensure passage. In addition, none of the chairs
of the relevant committees emerged as a policy entrepreneur. Because of
Obama's hands-off policy and the death of Senator Kennedy, then, there was
a vacuum in leadership, and that hurt the process. "Many Democrats said privately that if Kennedy had been driving the process, the bill would have been
more progressive, more bipartisan and more on schedule."[10] Perhaps this is
wishful thinking, but the fact remains that an active policy entrepreneur, engaged in the nuts and bolts of the legislation, could have helped.

Congress's Turn: Policy Formation and Legitimation

As we have seen, an open policy window is a necessary condition for passage
of a particular bill, but an open window provides no guarantee of passage.
Before turning to the twists and turns of healthcare in Congress, let us briefly
discuss the system in which the policy process operates.

The framers of the Constitution specifically and intentionally made it difficult for legislation to pass. This is not just because they expected there to be

IMAGE 4.2
House Speaker Nancy Pelosi (D-CA) speaks at a healthcare news conference on
Capitol Hill in Washington on Thursday, 2 October 2009. © Alex Brandon/AP/Corbis.

relatively few national issues before Congress. They certainly never expected the width and breadth of issues before Congress today. The framers made it difficult for legislation to pass because they understood that in a democracy, tyranny of the majority was as possible as tyranny of the one was in a monarchy. The framers accepted the idea of majority rule, but also insisted on the protection of minority rights. *Federalist No. 10* makes clear that Madison expected majorities to try to push legislation through Congress. The constitutional system put barriers in the way of those majorities. It is always dangerous to ask the question: What would the framers think of this or that policy? One could surmise that they would have been shocked at the government providing healthcare, but then, George Washington reputedly had wooden teeth. The world has changed in a variety of ways, and one could never know what Madison, Jefferson, or Washington might think about a given policy, if any one of them were living in the world today. The better question is this: Did the framers of the Constitution design a system that would encourage the passage of a broad, sweeping reform like healthcare? The answer is *absolutely not*. The framers didn't want quickly passed legislation, and they wanted to be sure that minorities had the right to block or stop such legislation. The system does not support sweeping change in the opposite direction, either (for example, a bill eliminating Medicaid and Medicare).

So in analyzing the passage of the healthcare bill, the first thing to realize is that the constitutional system is set up to make passage of just such a bill difficult. But there are extraconstitutional conditions that also impede the passage of broad bills. Among these are the committee system, the party system, and new rules and norms, especially in the Senate, which lead to what Barbara Sinclair has termed "unorthodox lawmaking." Although the first congresses considered each bill as it was introduced, setting up ad hoc committees as necessary, in a short time Congress found it necessary to set up permanent standing committees with jurisdiction over specific issues. These committees tend to decentralize policy making in Congress, and legislation can be stalled or die in committee. The party system organizes the House and Senate, with majority and minority party leaders vying for position and strategy in scheduling and considering bills. In the Senate, the increasing use of the filibuster (or often, the threat of a filibuster) means that in order for almost any piece of legislation to pass, it must have sixty votes. A cloture vote to shut down debate and end a filibuster requires a supermajority of sixty votes, so Senate leadership will not bring a bill to the floor unless they know they have sixty votes. To further complicate things in the Senate, a reconciliation bill is immune from a filibuster. A reconciliation bill is technically a budget-related bill to make authorizing legislation align with goals set in the budget bill. Only those parts of healthcare, or any bill, that are directly related to the budget may be passed as part of the reconciliation bill (under the Byrd Rule), and using a reconciliation bill as an end-run around the legislative process is generally frowned upon.

It is a wonder any legislation ever gets passed. And as we shall see later on, the increasing polarization of political parties adds another layer to the complexity of legislative passage.

One other important thing to note is that coalition building around particular policy issues is usually encouraged in the American presidential system of government. Compromise and accommodation are the routes to passage. Generally small, incremental changes are the rule of the day.

Obama's Congressional Strategy

President Obama's strategy with regard to healthcare was related to his vow to "change the way Washington works." His goal was to pass a bipartisan, widely accepted healthcare bill. He was to be (in the media's words, not his) "the post-partisan president." Obama learned from his campaign to start with his base (liberal Democrats) and then draw in moderates and independents with his themes of hope and change.[11] Translating this strategy to Congress would prove difficult, however. Obama was no longer courting voters, whose party identification was fluid, but members of Congress, whose own legislative careers were dependent in part on their party loyalty. He could probably count on his Democratic base in Congress, but congressional Republicans were strategic political actors in their own right. They were not voting for president, but crafting legislation that would affect their own careers. A post-partisan strategy was likely flawed from the start.[12]

What Obama and his advisors decided to do was to communicate in very broad strokes his priorities in healthcare. He would then let Congress do the work: creating the legislative details and negotiating with various players internally, while the White House would privately court interest groups.[13] At the end of the process, he would step in, both to "shape the final product" and claim credit for legislative success.[14] This plan had three advantages: it fit into his campaign promise to change the way Washington does business, it melded with his own personal style, and, from a cynical perspective, it allowed him to take credit while avoiding getting his hands dirty with the nuts and bolts of the legislative process. In this regard, Obama can be seen as a "contingency leader," who delegated White House policy making to his staff and allowed the leadership in Congress to take control over big-ticket issues (healthcare, energy, environment). This strategy is *transactional* rather than *transformative*, and seems to be at odds with his intention to change the way Washington works.[15]

Obama's style is cerebral, level headed, and professorial.[16] As opposed to President Bill Clinton's volubility and propensity to glad-hand, Obama is much more comfortable in the thought process and logical reasoning of policy issues.[17] Clinton would get knee-deep in intricate policy details, and chat away with anyone who shared his interest. Obama prefers to remain above the fray (some call him aloof), and offer broad policy prescriptions that show thoughtfulness and intellectual prowess. Diving into the congressional process and weighing in on specific proposals is not Obama's strong suit, nor did he pursue those tactics as president. Instead, he relied on what got him elected: his ability to motivate people through his gifted oratorical skills; for example, by giving a congressional address as healthcare legislation floundered in 2010. As many presidents have discovered in recent years, the intricate and specific details of the policy process do not mesh well with the broad-brush skills needed to get elected.[18] And in fact, while Obama's net-roots campaign (Obama for America) broke new ground in organizing through social media, his team's efforts to use the extensive database of names and e-mail addresses (renamed "Organizing for America" after the election) to garner support for healthcare reform fell far short.[19]

The first thing on the agenda, though, was to get a legislative success under his belt. Success breeds success, or so Obama's chief of staff Rahm Emanuel believed. Having served both in the Clinton White House and as a member of Congress, Emanuel had insight into the process from both angles. As much as anyone else, he wanted to avoid the mistakes of "Hillary-care," and he had specific ideas about legislative strategies. So in order to build political capitol, or at least breed the aura of success, the White House decided to pursue other legislative goals before turning to healthcare. Although some would argue that each legislative success spends political capital,[20] the Obama White House, and especially Emanuel, believed that legislative successes actually create political capital. Emanuel found support for that strategy both within the White House and in Congress, with Senators Charles Schumer (D-NY) and Byron Dorgan (D-ND) suggesting the administration focus on the economy first, and senior advisor to the president David Axelrod and others discouraging quick action on healthcare.[21] And so the Obama White House aimed for—and achieved—early legislative success: the Lily Ledbetter Fair Pay Act, the Children's Health Insurance Reauthorization, and the stimulus package (the American Recovery and Reinvestment Act) were all enacted in Obama's first months in office.

Congressional Committee Work

To say that the White House began with other legislation than healthcare is not to say that there was no early action on healthcare. In fact, as soon as the election was over in November 2008, congressional leaders began private talks with various interest groups, while the White House and then–HHS secretary-designate Tom Daschle met with grassroots supporters for a series of "coffees" to discuss healthcare.[22] President Obama mentioned healthcare in his inaugural speech on 20 January 2009. In February 2009, Congress, in a rather prescient move, began discussion about the process of health-care reform with a Senate Finance Committee hearing in which an elderly Senator Robert Byrd testified against using the reconciliation process (which fast-tracks the process by requiring only an absolute majority rather than a supermajority, as discussed previously) to pass a substantive law such as healthcare. In March, President Obama held a "healthcare summit" at the White House, to which he invited both Democrats and Republicans. By April, Kathleen Sebelius had been sworn in as secretary of the Department of Health and Human Services. And on 13 May, House Speaker Nancy Pelosi announced that healthcare legislation would be completed by July, and the Obama administration sent letters to the appropriate House and Senate committees that the bills should be finished in each house before the August recess, in preparation for an October signing.

The White House also worked behind the scenes with the insurance industry and pharmaceutical companies, forging "backroom" deals that would later inform the public view that healthcare was just more business as usual for Washington.[23]

But the "dance of legislation" doesn't begin until the committees get to work. Although Obama had made healthcare a priority, and everyone knew the basic parameters of his policy preferences, the White House did not submit legislation to Congress. Instead, congressional committees began the work with their own versions of healthcare reform. The more-or-less official starting point was a congressional document released on 8 June 2009, which included the public option, an individual mandate, and a ban on pre-existing condition exclusions. In June, hearings began in three House committees— Ways and Means, Education and Labor, and Energy and Commerce—and one Senate Committee, the Health, Education, Labor and Pension (HELP) committee, with Senator Christopher Dodd (D-CT) as its acting chair.

Having completed work on other Obama administration priorities, the committees devoted themselves full-time to healthcare once work began in June. The HELP Committee began markup on 18 June 2009.[24] Since Kennedy was a long-time champion of healthcare reform, the committee was ready and eager to begin the process. HELP considered a staggering five hundred amendments (including 160 from Republicans on the committee). The committee devoted thirteen working days, for a total of sixty hours, to healthcare markup.[25] In the House, the legislation was formally announced as HR 3200 on 14 July 2009. At 1,018 pages, and with a CBO-estimated cost of one trillion dollars, the massive bill was sent to the three House committees, which began markup shortly thereafter. At this point, things started moving quickly. The HELP Committee in the Senate finished markup and voted favorably on the bill on 16 July 2009. The House committees completed their markup quickly and moved to vote on the legislation. Here, the first snag occurred. On 16 July 2009, CBO director Doug Elmendorf testified before the Senate Finance Committee about the costs of the bill. Estimating it would cost over a trillion dollars, and that the cost was not offset in the bill, Elmendorf threw a wrench in the works, upending the Democrats' plan to push the bill through the House by the end of the summer. Fiscally conservative Blue Dog Democrats rebelled against the high cost of the legislation and sent a letter to Speaker Nancy Pelosi, asking her to take their fiscal concerns into consideration. Nonetheless, the House Ways and Means Committee and the Education and Labor Committee (which worked through the night of July 16) each approved their own version of the bill on 17 July 2009. The Energy and Commerce Committee's work was delayed by the Blue Dog Democrats' protests over the costs of the bill,[26] but the committee voted on the legislation on 31 July 2009.

Entering into the August recess, the deadline Obama had set long ago for passing healthcare reform in Congress, the bill had been voted on in all three House committees, and one of the two Senate committees. Remember, in order to pass, the bill needed not only to get out of all the relevant committees, but also to receive a favorable floor vote in both the House and Senate. As of July 2009, this was looking less and less like a probable outcome.

Senate versus House

You may have noticed that the foregoing discussion does not include mention of the Senate Finance Committee. This is because there was not a lot of action going on in the Finance Committee, at least not publicly. The Finance Committee was chaired by Senator Max Baucus (D-MT), who had close connections to the pharmaceutical industry, and who seemed to take the concept of bipartisanship very seriously, as he delayed the bill again and again, assiduously courting the Republicans on his committee. One of those Republicans was Olympia Snowe, a moderate Republican from Maine, who was often a swing vote in favor of Democratic initiatives,[27] so Baucus had at least some reasonable expectation of success. Baucus also showed the utmost deference to the committee's ranking member, Senator Charles Grassley (R-IA). Baucus and Grassley were old friends from across the aisle. Baucus felt that Grassley had treated him with respect when their roles were reversed and that he was honor-bound to return the favor. So throughout the winter and spring of

2009, Baucus went out of his way to make sure that Grassley felt included. He sought input from other Republicans as well, and eventually frustrated both Senate Democratic leadership and the Obama White House, who felt that his inclusiveness was going too far, and that he was being taken for a ride by Republicans on his committee, who had no intention of ever supporting healthcare, and instead wanted to hand the president a resounding defeat.

Committee Republicans, on the other hand, were insisting that the process was moving too quickly, and did, in fact, want to slow things down. This was partly a genuine search for middle ground and compromise, and also a delaying tactic to foil healthcare reform and hand President Obama a political defeat. Olympia Snowe, at least, seemed to be genuine in her attempts to find a compromise she could live with. Areas of disagreement included ways to cut the costs of the bill and how to set up the so-called public option. Snowe felt that the default for state implementation should be private insurance. If necessary, she believed, states should be able to opt *in* to a government-run plan. The Senate policy, however, included a government-run plan as one option that states would be required to implement, unless they opted *out* of that requirement. The arcane nature of the argument only added to the public perception that the bill was convoluted and cumbersome. Snowe and other Republican Senators agreed with Blue Dog Democrats in the House that the healthcare plan was too costly, and she and they were heavily swayed by Elmendorf's testimony in the summer of 2009. In fact, seeing that the process was moving so slowly, Rahm Emanuel had his staff write a "secret plan" to reform healthcare, a plan that ran eight hundred pages and never actually saw the light of day.[28] From the Democrats' perspective, the Republicans were the party of "no," who would delay and obstruct healthcare as part of a larger strategy to win back the White House and the majority in Congress.[29] From the perspective of this book's argument, the Republicans were doing exactly what the American system was set up to encourage.

The fact that the Senate was dragging its feet on the bill is not surprising, given that the framers had intended the Senate to act as a brake on the potentially quick and decisive action of the House of Representatives. However, it may be a bit surprising that Senate action eventually came about as a result of some questionable logrolling deals to gain *Democratic* votes. The "cornhusker kickback" (a deal negotiated by Senator Ben Nelson [D-NE] to have the federal government cover the costs of Medicaid expansion in Nebraska) and the "Louisiana purchase" ($100 million in healthcare funding for Louisiana, negotiated by Senator Mary Landrieu)[30] gave the bill an unseemly, indecorous gloss. But in the summer of 2009, the focus was on Republicans and on Baucus's attempts to win them over to his healthcare plan in the Senate. Time and again, Baucus missed his own deadlines, as Chuck Grassley brought up one or another reason to hold up the bill. Grassley was courted not only by his committee chair, but also by the White House, where he had several personal meetings with the president. White House staff, already annoyed with Grassley, eventually began to believe that he was merely enjoying the attention and wouldn't vote for the bill, no matter what compromises they offered him. As Baucus came under greater pressure from his own party, he had to admit that the Senate Republicans were not going to let him finish the bill within the timeframe that the Democratic leadership was demanding. Baucus finally brought the legislation to a vote in his committee after he had seen a fundraising letter from Grassley to his home state supporters, in which he explicitly criticized parts of the bill that he and Baucus had already agreed to.

The chance for bipartisanship had ended.

Floor Passage

While the House and Senate were on their August break, Democrats and Republicans were getting an earful from their constituents back home. Angry about the economic outlook, jobs, the housing crisis, and the increasingly partisan bickering in Congress, constituents let their Representatives and Senators have it in "town hall" meetings across the country, and the Tea Party (a loosely organized group of activists whose main goal is limited government and whose name harkens back to the Boston Tea Party protest against taxes) was born.

On 25 August 2009, Ted Kennedy died.

The House

Floor passage in the House was dependent on the discipline, power, and persistence of Nancy Pelosi, Speaker of the House. As Speaker, she consolidated power and kept close reins on what was going on in committees. Pelosi was born and bred to a life in politics. Her father had been mayor of Baltimore, and she remembers as a young girl seeing constituents come to their home for his help. This left a lasting impression on her, imprinting a view of politics as the art of quid pro quo. As Speaker, Pelosi made a study of understanding the needs of the rank and file, both in order to help them and to give her leverage. Pelosi's personal background and trajectory to office gave her an interesting mix of leadership qualities. Pelosi did not run for office until midlife. As a young wife and mother in California, she stayed home with her children, but she also stayed involved in Democratic Party circles, developing fundraising skills that would serve her well later on. "Pelosi's leadership style combined toughness, discipline and attention to detail with inclusiveness, a willingness to listen and attention to members' individual needs."[31]

As Speaker, Pelosi made "aggressive use of the institutional powers of speakership,"[32] and this showed in passage of healthcare. The biggest compromises she had to broker were a watered-down public option, and concessions to the pro-life contingent. Pelosi tried to walk a fine line between her pro-choice female colleagues in Congress and the Catholic bishops, whose support would put a gloss of bipartisanship on the bill. In the end, she supposedly had tears in her eyes when she told the Women's Caucus that she would have to allow the Stupak Amendment (restricting abortion coverage), or the bill wouldn't get passed.[33] Later on, when the Stupak Amendment created an obstacle to the House passing the Senate's bill (pro-life Democrats wouldn't sign on to a bill without it, abortion-rights Democrats wouldn't sign on to a bill with it). Pelosi was able to get "the nuns," representing the liberal Catholic Health Association and NETwork (a grassroots lobbying organization) to publicly assert that the Senate bill would *not* allow abortions,[34] a surprise announcement that gave pro-life Democrats cover to vote for the bill, despite the fact that the bishops and others in the pro-life movement did not agree with the nuns' assessment.

Pelosi's reining in of her party (she didn't even bother trying to get Republican votes) for healthcare votes was nothing short of masterful. According to a former Clinton staffer:

> On the final vote, the whipping process was intense and impressive. Democratic leaders I have known in the past have rarely played this kind of hardball, but some kneecaps were broken Saturday night to get these votes and the Speaker did a masterful job of doing every little thing that needed to be done. She gave no passes to people, and was very clear there would have been consequences to all who voted no. She got the job done.[35]

The Senate

The House passed the bill on 7 November 2009. Shortly afterward, the Senate began consideration of the healthcare legislation. The first test vote came on 21 November 2009, when the Senate took a procedural vote that would allow floor debate to begin. As the Democratic leadership struggled to garner the sixty votes needed to invoke cloture and begin floor debate, public negotiations with Senators Mary Landrieu (discussed above) and Blanche Lincoln (D-AK, who later lost her 2010 reelection bid) eventually resulted in the necessary sixty votes to move forward with consideration of the bill.[36] After consideration, yet another procedural vote was necessary to allow a vote on final passage. While passage of any legislation requires only a simple majority (i.e., fifty-one out of one hundred), a cloture vote with a supermajority of sixty is now generally required to even allow a vote on final passage. As the bill was debated, there were several obstacles to passage, including the public option and whether states could opt in or out; whether the bill, contrary to the Hyde amendment, provided for government funding for abortions; tax increases to pay for the bill; and reductions in Medicare spending. Senator Harry Reid, the majority leader, had difficult negotiations in order to garner the sixty votes necessary to proceed to passage. For example, if he got rid of the public option in order to get conservative support, liberal senators would vote against the bill. As a news report stated at the time, "crafting a version that pleases four centrists—Nelson and Sens. Mary Landrieu (D-LA), Blanche Lincoln (D-AK) and Joe Lieberman (I-CT)—and maintains the Democratic left flank may well take until Christmas."[37] And that points to another problem.

Republicans were concerned not only over issues, but also over the amount of time devoted to debate. They felt that the Senate should allow six weeks for debating the issue. While there was genuine concern over the rush to reform, it was also true that six more weeks would push the debate past Christmas, and thus into the next year, likely killing chances for passage.[38] As debate on the issue began, Republicans engaged in delaying tactics, while Democrats tried to cobble together both an acceptable bill and a sixty-vote majority to move to passage. On 15 December, Senators Snowe and Collins announced that they would not vote for cloture, saying that they wanted further debate on the bill. That same day, President Obama called a meeting of Senate Democrats at the White House, encouraging them to push ahead and pass the bill, though he acknowledged that "there are still disagreements that have to be ironed out. There is still work that has to be done in the next few days."[39]

Majority Leader Reid's deal making and arm twisting paid off. At seven o'clock on Christmas Eve morning, the Senate voted for passage of healthcare. Senator Reid and others invoked the memory of Senator Kennedy: "With Senator Ted Kennedy's voice booming in our ears," intoned Reid, "with his passion in our hearts, we say as he said, 'The work goes on, the cause endures.'"[40] Democrats were euphoric. The mood was dampened, however, by the fact that not a single Republican had voted for the bill. Senator Joe Lieberman (D-CT) expressed his regret: "There's a kind of bittersweet quality to it because a reform of this size shouldn't happen along partisan lines."[41]

The next usual step would be a conference committee to iron out the details of the legislation. In recent years, however, the House and Senate have increasingly foregone conference committees in favor of a sort of ping pong approach—one chamber amends the other's legislation and sends it back for a vote, and vice versa.[42] For healthcare, House and Senate leaders decided to meet together and with the White House to forge a compromise behind closed doors, causing complaints from C-SPAN that the process was not conducted in the open.[43] After the deals were made, the intention was to have the House vote to amend the Senate bill, and then send the amended version back to the Senate for its approval. Over the Christmas break, House Democrats began negotiations by telephone, and Speaker Pelosi, Majority Leader Hoyer, Finance Committee chair Max Baucus, and acting HELP Committee chair Christopher Dodd met with the president.

The political environment was about to change drastically.

The Election of Scott Brown and Legislative Maneuvering

On 19 January 2010, Republican state senator Scott Brown defeated Democratic attorney general Martha Coakley in Massachusetts to fill the Senate seat vacated by Senator Kennedy's death. The political world was turned on its head. Not only was it unthinkable that a Republican upstart could replace Kennedy, but the Senate Democrats lost the sixty-vote majority needed for the legislative maneuvering that was now required to pass legislation. And, in addition, Democratic senators and representatives feared that Scott Brown's election was a harbinger of things to come. Town halls and Tea Partiers were signs of decreasing public support for healthcare reform that might make it politically unpalatable for Democrats to vote for healthcare legislation. If a Republican could win on the issue of healthcare (people chanted "Forty-one" at Brown's political rallies, indicating that he would be the forty-first vote, blocking healthcare passage) in liberal, Democratic Massachusetts, of all places, then every Democratic member of Congress was in trouble. The euphoria among Democrats was now turning to gloom. Despite the fact that healthcare had already passed both the House and the Senate, under the American system of checks and balances, a law must be passed in *identical form* by both chambers before it can be sent to the president for his signature. As noted above, there were significant differences between House and Senate bills. Immediately following the election, there was much talk from the White House and House and Senate Democrats of scaling back the bill. Both Nancy Pelosi and presidential advisor David Axelrod expressed optimism that the bill could still pass, although most observers realized that passage would require threading a very narrow needle.[44] Privately, Nancy Pelosi expressed her frustration with what she saw as Obama's lack of understanding of how the House works. "Does the president not understand the way this game works? He wants to get it done and be beloved and you can't have both—which does he want?"[45]

House and Senate leaders decided to try to thread that very narrow needle. The problem was twofold: The Senate could not pass any healthcare revisions

IMAGE 4.3
U.S. Republican Senator-elect Scott Brown of Massachusetts celebrates with his daughter Ayla (R) and other family members and supporters at his victory rally in Boston on 19 January 2010, after defeating Democrat Martha Coakley in the U.S. Senate race to replace the late U.S. Senator Ted Kennedy. © BRIAN SNYDER/ Reuters/Corbis.

the House sent to it without sixty votes, and the House would absolutely not accept the Senate version as is. That left two competing versions of healthcare, instead of one bill to go to the president. Although Pelosi was adamant with the president and his advisors that there was no way the House would vote for the Senate bill because of its objectionable provisions, there just might be a way to get the legislation passed.

As we mentioned earlier, according to Senate rules, *reconciliation* bills are not allowed to be filibustered, and thus can be passed with a simple majority (fifty-one out of one hundred instead of sixty out of one hundred). These bills have a very specific purpose: to reconcile budget goals with authorizing legislation. They are not, in theory, to be used for passing new laws. But what if the portions of the healthcare act dealing with spending (a budget issue) were separated out and included as part of reconciliation? Any senator could move to strike out provisions that are not budget issues, yes, but the Senate parliamentarian gets to rule on the point of order.[46]

So the plan went like this. First, the House would pass the Senate bill, as is. This would require a lot of arm twisting by Speaker Pelosi and the president.

Second, the House would make changes to the Senate bill and include those changes as part of a reconciliation bill. The Senate could then pass reconciliation with a simple majority, and healthcare would be law. Democratic leaders decided to try this strategy, and Nancy Pelosi's legislative prowess was again on the line. This was not your typical textbook version of how a bill becomes a law.

TABLE 4.2
How the Healthcare Bill Became a Law: The Textbook Version

HOUSE		SENATE
Bill introduced, referred to committees	**June 2009**	Bill introduced, referred to committees
	Committee Consideration	
Hearings begin in House committees	**17 June 2009**	
	19 June 2009	HELP Committee considers healthcare legislation
	15 July 2009	HELP approves healthcare bill
Education and Labor, Ways and Means, and Energy and Commerce begin markup of healthcare bill	**16 July 2009**	CBO Director Elmendorf testifies to Senate Finance Committee
Ways and Means and Education and Labor approve the bill	**17 July 2009**	
Energy and Commerce approves the bill; bill placed on House Union Calendar	**31 July 2009**	
HOUSE IN RECESS	**August 2009**	*SENATE IN RECESS*
	Floor Consideration	
Rules Committee issues rule	**November 2009**	Senate Finance Committee completes markup of bill
House floor debate and passage	**7 November 2009**	
	11 November 2009	Senate invokes cloture
	24 December 2009	Senate final passage
	Conference Committee Action	
House leaders negotiate with Senate	**December 2009– January 2010**	Senate leaders negotiate with House
	Final Action	
House approves Senate bill	**21 March 2010**	
	23 March 2010	
	President Obama signs the Patient Protection and Affordable Care Act	

TABLE 4.3
How the Healthcare Reform Bill Became Law: The Real Story

8 November 2008	Barack Obama elected president; healthcare is a major issue in his platform
November 2008– January 2009	Senate Finance Committee and Senate HELP Committee quietly hold meetings with healthcare lobbyists on all sides
19 January 2009	Barack Obama is sworn in as president
February 2009	Byrd testifies at a Senate Budget Committee hearing, saying healthcare should not be passed through the reconciliation process
March 2009	Healthcare Summit with various interests; Obama presents his plan as a budget cutting measure; members of Congress are already discussing using budget reconciliation as the means to get healthcare reform passed
28 April 2009	Sebelius is confirmed as HHS secretary by the Senate
13 May 2009	Pelosi announces that House will complete healthcare reform by July
2 June 2009	Obama letter to Senate Finance and HELP: pass bills before August, final version by October
8 June 2009	House releases healthcare framework, including public option and individual mandate, ban on exclusion of pre-existing conditions
June–July 2009	Baucus holds series of meetings with Republicans on Finance Committee
15 June 2009	Obama gives healthcare speech to American Medical Association
17 June 2009	HELP Committee begins markup: 500 amendments (160 from Republicans), thirteen working days, sixty hours
19 June 2009	Hearings and markups begin in House committees
9 July 2009	Blue Dog coalition letter to Pelosi: control costs, don't put onerous burdens on small business
14 July 2009	HR 3200, 1,018 pages, released by House Democrats, sent to Ways and Means, Education and Labor, Energy and Commerce; CBO estimate: $1 trillion
15 July 2009	HELP approves healthcare bill: individual mandate, public option, preventive care, covers uninsured; still waiting for Senate Finance committee bill
16 July 2009	Elmendorf, CBO, testifies to Finance Committee that the plans (HELP and House committees) would increase healthcare spending; later that same day, House Ways and Means committee marks up healthcare bill; Education and Labor begins markup, works through the night on the bill; Energy and Commerce begins markup, stalled by Blue Dog Democrats' efforts to cut costs
17 July 2009	Ways and Means (23–18), Education and Labor (26–22) approve HR 3200; Olympia Snowe and others send letter to Senate leadership urging them to "resist timelines" for healthcare legislation

31 July 2009	House Energy and Commerce (31–28) approves HR 3200 (including Lois Capp's amendment on abortion)
August 2009	House and Senate go on recess, thereby missing a deadline for passing healthcare reform; in their Districts, House members hear from angry constituents at town hall meetings
25 August 2009	Ted Kennedy dies
9 September 2009	President Obama addresses a joint session of Congress; weighs in on individual mandate, employer mandate, insurance exchange, public option, pre-existing conditions, malpractice, funding (reducing fraud and waste in Medicare and Medicaid, charging insurance companies a fee)
September–October 2009	Senate Finance Committee markup of S 1679
29 September 2009	Public option is voted down in Senate Finance Committee
30 September 2009	Senate Finance Committee votes down abortion amendment
2 October 2009	Senate Finance Committee completes markup
7 November 2009	House passes HR 3590, healthcare legislation (only one Republican votes in favor: Rep. Anh "Joseph" Cao of Louisiana)
21 November 2009	Senate invokes cloture on motion to proceed to consideration of HR 3590 (Saturday vote)
24 December 2009	Senate, in early morning vote, approves the healthcare bill
Late December 2009	House and Senate Democrats begin discussions with the White House on reconciling the House and Senate bills
19 January 2010	Republican Scott Brown is elected senator from Massachusetts, replacing Ted Kennedy and denying the Democrats the sixty-vote margin needed for procedural votes
27 January 2010	Obama's State of the Union address announces his intention to go forward with healthcare reform
January–February 2010	Congressional Democrats strategize with the White House on healthcare reform, decide to proceed (rather than scale back), and choose the reconciliation process as the vehicle for passage
3 March 2010	Obama announces his healthcare plan, push begins for votes
21 March 2010	House votes on Senate bill and reconciliation changes, Senate votes on reconciliation changes
23 March 2010	President Obama signs the Patient Protection and Affordable Care Act into law
25 March 2010	Senate votes on reconciliation bill (including changes to healthcare legislation made in the House) Health Care and Education Reconciliation Act of 2010; House votes on and passes Senate reconciliation bill changes
30 March 2010	President Obama signs the Health Care and Education Reconciliation Act of 2010 at Northern Virginia Community College

On 3 March 2010, Obama announced "his" healthcare plan, and the full-court press on healthcare began. Obama and Biden used a White House cocktail party celebrating pay-go legislation (requiring new spending to be offset by revenue from new taxes or savings) as a way to gently persuade fence-sitting House members to support healthcare as a cost-cutting measure. Obama gave speeches and went to rallies, blasting the healthcare industry that he had so assiduously courted at the start of the process. His cabinet wrote opinion pieces in support of healthcare. The president put personal pressure on several members of Congress, and brought Representative Dennis Kucinich (D-OH) on Air Force One with him. Rumors swirled that Obama was offering him a cabinet post, or money for pet projects. Eventually, Kucinich gave in, and his vote started a "roll" in Congress, with other Democratic fence sitters promising to vote for the legislation as well. "Arm twist after arm twist, deal after deal, these last days played out so publicly that at some point amid the news conferences and speeches it started to feel like a compressed, frenetic rehash of the fourteen-month fight."[47]

The vote was scheduled for 21 March. Thirty-four Democrats joined the entire Republican caucus in opposition, but the House approved the Senate version of healthcare with a vote of 219–212 and then approved the separate reconciliation package (making changes to the Senate bill) on a vote of 220–211. Reconciliation was sent to the Senate, which voted on the package on 24 March 2010. It passed with a vote of 56–43; three Democrats (Ben Nelson [NE], Blanche Lincoln [AR], and Mark Pryor [AR]) voted against. Senator Joe Biden presided over the Senate in his constitutional role. Again, Ted Kennedy was invoked as majority leader Harry Reid asked for a moment of silence in his memory. "The chamber was so quiet that the whir of computers and electronic devices on the dais could be heard, as could the ambient noise outside the chamber."[48]

The bill was sent back to the House, where it hit a snag in the form of Representative Bart Stupak (D-MI), who had held out on an earlier version for a guarantee that federal funds would not pay for abortions. Heralded at the time by the right as an anti-abortion hero, in March of 2010, he acceded to Pelosi's demand that he remove the so-called Stupak Amendment, and in return was promised an executive order from the president specifying that no federal funds would be used for abortion. Stupak became a pro-life pariah and was called a "baby-killer" on the House floor.[49] With one last compromise out of the way, the bill finally won by a 225–199 vote (with twenty-five Democrats voting against, and no Republicans voting for).

Healthcare legislation was sent to the president for his signature, without a single Republican vote for final passage. And so, the healthcare fight was over, and the Democrats had won . . .

Welcome (Again) to the World of Checks and Balances

. . . Except that it wasn't, and they hadn't. In the elections of November 2010, Republicans—running against healthcare reform and vowing to repeal it—took over control of the House and made significant gains in the Senate. So the Democrats had a major legislative accomplishment, passing comprehensive healthcare for the first time in history, and immediately afterwards, in the words of the president, "took a shellacking." What happened?

Welcome to the world of checks and balances.

Earlier, this chapter pointed out that broad, sweeping reform is not common in our presidential system, nor is it what the framers intended. The constitutional system is designed to protect minority rights and thwart majority rule. In one sense, then, healthcare reform defied the odds, and illustrates that a majority faction *can* get something done. Despite all the favor the system gives to the minority, in this case, the majority won. At least, the majority won, at one point in time, in two branches: Congress (which passed the bill) and the presidency (Obama signed it). But the system of checks and balances separates power in several ways. First, the House in particular is dependent upon and highly reactive to the will of the people. And while the 111th Congress interpreted their will to include the passage of healthcare, the 112th Congress got the message—loud and clear—that a well-organized, Tea Party–dominated electorate did not want this version of healthcare reform. Second, power is dispersed among the legislature, the judicial branch (discussed below), and the executive branch. Once healthcare passed Congress, the Department of Health and Human Services had to get down to the nuts and bolts of the policy and figure out specifics such as how to execute (and fund) the required insurance exchanges and whether and how increased benefits might lead to higher health insurance premiums. HHS has also stepped into some thorny issues on its own, such as expanding mandatory preventive coverage to include birth control. In July 2013, the administration announced that the employer mandate (the requirement that employers provide healthcare coverage) would be delayed from its original start date in 2014, to a 2015 date, which, conveniently, would occur after the midterm elections in 2014.[50]

Separation of powers also refers to the system of federalism, in which government is split between national (federal) and state governments. States (Republican states, anyway) did not like healthcare and balked at implementing it. This caused problems for the insurance exchanges that states were supposed to create and maintain. Twenty-six states even signed on to a lawsuit declaring the law unconstitutional. This brings us to the third branch of government: the judicial branch. The Supreme Court was given the opportunity to overturn the individual mandate, and perhaps strike down the entire law, as unconstitutional. In a somewhat surprising move, the Court upheld the law as constitutional in a 5–4 decision, but only because of the argument that the law's requirement that Americans buy health insurance constituted a tax—an argument that the administration's lawyers had specifically rejected, at least in part. Even a Supreme Court decision is not the end of the line for healthcare. Republicans in Congress have repeatedly passed legislation repealing the healthcare law—legislation that had zero chance of being approved by the Senate. And in July 2013, some Republicans announced their plans to veto any continuing resolutions that would fund the Affordable Care Act, setting the stage for a government shutdown in the fall of 2013.[51]

Perhaps a comparison to the 1994 Contract with America is apt here. Like Obama and the Democrats in Congress, the 1994 Contract Congress achieved its promises. The 104th Congress, too, was blocked by checks and balances, but at a different stage. The Contract Congress got each and every one of its proposed bills voted on in the House; most passed. (And, notably, the Contract only promised to bring bills to a vote in the House.) *Then* checks and balances set in: the Senate sat on bills, the president vetoed them, and the Supreme Court weighed in. The Contract Congress had what was then called "rare" party unity: party-line voting on most issues, though Democrats did cross over and vote for some of the Republican legislative proposals. Obama's healthcare, on the other hand, was passed without a single Republican vote in the House or Senate and signed by the president. With the Contract Congress, legislation stalled, and cries of gridlock went up. With Obama's healthcare plan, a law was passed, and cries of government intrusion were heard. But in both cases, quick and decisive action was limited (before or after the fact) by the institutional makeup of the American system of government.

There were certainly many differences between 1994 and 2008. The Contract Congress was more like a parliamentary system: representatives ran on a very specific party platform. Obama's election was purely presidential: voting for a charismatic personality with a promise that was, on its surface, vague enough for everyone to agree with—change and hope. Voters may or may not pay attention to the details, but there is a difference between having a specific contract, as the Republicans did in 1994, and the usual personality-driven presidential campaign. In addition, Obama ran on a promise to change the way *Washington* gets things done. Part of the Contract's promise was to change the way *Congress* gets things done. This was certainly more achievable: they were running for Congress. The first thing the new Republican majority did in 1994 was to change the rules of the House. Obama's promise, however, required others to go along with him, and you can't make a promise that someone else—particularly your political opponents—will do something. For better or for worse, the American political system is based on two entrenched political parties. Having only two parties (as opposed to multiparty parliamentary systems) means that issues become bifurcated. So it is hard to be post-partisan without completely eliminating or drastically changing the party system. And beyond political parties, the framers set up a system that makes it difficult to get things done. Changing the system to any large degree would require fundamental, constitutional change.

Students of the Contract with America Congress noted how similar the 1994 election was to a parliamentary election: it was more based on issues (at least on the part of the people running for office) than American elections normally are, and it was also nationalized.[52] And once the Republicans took over Congress, they voted en bloc to pass their legislative promises. Because of the United States' separation of powers, the similarity to a parliamentary system stops there. But for purposes of argument, let us take a moment to look at some advantages of a parliamentary system: there are clearly defined party platforms, coalition building exists around a party platform (in a presidential system, coalition building is done around each issue), it is easier to get things done, and there is no competition between the executive and the legislature. Looking at healthcare from that perspective, it would certainly be easier to get legislation passed in a parliamentary system. For one thing, voters are less likely to vote for charismatic personalities and are more likely to focus on the specific policy differences between the parties. For another, coalition building begins *before* the new government starts its work. Multiple parties (and we have only two) will broker deals and adjust policy goals in order to form a majority coalition government. And the executive branch doesn't have to convince the legislative branch to get things done, since the executive and cabinet members come directly from Parliament. One can see how healthcare, or any policy, for that matter, would have a much easier route to passage under such circumstances. And, if a policy were too controversial, too big, too overreaching, it would likely be abandoned in that earlier coalition-building process, before the lawmaking even began. So, if we had a parliamentary system, then, healthcare as a specific policy goal would have been presented as part of a party platform, debated in the process of coalition creation, and then, perhaps, would be accepted when it was written into law and then implemented.

Or perhaps not. Institutions matter, but so does political culture. And we have the institutional framework that our political culture demands. America's founding principle was suspicion of government. Our rallying cry was "No taxation without representation." From our earliest history, we have fought about the proper role of federal government, and despite the framers' concerns about political parties, our party system has long been built around the tension between too much and not enough government.[53] There are some advantages in a presidential system, as well, and these advantages suit our culture. For one thing, minority rights are enshrined in our separated system, and these minority rights protect against tyranny of the majority. Despite Republicans' loud arguments of majority tyranny, minority rights are alive and well in the United States. Especially in Congress, when the minority feels that its rights have been trampled upon—as the Republicans felt in the 2010s—it has other outlets to reassert them, and that is what happened with respect to healthcare. Coalition building in our system occurs around specific issues, and, again, that's the way we like it. Americans, like helicopter parents, want to be able to second-guess every move the government makes, and redirect it when necessary. Our system is based on compromise and bargaining over issues, and it leads to *incremental* rather than *comprehensive* change. Comprehensive change is not impossible, but it is not easy, either.

So does all this mean the system is fine just the way it is? Of course not. Healthcare illustrates the highly polarized nature of the current party system, and the increasing use of extraconstitutional maneuvers and parliamentary tactics to get things done. Healthcare reform is a problem because it wasn't

IMAGE 4.4
U.S. President Barack Obama waves to the audience after signing the comprehensive healthcare reform legislation during a ceremony in the East Room of the White House in Washington on 23 March 2010. With Obama on stage are Vice President Joe Biden (L), Speaker of the House of Representatives Nancy Pelosi (2-R), and Senate Majority Leader Harry Reid (R). © JASON REED/Reuters/Corbis.

incremental, and it wasn't bipartisan. While the 104th Congress was notable for its party-line voting, partisan voting in Congress has become increasingly prevalent since then. There are no longer incentives for Republicans to work with Democrats, and vice versa. Policy making has become a zero-sum game, with each party trying not only to get its own legislative successes, but—with an eye to the next election cycle—also to ensure that the other party fails.[54] Perhaps Republican Jim DeMint illustrated this cynical view best when he described a potential defeat of healthcare as President Obama's "Waterloo." This hyper-partisanship is not just about political maneuvering. The two parties genuinely do have different views of government. Those views are increasingly divergent: *Government can and should solve societal problems*, OR *Government IS the problem*. There is no room for middle ground.

Conclusion: Lessons from the Past

Going back to the lessons from chapter 3, we can see that the exception does in fact prove the rule. Francis Fukuyama has usefully observed that:

> The American system . . . is deliberately designed to place many more veto gates—what Americans call checks and balances—in front of executive decision-making, by adding separated powers, bicameralism, federalism, weak party discipline, and judicial review. The only important feature of the US political system that increases rather than decreases decisiveness is its single-member plurality voting system. A British Prime Minister's budget is approved within days of its being submitted to parliament; an American budget, by contrast, takes the better part of a year to pass, and never survives in the form proposed by the president.[55]

In contrast to a parliamentary system, the American presidential system makes it exceptionally difficult—thought not impossible—for broad, comprehensive legislation to pass. Let us revisit the lessons from 1994 to see how they apply to 2010.

The Legislative Process Is More Open

The legislative process is, in fact, more open in a presidential system than in a parliamentary one. Although the system for healthcare reform might not seem open from an American point of view (decisions and deals were made behind closed doors), from a parliamentary perspective, the system is more open to input, all along the way. Democrats had to deal with obstruction from Republicans at all stages of the process, from committee hearings to floor debates and final passage. Interest groups played a substantial role in the process, as did public opinion, particularly in the form of Tea Party activists at town hall meetings. In addition, healthcare policy was directly affected by a special election in the middle of the 111th Congress, something that would never have happened in a parliamentary system. Finally, Democratic leaders had to deal with difficult amendments from their own party, leading us to the second conclusion.

Party Discipline Is Fleeting, at Best

In a parliamentary system, party leaders expect their rank and file to vote with them. As noted in the Contract with America chapter, coalitions are built before the government is formed, not as legislation is being considered. Healthcare coalition building was somewhat unique, in that it was intraparty rather than interparty. The Affordable Care Act was passed without Republican votes, and Democratic leaders were left in the awkward position of having to bargain with, compromise with, make promises to, and otherwise coerce various individuals and factions *within their own ranks*. The Affordable Care Act was similar to legislation passed in a parliamentary system, in that it received votes only from the majority party. Where it was different was that those votes were *not* automatic, but rather, hard-fought and tenuous.

Accountability Is Limited

In the case of the Affordable Care Act, accountability seems very clear: it was a Democratic initiative, sponsored by a Democratic president, and passed by a Democratic Congress. As President Truman used to say: "The buck stops here." However, because of the very openness of our system, the buck never really stops. Congress passes a law that is implemented by federal agencies. Delays occur when those agencies move from the generalities of creating legislation to the specificities of executing it, and the administration finds that implementation may take longer than originally planned. States, too, play a role in implementing policy, and the courts can be called in to answer questions of constitutionality. When all else fails, a law can be repealed, or, short of that, Congress can refuse to fund it.

For healthcare, the issue is not so much accountability as responsibility. Decision points are many, and the opposition can put up obstacles at many different points. Accountability is limited in the sense that it is fluid: passing the law, implementing the law, and interpreting the law are all done by different entities in our separated system. The question, then, may be one of legitimacy: it may just require more effort in our presidential system to convince the losing side that a law is legitimate (that is, valid and acceptable), and the minority has the ability to be obstructive even after the law is passed (witness the dozens of House votes to repeal healthcare legislation, and the Republican attempt to defund the legislation, rsulting in a government shutdown in Fall 2013).

Policy Windows Only Remain Open for a Short Time

As with the Contract with America, Democrats in the 111th Congress had only a short amount of time in which to pass healthcare policy. The Democratic majority in Congress was short lived, the compromises leadership made to garner votes had a tendency to unravel, and something as simple as the death of a single senator set off a string of events that very nearly undid two years' worth of work on healthcare. If healthcare had not passed when it did in 2010, it most probably would not have passed within the remainder of Obama's two terms of office.

Finally, the legislative process for healthcare reform illustrates some of the same issues as the process for the Contract with America, including openness, minority rights, and bargaining (though in 2010, bargaining was intraparty rather than interparty). Unlike most Contract tenets, healthcare reform passed, but not in the unencumbered way legislation might pass in a parliamentary system.

Like the 104th Congress, the 111th Congress illustrates the strengths and weaknesses of our system, and also like the 104th Congress, the 111th Congress is both an anomaly (in that comprehensive change was passed) and characteristic of the way Congress works (in that the outcome, like that of the Contract, was not foreordained, that work had to be done within a policy window, and that all parts of the separated system had to weigh in).

Plus ça change, plus ç'est la même chose.

Notes

1. See, for example, James Anderson, *Public Policymaking*, 7th ed. (New York: Wadsworth, 2010).

2. John Kingdon, *Agendas, Alternatives, and Public Policies*, with an epilogue on healthcare, 2nd ed. (New York: Longman Classics in Political Science, 2010).

3. Deficits are when the government spends more money than it receives in a given year. Debt is the sum of the deficits from year to year.

4. Center for Budget and Policy Priorities, "Where Do Our Federal Tax Dollars Go?" 12 April 2013, www.cbpp.org/cms/index.cfm?fa=view&id=1258.

5. Social Security Advisory Board, *The Unsustainable Cost of Healthcare*, September 2009, 2. www.ssab.gov/documents/TheUnsustainableCostofHealthCare_508.pdf. See also Center for Budget and Policy Priorities, "Where Do Our Tax Dollars Go?"

6. For example, in Newport News, Virginia, on 8 September 2008, Obama talked about his mother's struggle with healthcare and the numbers of Americans who had to file for bankruptcy because of the high cost of treating long-term healthcare problems.

7. "Blue Dog" is an expression used to mean moderate, usually fiscally conservative Democrats. It is a play on the old expression, "yellow dog" Democrats, which was used to describe a Southern Democrat who would vote for any Democratic candidate, even a yellow dog. The expression "blue dog" supposedly was coined when a group of moderates was meeting in the office of Billy Tauzin (D-LA, now a pharmaceutical lobbyist who became involved in the healthcare bill) under a painting of blue dogs by Cajun artist George Rodrigue. Jonathan Alter, *The Promise: Obama, Year One* (New York: Simon and Schuster, 2010), 406.

8. The old saw goes that one doesn't want to watch either sausage or legislation being made.

9. While many people, including Martha Coakley, the Democrat running against Brown, were truly surprised by the results, the election of Brown was probably not as unbelievable as one might be led to believe. Massachusetts has a history of electing Republican governors, including recent presidential candidate Mitt Romney. While Coakley ran a poor campaign (including calling Curt Schilling—the great Red Sox pitcher and hero of the 2004 World Series Championship, who was also a supporter of Scott Brown—a Yankee fan, on the WBZ-Boston evening talk radio show, "Nightside with Dan Rea"), that doesn't fully explain the election. Brown ran a good campaign, hitting on populist themes to a receptive audience. His campaign, as many in the media correctly predicted, was a harbinger of the 2010 election that gave the House back to the Republicans.

10. Alter, *The Promise*, 255.

11. James Thurber, "An Introduction to an Assessment of the Obama Presidency," in *Obama in Office*, ed. James Thurber (Boulder, CO: Paradigm Publishers, 2011), 2–3.

12. John E. Owens, "A 'Post-Partisan' President in a Partisan Context," in Thurber, *Obama in Office*, 124.

13. Ibid., 121.

14. Barbara Sinclair, "Congressional Leadership in Obama's First Two Years," in Thurber, *Obama in Office*, 97; Owens, "Post-Partisan President," 115.

15. Thurber, "An Introduction," 7. See also Stephen Wayne's chapter in the same book.

16. Owens, "Post-Partisan President," 112: "He cultivated a reputation as a deliberative, fair-minded intellectual."

17. See David Maraniss's op-ed, "Clinton and Obama: Presidential Parallels," in *The Washington Post*, 25 March 2012.

18. See, for example, Sam Kernell, *Going Public: New Strategies of Presidential Leadership*, 4th ed. (Washington: CQ Press, 2006).

19. Alter, *The Promise*, 398. See also Thurber, "An Introduction," in which the author notes that the new media mobilizes *voters*, not policy support.

20. See Paul Light, *The President's Agenda: Domestic Policy Choice from Kennedy to Clinton*, 2nd ed. (Baltimore: Johns Hopkins University Press, 1998).

21. Alter, *The Promise*, 45.

22. Rebecca Adams, "Healthcare Overhaul Still in 'Happy Talk' Stage," *Congressional Quarterly Weekly Reports*, 19 January 2009, library.cqpress.com/cqweekly/document.php?id=weekly report111-000003012941&t. Note that Daschle, who was originally supposed to be both the healthcare "czar" and head of HHS, eventually withdrew his name from consideration for both when significant personal finance problems were revealed. Nancy Ann DeParle replaced him as the White House point person on healthcare, and former governor Kathleen Sebelius (D-KS) replaced him as secretary of HHS.

23. Alter, *The Promise*, 254. The author states: "There was cunning here. The idea was to keep interest groups on board long enough so that when the president blasted them and they went into active opposition (as the insurers and hospitals inevitably did) it would be too late to derail the bill, or so they thought at the time."

24. Markups are when the actual legislative work is done in committee. The bill is considered line by line, and any changes committee members desire to make are submitted as amendments, which are then voted on by the committee. Hearings, on the other hand, are usually more for public display. Officials, interest groups, or constituents may come to testify in favor of or against a bill, or about an issue in general.

25. Drew Armstrong and David Clarke, "Panel Advances Health Overhaul," *Congressional Quarterly Weekly Reports*, 20 July 2009, 1708, library.cqpress.com/cqweekly/document.php?id=weekly report111-0000031705090&t. See also "Health Committee Opens Markup," *Congressional Quarterly Weekly Reports*, 1444.

26. Adriel Bettelheim, "Overhaul Hard to Steer Using Hands-Off Approach," *Congressional Quarterly Weekly Reports*, 10 August 2009, 1894, library.cqpress.com/cqweekly/document.php?id=weekly report111-000003189437&t.

27. Senator Snowe announced her retirement in March 2011, citing the increasingly polarized and partisan atmosphere of the Senate.

28. Alter, *The Promise*, 266.

29. See Charles Mahtesian and Patrick O'Connor, "GOP at Risk of Becoming Party in the No," *Politico*, 26 February 2009, www.politico.com/news/stories/0209/19346.html.

30. Ibid., 411.

31. Sinclair, "Congressional Leadership," 98.

32. Ibid.

33. Ceci Connolly, "61 Days from Near-Defeat to Victory: How Obama Revived his Healthcare Bill," *The Washington Post*, 23 March 2010.

34. Gail Russell Chaddock, "Inside Pelosi's Realm," *The Christian Science Monitor*, 19 July 2010.

35. Mike Lux, "One More Step," *The Huffington Post*, 9 November 2009, www.huffingtonpost.com/mike-lux/one-more-step_b_351269.html.

36. Dana Milbank, "Sweeteners for the South," *The Washington Post*, 22 November 2009, www.washingtonpost.com/wp-dyn/content/article/2009/11/21/AR20091121 02272.html. See also Manu Raju and Chris Frates, "Lincoln's Long Walk to 60th Vote," *Politico*, 22 November 2009, www.politico.com/news/stories/1109/29824_Page2.html.

37. Carrie Budoff Brown, "Dems Seek Deal as Senate Debate Begins," *Politico*, 29 November 2009.

38. Alter, *The Promise*, 416.

39. "Obama Gives Senate Democrats Another Push on Healthcare," *Congressional Quarterly Weekly Reports*, 15 December 2009, www.cq.com/doc/nes -3267710?print=true.

40. Drew Armstrong, "Senate Passage of Health Bill Sets Stage for Talks with House," *Congressional Quarterly Weekly Reports*, 24 December 2009, www/cq.com/ doc/news-3273233?print=true.

41. Quoted in Armstrong, "Senate Passage."

42. See Barbara Sinclair, *Unorthodox Lawmaking: New Legislative Processes in the U.S. Congress*, 4th ed. (Washington: CQ Press College, 2011).

43. Drew Armstrong and Alex Wayne, "Tentative First Steps Toward a Deal on Healthcare," *Congressional Quarterly Weekly Reports*, 11 January 2010, 138.

44. Carrie Budoff Brown and Patrick O'Connor, "Fallout: Dems Rethinking Health Bill," *Politico*, 21 January 2010.

45. Quoted in Alter, *The Promise*, 397.

46. Kerry Young, "Healthcare Bill Could Hinge on Byrd Rule," *Congressional Quarterly Weekly Reports*, 14 September 2009, 2014, library.cqpress.com/cqweekly/ document.php?id=weekly report111-000003200762&t.

47. Connolly, "61 Days from Near-Defeat."

48. Alex Wayne, Kathleen Hunter, and Jennifer Scholtes, "Senate Passes Reconciliation, Returning It to House for Final Vote," *CQ Today Online News*, 25 March 2010, www.cq.com/doc/news-3622652?print=true.

49. Clea Benson, "A New Kind of Abortion Politics," *Congressional Quarterly Weekly Reports*, 29 March 2010, 740, www.cq.com/doc/weeklyreport -3634203?print=true. Stupak was later defeated in his reelection bid, and the right-to-life movement was further angered when the administration's rules included a requirement that all employers, including most Catholic schools and hospitals, pay for contraceptive coverage.

50. Zachary A. Somashekhar, "Health-Care Rule Is Delayed a Year," *The Washington Post*, 3 July 2013.

51. Jonathan Easley, "GOP Support Grows to Force Shutdown over Funding ObamaCare," The Hill, thehill.comvideosenate312497-sen-lee-threatens-shut down-to-block-obamacare-#ixzz2a4MH2kNF.

52. See Paul Manuel and Anne Marie Cammisa, *Checks and Balances: How a Parliamentary System Could Change American Government* (Boulder, CO: Westview Press, 1998).

53. See, for example, Edward J. Larson, *A Magnificent Catastrophe: The Tumultuous Election of 1800, America's First Presidential Campaign* (New York: Free Press, 2007) for an account of a highly partisan presidential election contest early in our history, and note the familiar debate over what role government should play.

54. Ezra Klein, "The Unpersuaded: Who Listens to a President?" *The New Yorker*, 19 March 2012, www.newyorker.com/reporting/2012/03/19/120319fa_fact_klein#ixzz1qzYA96Pf.

55. Francis Fukuyama, "Do Defective Institutions Explain the Gap between the United States and Latin America?" *The American Interest*, November/December 2006, www.the-american-interest.com/article.cfm?piece=198.

5

What if American Democracy Were on a Different Path?

If the United States were to adopt a British-type parliamentary system, the government would be accorded more power and be better able to respond to the demands of the electorate. At the same time the legislative majority in Washington, free from the various institutional limitations on its power, could imperil the rights of the minority out of power. At the Constitutional Convention in Philadelphia, the framers decided that it was better to enable the minority with legislative means to block the initiatives of the majority rather than to risk the tyranny of the majority in power.

—Seymour Martin Lipset

Remember, the political battle surrounding the debt ceiling is actually impossible in a parliamentary system because the executive controls the legislature. There could not be a public spectacle of the two branches of government squabbling and holding the country hostage.

—Fareed Zakaria

How a British-Style Parliamentary System Could Change American Politics

THIS CHAPTER ASKS WHAT things might look like if the United States were on a different ideational and institutional path. What if the United States had instead adopted a parliamentary regime in 1789, as was actually proposed in the Virginia Plan (i.e., the legislature would elect the executive)? How would politics and policy outcomes have been different if American government functioned under a British-style parliamentary system, in which there are no checks and balances? Would a British parliamentary regime make American democracy more responsive? Would it solve legislative gridlock once and for all? What problems might such a system raise?

Expanding on the model set forth in an essay by Joy Esberey,[1] this chapter seeks to examine how a British-style parliamentary system might have changed the course of American politics. Following a review of some of the main characteristics of this imagined American parliamentary regime, this chapter will analyze the alterations to American political culture that would result from such a regime: if American government could be more representative, if there could be more effective responses to political scandals, and how selected elections could have been different. Taken in aggregate, this hypothetical inquiry seeks to illustrate how a parliamentary arrangement could have changed the path of American political development. It will conclude with a review of some possible institutional reforms to the constitutional system.

An Alternative Constitutional Convention

To begin, let us assume that a parliamentary system was introduced into the United States after the American Revolution.[2] In such a case, a different set of agreements would have been reached at the Constitutional Convention in Philadelphia. We have decided to dub our imaginary constitutional compromise, leading to the establishment of an American form of parliamentarism, "the Westminster Compromise" after the British parliamentary system. Under the terms of this Westminster Compromise, the framers would have opted for three points that were actually under discussion at the Constitutional Convention in Philadelphia: from the Virginia Plan, the executive would be chosen from the legislature, and legislative representation would be based on population, not geography; from the New Jersey Plan, there would be one representative assembly, a unicameral legislature rather than our bicameral one. The net result of this arrangement would have been the implementation of a parliamentary form of government in 1789. As discussed in chapter 2, Robert Dahl has observed that the actual debate over the Virginia Plan brought the framers to the brink of inventing a form of a parliamentary system because this discussion advanced the idea that the executive be chosen by the national legislature.[3]

For the sake of simplicity, we envision four key alterations to the American system of government under this Westminster Compromise. First, there would be no separation of powers. Rather, executive and legislative powers would be fused and sovereign. Second, there would only be one legislative chamber, not two, and it would be called the National Assembly. Third, the internal operating rules of this unicameral legislature would follow the Westminster system: the unicameral National Assembly selects the prime minister, and delegates to that executive official the task of national administration and the authority to direct the legislative branch. Fourth, the prime minister chooses a cabinet from among the ranks of the majority party in the legislature and is able to dominate the parliament, and there are no legal limitations on the actions of the legislature. As is the actual case in the United Kingdom, as long as the government has a legislative majority, it can expect to have all of its legislation passed without any revisions from the opposition. These four broad changes (explicitly rejected by the actual constitutional convention) could have significantly altered American political development.

How the United States Could Have Ended Up with a Proportional System

Our Westminster Compromise is based both on actual alternatives discussed at the American Constitutional Convention and on a British-style parliament. For purposes of argument, we would like to include one additional change: the use of a proportional system of elections, rather than the single-member districts currently used by all fifty states. This change was not discussed at the Constitutional Convention, nor is it part of the British system, which, like the American system, relies on winner-take-all elections. Yet such a change could have significantly altered election outcomes, as will be discussed later in the chapter. Since we are creating our own imaginary form of government, we would like to include proportional representation. And it is conceivable that our system could have evolved in that direction.

The American Constitution does not require the use of single-member districts to elect representatives to the House. The Constitution specified only that representation would be determined by population, not that each state would have the same number of congressional districts that it has seats in the House. In other words, the framers of the Constitution did not specifically rule out proportional representation. The framers never expected the United States to adopt proportional representation, but in like fashion, they also never expected American politics to be dominated by political parties. (In fact, the framers were actually opposed to political parties.) The United States more or less invented political parties in the 1790s with the creation of the Federalist Party and the Democratic (or Jeffersonian) Republicans. The United States would not have had to invent proportional elections (the idea existed prior to the founding of the United States), but it could have developed its own proportional system as it adapted to the increasing importance of political parties.

The history of political parties in the United States involves both struggles for domination between the parties and factionalization within parties. It is conceivable that at some point, a proportional system could have been institutionalized as a way for some of the less-dominant parties and factions to gain political control. For example, in the late 1800s, political parties represented urban interests, which dominated national politics. Several rural parties were formed in the late 1800s, including the Greenback Party and the People's Party (also known as the Populists) to counter the power of the urban parties. They were ultimately unsuccessful, although William Jennings Bryan, representing the Populist Party, came close to getting elected in 1896. A proportional system of elections would have given the newly formed agrarian parties more power in Congress. A parliamentary system could have forced the dominant parties to form a coalition with the agricultural parties.

By the turn of the century, the progressive movement emerged, trying to eliminate political corruption and reform the party system. Although progressives questioned the usefulness of political parties, and even favored nonpartisan elections, it is possible to imagine slightly different tactics for the progressive movement under a parliamentary system. Knowing that the majority party selects the prime minister in a parliamentary form of government, the progressives might have attempted to take control of the legislature by entering into a coalition with other interests, such as the rural parties. As it was, progressives favored changes to the political system, including the end of patronage and the institution of primary elections. Both of these reforms attempted to limit the power of political parties. In fact, the progressives would have liked the elimination of political parties, but found that goal impossible to achieve. Instead of eliminating political parties, the progressives might have attempted to dilute the power of political parties through proportional elections. The progressives could have lobbied for this change (as they did for others) at the state level, and may have changed the American electoral system in even more profound ways.

How American Political Development
Could Have Been on a Different Path

Obviously, political institutional arrangements do not control or determine all aspects of a nation's political life. However, under the terms of this Westminster Compromise, one can assume that there would have been some modifications to the path of political development in the United States. Arguably, there may have been some changes to the party system and to the political behavior of interest groups, the relationships among key government policy makers would change, and the power of the majority party in the legislature would be increased.[4] Let us focus our inquiry on three main areas:

- alterations to American political culture,
- whether a proportional representation system could provide for better representation in the legislature, and
- the issue of effective responses to political scandals.

Alterations to American Political Culture

A political culture may be defined as the set of attitudes, expectations, feelings, and values held by a people about how political life in their society ought to be carried out. In particular, and for a wide variety of political, social, economic, and cultural reasons, Americans have historically been preoccupied with their rights and with freedom from government restraints. One important contributing variable to this widespread distrust of government at the beginning of the American republic was the dominance of Protestant religious belief in American society. Specifically, the Protestant work ethic—which holds that a person should advance in society solely based on his or her individual abilities and hard work, and not due to family connections or class position—is hostile to governmental intrusions that seek to aid segments of the population.[5] Thus, among the world's peoples, Americans tend to be more concerned about limiting governmental intrusions, save in certain critical areas. This generalized suspicion of government resonates with the constitutional guarantees of the inalienable rights to life, liberty, and the pursuit of happiness for every person, as well as with the protections of individual freedoms in the Bill of Rights. Accordingly, the ideas of liberty and individualism are pronounced features of American political culture, and have generated certain hostility toward government among people of varying political convictions. For example, many liberals are concerned about the government's involvement in defense and military activities, saying that government should limit itself to social problems such as poverty and injustice. More conservative critics would charge that such social programs themselves create unnecessary governmental intrusion into people's lives. Still others are concerned about limiting the government's role in individual decisions about such issues as religion, sexual activity, and childbearing. All sides have a political cultural bias that is deeply suspicious of government intrusion.

Under the terms of the Westminster Compromise, this pronounced suspicion of government might have been somewhat mitigated. Had the framers opted for the Westminster Compromise, they would have decided to place the responsibility of governing squarely in the hands of the majority: there would have been no constitutional provisions hindering the rule of the majority, which would have been given the power and the authority to effect changes. As such, the majority in our fictional National Assembly could act swiftly to make a real difference. As Seymour Martin Lipset points out in the quote at the start of this chapter, American national government would be accorded more power and be better able to respond to the demands of the electorate under a parliamentary system. At the same time, this legislative majority could imperil the rights of the minority out of power. Under the terms of our Westminster Compromise, the framers would have decided that it is better to enable that majority to rule than to hinder majority rule for the sake of protecting minority rights. They would have designed the legislative chamber to reflect and be responsive to the people. In a way, then, this could have happened, had the Antifederalists' arguments won out over the Federalists, who were most afraid of tyranny of the majority.

Perhaps our Westminster Compromise system might enable the government to be viewed more positively as an instrument for change rather than as a perpetual threat to individual liberty, as Joy Esberey has noted:

> Under a parliamentary system of government, it is unlikely that Americans would be as suspicious of government as they are, even considering that many who came to this country did so to escape repressive regimes. They could not have equated democratic government with the autocratic governments they left behind; it is far more likely that they would have seen in democracy an opportunity to improve their conditions.[6]

Finally, under the Westminster Compromise, when groups in society were not treated equally, the government would have the power to quickly intervene to ensure equal opportunity. Such rapid response to societal ills could have won staunch supporters of governmental actions, and diminished some of the current distrust of government. On the other hand, it might also have provoked a serious reaction against the national government, whose swift and decisive actions might have been viewed suspiciously. Indeed, such a strong national government might have led to calls for secession early on in American political development. Whatever the system of government existing in the United States, American society would probably still be more distrustful of government than other societies are. It is also possible that Americans might be even more suspicious of government than they are now if the framers had adopted the Westminster Compromise, which would have granted the government more power than it currently has.

A More Representative Polity?

The question of representation is at the heart of the institutional question. As we discussed in chapter 2, the United States' system of single-member districts inhibits the ability of new political parties to win elections.[7] American elections are won one district at a time, usually in contests between only two political parties. A proportional system, on the other hand, would create multimember districts and create room for third parties. In the United States, a party that can garner just 20 percent of the vote has virtually no chance of representation in the legislature; that party could make up 20 percent of the legislature in a proportional system. Further, one can imagine under the Westminster system the formation of minority parties made up of labor, blacks, or other groups.

It is not unreasonable to assume that a system that accords seats on the basis of the proportion of votes received would have led to the development of a third party, and/or several regional or ethnic parties, at some point over the past two hundred years. Under those electoral rules, it is easy to imagine a third party starting in the early part of the twentieth century. As millions of people emigrated to the cities from abroad, as well as from rural areas, they could quickly have formed a mass-based party, like the Labour Party in Great Britain. Other parties might have formed as well, including agrarian-based parties, progressive or reform-minded parties, and socialist, libertarian, anarchist, ethnic Catholic, Christian conservative, black, Hispanic, and militia formations. In such a system, the Democratic and Republican parties would have faced a great deal of competition from significant minorities. The Tea Party would be an actual party, rather than a reformist movement within the Republican Party.

The Westminster Compromise could have resulted in a very different legislative history for minorities in American history. Whereas the present single-member district plurality system favors the majority ethnic groups, it is reasonable to assume that there would be greater numbers of minorities in the National Assembly under a proportional representation system. For instance, under this scenario, African American leaders could have formed a separate political party, and charged into Washington with much influence.[8] The Democrats would not have been the majority party throughout much of the early twentieth century, and a third political party representing the interests of African Americans could have had much more sway in negotiating with Democratic and/or Republican leaders for specific programs in exchange for their legislative support. This could have been a much better situation for blacks, who historically have voted in large numbers for the Democratic Party, but themselves do not make up the majority of the party. Democrats can count on the "black vote," but do not necessarily have to do much to court it. Blacks in the Democratic Party may feel that the party neglects them, but lament that they have nowhere else to go. The Republican Party does even less to court blacks as a group, and if the group were to form its own political party, it would not have sufficient numbers to win elections. The case could be different in a parliamentary system with proportional representation, as Esberey notes:

> At various times this century in which American blacks were denied their con-
> stitutional rights, presidents, Congress and the Court tried to do something to
> change the situation. On each situation they were frustrated by the checking
> power of the other branches. This situation would not arise in our parliamentary
> America. If we consider how much was achieved with everything in the political
> system working against the change, there can be no doubt that, with a system
> which facilitated change, the position of minorities would have been improved.[9]

Critics have noted, however, that if African American political influence were wholly depended on a separate black political party, issues important to African Americans would never have gained the attention of the majority parties, nor would a black political party have been able to make significant progress in civil rights legislation. Perhaps true, but on the other hand, the existence of a separate black party could have been advantageous in one key area: it could have enabled the African American legislative leadership to strike alliances with the leading majority parties in return for specific legislative goals. And even if there were not more African American representatives under this fictional system than there actually are under the present system, one could still argue that the Westminster Compromise could have enabled African Americans to be elected to the National Assembly, and could have enabled those representatives to coerce the majority party in our fictional National Assembly to confront the problems of racial injustice much earlier than was actually the case.

More Effective Response to Political Crises and Scandals?

It is also possible that the mechanisms available under a British-style parliamentary system would have enabled the American National Assembly to deal more easily with scandals. Let us look at how the Westminster Compromise would have handled some twentieth- and twenty-first-century political scandals.

Watergate occurred during the Nixon administration and resulted in a constitutional crisis for the office of the presidency. In 1972, a group of operatives working for the Republican Party and known as "the plumbers" was caught breaking into the Democratic National Committee headquarters in the

Watergate Office Building. They were apparently trying to get information on the Democratic strategy to win the presidential elections later that year. The investigation of this crime produced evidence that indicated that President Nixon may have ordered the break-in, or at the very least obstructed justice by covering up the crime. Democrats in Congress led the charge against President Nixon, and impeachment proceedings were initiated in 1974.

The nation was glued to televised coverage of the congressional impeachment proceedings, which were slow, painful, and difficult. One area of the congressional investigation focused on the White House tapes. These were tape recordings that the president had made for historical purposes of all discussions in the Oval Office. The investigators wanted to hear these taped conversations, because they believed that the conversations held clues as to the guilt or innocence of the president. President Nixon, however, refused to release private tape recordings of White House meetings, citing the principle of executive privilege. The president argued that, by virtue of his office, he was not required to release the tapes. Releasing the tapes, according to Nixon, would set a bad precedent and threaten national security. This legislative-executive deadlock was settled by the unanimous decision of the Supreme Court that the president was obliged to release the tapes. Once this was done, the information they contained implicated the president in the cover-up. Before the impeachment proceedings were over, Nixon resigned the presidency, and Vice President Ford was sworn in as president.

Under a British-style parliamentary system, Congress could have rid the nation of Nixon in 1974 with a simple vote of no confidence. The Watergate crisis, dubbed "our long national nightmare" by President Gerald Ford, could have been dealt with swiftly and decisively, and a new government instituted immediately. Rather than having President Ford serve out an essentially lame-duck presidency without the legitimacy of having been elected, the country could have seen a new leader emerge with the consent of the parliament. The adversarial relationship between the president and Congress—exacerbated by the Watergate scandal—would not exist under our Westminster system. However, it is also important to note that a parliament controlled by a Prime Minister Nixon could have had a negative side. The prime minister might have been able to prevent the National Assembly from acquiring the information necessary to institute impeachment procedures. As leader of both the party and the government, a Prime Minister Nixon could have exerted even more control than did President Nixon, and would not have faced institutional checks on his power.

The Iran-Contra affair, which occurred during the Reagan administration, is another case in point. The conservative Republican administration's adversarial relationship with the liberal Democratic Congress was a major

IMAGE 5.1
A woman at Washington National Airport reads a copy of the *Washington Star-News* on 8 August 1974, with "Nixon Resigning" as the headline on the front cover. A parliamentary system may have been better able to end America's "long national nightmare" swiftly and decisively. © Owen Franken/CORBIS.

component of the scandal. In 1979 an armed left-wing rebel movement in Nicaragua, known as the Sandinistas, defeated the American-supported right-wing dictatorship under Anastasio Somoza Debayle. At first, President Carter welcomed the victory of the Sandinistas, in the hope that they would bring about more respect for human rights than had been the case under Somoza. When Reagan came to office in January 1981, however, relations quickly cooled between Nicaragua and Washington. Reagan accused the Sandinistas of attempting to force Marxism on the Nicaraguan people, and of fomenting revolution in the neighboring country of El Salvador. In the early 1980s, a group of anti-Sandinista Nicaraguans, agreeing with Reagan, decided that the only way to defeat the Sandinista leadership was by armed struggle, and so a civil conflict broke out. These rebels were against (or "contra," in Spanish) the Sandinistas, and thus became known as the contras. The Reagan administration was very supportive of the contras and sought to arm them. Nicaragua still had some support in the Democratic-controlled Congress, which sought to block Reagan's political and military initiatives against the country. It passed a law forbidding the administration to sell arms to the Nicaraguan contras. Since Congress controls the purse strings, the Reagan administration was legally unable to help the contras. With or without the president's knowledge, people in his administration, including Oliver North, resorted to illegal means to raise funds, purchase arms, and send them to the contras. In a rather complicated plan involving Iran, administration officials privately raised funds to arm the contras. Once the news of this illegal activity broke, there was talk of impeaching the president. Investigative hearings, much like those during the Watergate crisis, were held in Congress.

At first glance, had our Westminster Compromise been in place, the governmental crisis could have easily been solved by a vote of no confidence in a Prime Minister Reagan. The larger point here is that the adversarial relationship between the executive and legislative branches would not have existed under the Westminster Compromise. In that case, the scandal would probably never have occurred. A Prime Minister Reagan, as leader of the majority party in the National Assembly, would have been able to arm the contras through legal means and with parliamentary support. There would be no need to resort to illegal and covert means to accomplish the goal of arming the contras. Of course, many Americans were glad that Democrats in Congress provided opposition to Reagan's plan to arm the contras. Under a parliamentary system, such opposition could have been muted, and there would have been no effective check on a Prime Minister Reagan's power.

The Clinton presidency was also plagued by scandal, and President Clinton, like President Nixon, faced impeachment charges in the House of Representatives after a series of charges and investigations into his personal life and financial dealings. Under investigation, President Clinton lied under oath about his relationship with an intern, and that almost proved his undoing. The main scandal was known as Whitewater, a questionable Arkansas financial deal in which the president and Mrs. Clinton were involved. Using a law created in response to the Watergate scandal, Attorney General Janet Reno appointed an independent counsel (also known as a special prosecutor) to investigate Whitewater and related charges. The independent counsel, Kenneth Starr, conducted an investigation of the president, acting as an additional check on the executive branch. The independent counsel must be appointed by the attorney general and approved by Congress. In this way, Congress is able to exert some control over an executive who may be abusing power.

How would the situation differ in a parliamentary system? An independent counsel would not be necessary, for at least two reasons. First, the parliament automatically has control over the chief executive, since the prime minister is selected from its majority party. An American National Assembly would not need the additional check of an independent counsel to maintain control over the chief executive. Second, a vote of no confidence could send a prime minister from office. The United States has a long and cumbersome impeachment process that allows for removal from office only in the case of criminal activity. The president cannot be removed before his term of office ends simply because he is politically unpopular or has the taint of scandal. Thus, a special prosecutor is needed to discover if there are any criminal charges to be made and that a basis for impeachment thus exists. Of course, the problem is the perception that the special prosecutor is bent on finding anything that he can hang charges on. This perception dogged special prosecutors in the Nixon, Reagan, and Clinton administrations.

President Clinton's investigation, like President Nixon's, led to impeachment proceedings in the House of Representatives. As had happened with Nixon, a rapt television audience watched as the president was impeached by the House of Representatives (basically indicted, or charged with a crime) in the fall of 1998 and then faced a trial in the Senate. The Senate, always the cooler-headed body, acquitted the president of the impeachment charges in early 1999, and a much-weakened president faced his final two years in office, having barely missed being removed from office.

In a parliamentary system, these investigations and the subsequent impeachment proceedings would not have happened. Instead of a four-year inquiry by independent counsel Kenneth Starr into President Clinton's financial and sexual dealings, these situations could have been dealt with quickly. If the National Assembly felt that Prime Minister Clinton had lost, in the eyes of the American people, the legitimacy needed to continue to govern effectively, it could remove him by a simple vote of no confidence. If, on the other hand, the National Assembly felt that too much was being made of these situations, and that they did not negatively influence Clinton's ability to govern, it could simply ignore these matters. Either way, this problem would not have resulted in long, drawn-out deliberations with divisive results. Republicans were angry that the president was still in office; Democrats were angry over the intense scrutiny he had faced.

There have also been a slew of scandals plaguing the Obama administration.[10] Some of the most serious questions have focused on how the administration responded to a terrorist attack on the American embassy complex in Benghazi, Libya, on 11 September 2012, when Ambassador Christopher Stevens and three other Americans were killed by radical Islamists—perhaps affiliated with the Al Qaeda global terror network. Many have wondered what the president knew, when he knew it, and what he decided to do; but no clear answers were immediately provided.[11] President Obama did not face an investigation by a special prosecutor, as did Nixon and Clinton, and the Benghazi scandal did not cause the same kind of public outcry that Nixon and Clinton faced. In fact, though Obama's Republican opponent, Mitt Romney, did bring up the Benghazi scandal during the 2012 election, the scandal itself seemed to have little impact on the outcome. Other scandals include revelations that the Department of Justice secretly seized the phone records of the Associated Press as well as the phone records and personal e-mails of news reporters, angering the media, whom the right had been claiming for some time had given Obama a free pass on the scandals affecting his administration.[12] Perhaps most disturbing to many were the reports that the National Security Agency was spying on the American public, and that the Internal Revenue Service had targeted conservative political groups for investigation and audits. Regarding the IRS scandal, Joe Klein has noted that it was broader and more problematic than the other scandals plaguing the president:

> The IRS's targeting of Tea Party groups is, however, an actual full-blown scandal. In fact, it is several scandals. The most obvious one was the lunkheaded effort by midlevel IRS employees to use an ideological shortcut—auditing groups with Tea Party and Patriots in their names—to find out whether they were engaging in political activity, which is illegal for "social welfare" groups under the 501(c)(4) provision of the tax code.[13]

There have been a variety of calls for a Watergate-style independent prosecutor to get to the truth behind each of these situations, rendering the policy environment in Washington toxic.[14] Republicans are furious and frustrated with the administration for its perceived obfuscation and arrogance; Democrats claim that each of these situations involves policy differences, for the most part, and argue that the president's opponents have misrepresented the facts and that a special prosecutor is not necessary. In lieu thereof, Congressman Darrell Issa, chair of the House Oversight and Government Reform Committee, has been a thorn in the Obama administration's side, holding hearings on the various scandals, subpoenaing documents, and otherwise trying to keep attention focused on the issues that have angered Republicans. Congress, dominated by Republicans, won't give up on badgering a Democratic president whom they feel has, at best, overstepped his bounds.

The result: gridlock remains in force. It appears that Washington will have to wait for a unified government before any serious legislative work can recommence. In the meantime, Americans are stuck with the old-fashioned blame game that is typical of a separated political system of checks and balances.

Under the terms of our fictional Westminster Compromise, however, the American National Assembly would have had the power to quickly investigate and resolve any of the scandals, at any point holding a vote of confidence in the Obama administration. If he won, he would remain in office and be strengthened politically. If he lost such a vote, the chief executive would be forced to resign, which would cleanse the scandal-ridden political environment and usher in a new beginning. Such a parliamentary institutional mechanism would help American presidentialism overcome gridlock. The chief executive would not then continue to face a Congress dominated by his opposition party, intent on discovering and exposing problems or inappropriate actions. Nor would the chair of a powerful committee focus his energies on investigating the prime minister—under a parliamentary system, if the prime minister loses a vote of confidence, such a committee chair would be out of power, too. A special prosecutor, independent counsel, or aggressive chair of the Oversight and Reform Committee does make life difficult for the president, who may face embarrassing inquiries into his political and personal life, both past and present. Republicans and Democrats can all agree that sometimes it seems as if a special prosecutor is acting out some kind of a vendetta, trying to discover dirt on his political enemies. The post of special prosecutor does reveal something about American politics: the citizens' basic distrust of government. The United States would rather err on the side of too much investigation of the president than risk the possibility of his taking on excessive powers. While a parliamentary system could easily remove a president from office, there is no guarantee that it would: What if the scandal or political crisis involved not only the prime minister, but also his or her party in parliament? There would then be no incentive to remove the prime minister from office, or to bring forth information that might be damaging to the party. Americans would rather have an adversarial system with built-in checks than allow for excessive political power.

A parliamentary system would certainly have handled political scandals differently; it would have had different electoral results as well. In the next section, we examine how a proportional voting system might have led to radically different election results, both in terms of the majority party in Congress and the actual person who became chief executive.

How Selected Election Outcomes Might Have Been Different

Recall that the framers never anticipated a single direct national election for the president; according to Article II, Section 1, Clause 2 of the Constitution, each state legislature decides how electors are appointed to the Electoral College:

> Each state shall appoint, in such manner as the Legislature thereof may direct, a number of electors, equal to the whole number of Senators and Representatives to which the State may be entitled in the Congress: but no Senator or Representative, or person holding an office of trust or profit under the United States, shall be appointed an elector.[15]

Thus, the framers designed a system in which the states would decide how to choose electors, who would subsequently convene to vote for the president. The national popular result of the presidential election was not to be tallied into one controlling final result; the elections were to stay close to the state level, as a check on both the possible tyranny of the majority and on national power. But how could a pure proportional voting system have changed American politics? Let us investigate some of the electoral outcomes in the twentieth century.

Such a reinterpretation of electoral results is a challenge: obviously, if a different system were in place, each election would have followed a different trajectory. Path dependence implies that an early change in political direction may have subsequent multiplying effects. Therefore, as we revisit each electoral outcome, we must also assume that in each case there were not past influences or trajectories. In other words, when we consider Ronald Reagan's legislative program of the 1980s, we will not assume that any earlier period of Republican rule had already implemented Reagan's conservative agenda. Nor will we assume that a welfare state had been created by Teddy Roosevelt and was already in existence by the time his distant cousin became president.

As we begin this inquiry, one big caveat is in order: It actually may be impossible to meaningfully reinterpret electoral results garnered under a presidential system for the purposes of exploring what would have been the case if a parliamentary system had been in place. One could try to examine the national aggregate totals of the congressional elections for this purpose as well, but in most cases, congressional elections in the United States are dominated by local pork barrel concerns. In fact, the general consensus is that congressional elections are local elections won or lost on local issues. On the other hand, presidential elections do tend to focus on national issues, but in actuality, presidential electoral results are the product of both local and national concerns. These factors are so tightly interwoven in the United States that it is almost impossible to tease out which presidential outcome was decided on national issues. The presidential results are the only national elections held in the United States, and will have to do. Of course, a "what if" exercise can be fun, but we caution the reader that the following is an exercise of pure fancy in the effort to illustrate that institutional arrangements can change policy outcomes.

For the sake of simplicity, we will assume that representation in the unicameral National Assembly is based on a pure proportional representation system drawn from the actual national vote totals from the presidential elections, which is the one true national vote we presently have for the head of government. Thus, presidential elections results serve as a "proxy" for a national vote in a parliamentary system.[16] Such a proxy is, naturally, incomplete;

presumably, voters' decisions would be affected by whether they were voting for an individual to serve as president or a party to serve as government. Further, we will assume that the vote totals for the presidential elections were for a party list of candidates for the unicameral National Assembly, and ignore the actual results of the local elections. Let us now turn to the elections.

Case One: The Presidential Election of 1912

TABLE 5.1
Case One: 1912

1912 National Vote Percentages
  Democratic: Woodrow Wilson, 41.84%
  Progressive (Bull Moose): Theodore Roosevelt, 27.4%
  Republican: William Harding Taft, 23.17%
  Socialist: Eugene Debs, 6%
Makeup of 63rd Congress
  House: Democrats 291, Republicans 127, Other 17
  Senate: Democrats 51, Republicans 44, Other 1

We start our what-ifs with the election of 1912. That election is an appropriate starting point for at least two reasons. First, it involved the Progressive Party, which we have already imagined could have been the impetus for the institution of a proportional electoral system in our imaginary Westminster system. Secondly, the 1912 election was notable in that it involved one of the few serious third-party challenges in American history, this one waged by former president Theodore Roosevelt. To begin, it is important to remember that although the 1912 election was an atypical occurrence in the United States, the presence of a third-party candidate for the presidency does make it an interesting case for this exercise. (It may also demonstrate how presidential elections would have occurred if, in fact, the Westminster Compromise had been adopted, along with a proportional representation system!)

Theodore Roosevelt, a Republican, was president from 1901 to 1908. He had been William McKinley's vice president; when McKinley died early in his second term, Roosevelt inherited the office. He then ran on his own in 1904, and, following precedent, did not run for a third consecutive term. William Howard Taft ran and won as the Republican candidate in 1908, and decided to run for reelection in 1912. Taft and Roosevelt disagreed politically, and eventually became personal and political enemies. Roosevelt remained popular with the public, decided to challenge Taft for the Republican nomination, and won several primaries. The old guard Republicans distrusted Roosevelt's reform ideas, and decided to support the more reliably conservative Taft at the Republican National Convention in Chicago. This enraged Roosevelt; he withdrew his name from consideration before the first ballot, and decided to leave the Republican Party.[17]

Theodore Roosevelt then found a home in the progressive movement. He told his supporters that he felt "strong as a bull moose," and the nickname Bull Moose was then applied to him and the new Progressive Party. The term took on legendary proportions when, following an assassination attempt by John Schrank in Milwaukee on 14 October 1912, Roosevelt told the assembled crowd:

> Friends, I shall ask you to be as quiet as possible. I don't know whether you fully understand that I have just been shot; but it takes more than that to kill a Bull Moose. But fortunately I had my manuscript, so you see I was going to make a long speech, and there is a bullet there is where the bullet went through—and it probably saved me from it going into my heart. The bullet is in me now, so, that I cannot make a very long speech, but I will try my best.[18]

Roosevelt gave his speech to the crowd, and then agreed to go to the hospital over an hour later. For the election of 1912, the Progressive bull moose took its place alongside of the Republican elephant and the Democratic donkey.[19]

In his campaign, Roosevelt promised significant political and economic reforms, including the idea that property rights be held secondary to human rights, and plans to tax the wealthy to provide programs for the poor and unfortunate, increase the power of the national government, and create a welfare state. The former president delivered a fascinating speech before the Progressive Party's national presidential nominating convention on 6 August, dubbed his political "confession of faith." His comments give a clear idea about what he would have done in office. He stated clearly that "the time is ripe, and overripe, for a genuine Progressive movement, nation-wide and justice-loving,"[20] further observing:

> Now, friends, this is my confession of faith. . . . I believe in the larger use of the governmental power to help remedy industrial wrongs, because it has been borne in on me by actual experience that without the exercise of such power many of the wrongs will go unremedied. I believe in a larger opportunity for the people themselves directly to participate in government and to control their governmental agents, because long experience has taught me that without such control many of their agents will represent them badly.[21]

The conservative Republican establishment feared that these plans by their former president would lead to mob rule, and a generalized attack on property rights and social status. In response, the Republican candidate, President Taft, adopted some progressive measures, including provisions to protect working men, widows, and children. The thrust of the Republican message was that change had to be controlled and limited. The divided Republican Party gave Woodrow Wilson, the Democratic Party candidate, an opening. Wilson campaigned for some reforms as well. He supported the introduction of an income tax and the direct election of senators, and he promised to protect labor. Eugene Debs, representing the Socialist Party, presented a far-left political program, providing for the nationalization of most industries.[22]

Debs did not have enough votes to present much of a threat. The battle was fought between three candidates: Woodrow Wilson, representing the Democratic Party; William Howard Taft, the Republican candidate; and Theodore Roosevelt, the progressive Republican representing the Progressive (Bull Moose) Party. Roosevelt split the Republican vote, allowing Wilson to be elected. The Democrats controlled both the White House and the Congress. The Wilson administration, although Democratic, ended up enacting much of the Progressive Party's platform, leaving the Progressive Party without much reason for opposition. The Republicans were the minority party in Congress, and the Bull Moose progressives eventually broke up. Theodore Roosevelt left the public scene, and the worst fears of the conservative Republicans never materialized. Further, as noted by George Mowry, "even though Debs had raised the total Socialist strength by over a third from that of the previous elections, his votes did not materially affect the results."[23] Congress remained dominated by two political parties, despite the strong showing of the Socialists. The political results in Congress were in favor of stability and against change; the actual electoral results, however, indicate that the American population was in the mood for greater change. The Republican Party led by William Howard Taft, which stood for stability and the status quo, was clearly rejected by the electorate.

How could these electoral results have played out under the terms of the Westminster Compromise? One can envision a much different political situation. A proportional representative system would have allocated seats in the National Assembly in proportion to the votes received. As the head of the party receiving a plurality of votes, Wilson would have presided over a minority government with 41.9 percent of the seats. On the other hand, it might have made more political sense for Wilson to form a coalition government with Theodore Roosevelt's Progressive Party, which received 27.4 percent of the seats. Perhaps he could have also included Eugene Debs's Socialist Party, which had won 6 percent of the seats, in the coalition. Arguably, the parties involved in the formation of this coalition government would have made some deals. Perhaps Wilson would have had to accept portions of the other parties' platforms in exchange for their support. In addition, Theodore Roosevelt and Eugene Debs could have been appointed to prominent cabinet posts.

However the accommodation was reached, this coalition government would certainly have been very powerful, and would have diluted the power of the Republicans in Congress. Holding on to a combined 75 percent of the seats in the National Assembly, Woodrow Wilson could have presided over an effective government: it is not difficult to imagine that Wilson would have shepherded some reform legislation through the American National Assembly in the 1912–1916 legislative term, including a tax system predicated on the wealthy providing the money for poverty programs and the creation of a welfare state. Based on the actual actions of Theodore Roosevelt when he was president (1901–1909) and the public statements of the socialist leader Eugene Debs, one can imagine that a cabinet including them would have sought antitrust laws limiting the power of large monopoly groups. Also, it would most likely have been a strong supporter of workers' rights, including increased compensation, benefits, and the right to strike. This cabinet would probably have sought a pro-conservation agenda as well. Other reforms could have involved the abolition of child labor, improved working conditions, and women's suffrage. Indeed, even if this coalition government were restricted to Wilson and Roosevelt, it would still be safe to assume that the net result of a shift in the American institutional structure from a presidential to a British-style parliamentary system would certainly have created a different—and more progressive—political trajectory in the United States following the 1912 elections.

The American system limited the power of an outsider candidate like Roosevelt. The entrenchment of two parties meant that there was little room for a third party to take hold. Teddy Roosevelt's Progressive Party candidacy did, however, have an impact on the American political system. Both major parties, fearful of the popular appeal of Roosevelt's ideas, adopted some progressive platforms for their candidates. As president, Wilson instituted some, but not all, of Roosevelt's proposed reforms. American government, with its checks and balances, did not experience dramatic change as a result of the election of 1912. The system did allow a somewhat modified version of Roosevelt's ideals to be absorbed into the existing parties. Perhaps the framers would have feared the populist nature of Roosevelt's Bull Moose Party and the coalition that might have resulted from a proportional system of election in 1912. A coalition with 75 percent of the popular vote might have represented the tyranny of the majority that the framers were trying to avoid.

Case Two: The Presidential Elections of 1932 and 1936

TABLE 5.2
Case Two: 1932 and 1936

1932 National Vote Percentages
Democratic: Franklin Roosevelt, 57.4%
Republican: Herbert Hoover, 39.6%
Socialist: Norman Thomas, 2.2%
Makeup of 73rd Congress
House: Democrats 311, Republicans 117, Other 5, Vacant 2
Senate: Democrats 60, Republicans 35, Other 1
1936 National Vote Percentages
Democratic: Franklin Roosevelt, 60.8%
Republican: Alf Landon, 36.5%
Union: William Lemke, 1.9%
Socialist: Norman Thomas, 0.4%
Makeup of 75th Congress
House: Democrats 322, Republicans 103, Other 10
Senate: Democrats 70, Republicans 23, Other 2, Vacant 1

Let us now consider the results of the historic 1932 and 1936 presidential elections together. Franklin Roosevelt's victory in 1932 was solidified by his landslide reelection in 1936. In 1932, the public clearly showed its lack of confidence in Herbert Hoover, who appeared to believe that the Depression would work itself out without government intervention. Although it was not clear what exactly Roosevelt would do once in office, the public obviously believed he would do something, and that was more than they expected of Hoover.[24] Once elected, President Roosevelt sought immediate relief from the Depression by pushing Congress to pass new "big government" programs. By the time the 1936 election took place, the vote was considered a referendum on the New Deal, which was ratified overwhelmingly.[25] The difference between the two major political parties, which had been relatively indistinct in 1932, was now clearly delineated: Republicans wanted weak national government, and Democrats wanted strong national government. Big government won.[26]

According to the Democratic platform adopted in 1936, the Roosevelt administration planned an active governmental agenda. Their promised actions included the creation of a structure of economic security for all beyond the existing Social Security program, to secure for the consumer fair value and a fair spread between the price charged for a product and its cost, decent adequate and affordable housing for all Americans, enforcement of antitrust regulations, guaranteed work supplied by the government when businesses fail to provide adequate jobs, and equal rights for all.[27] Many observers noted that the stakes were high for the 1936 elections: the issues included whether or not the Democrats could become America's majority political party, whether Americans would accept big government, and how extensive the welfare state would become. The Democrats did become the majority party, Americans did at least partially accept big government, but the welfare state did not become as extensive as those that evolved in Europe. In spite of the Democrats' best efforts to expand big government, the Republicans managed to slow down some of their initiatives. That is, the structure of Congress, which encourages minority rights, compromise, and inaction, hindered Roosevelt in creating a true welfare state.

In fact, President Franklin Roosevelt managed to create a new and expansive role for the federal government. He increased its regulation of business, he used public funds to provide immediate relief to persons out of work, he implemented a progressive income tax (whereby the rich pay a greater percentage than the poor), and he signed the Wagner Act into law, which gave workers many advantages over management in labor negotiations. In addition, Roosevelt proposed and implemented the Social Security system. As the above accomplishments clearly indicate, he presided over a very active and progressive presidency.

Under parliamentary rules, Roosevelt could have done even more. He would not have encountered any meaningful opposition from the Republicans. With such a wide margin in the National Assembly (57 percent in 1932 and 62 percent in 1936), Roosevelt would have had little problem getting broad new social programs passed. In addition, it is possible that the Democrats would have formed a coalition government with a socialist or workers' party. Under a presidential system, the 2 percent of the national vote that those parties received reduced them to the status of a footnote on election results. Under a parliamentary system, 2 percent of the national vote would give such a party a toehold in the legislature, perhaps creating a launching pad for future gains. At the very least, a National Assembly in which 2 percent of the membership was Socialist would have given some voice to an American leftist movement. Further, in coalition with the leading Democrats, it is also possible that Roosevelt would have appointed one or two Socialists to his cabinet.

While the New Deal actually resulted in something far less expansive than the European welfare state, a parliamentary system controlled by Rooseveltian Democrats could have resulted in much more extensive social programs, increasing federal government involvement in the economy and the lives of its citizens to a much greater extent than was actually the case in the New Deal. The Republican Party, which favored less government control, would not have had much power to stop the Democrats in a parliamentary system. A parliamentary system would not have had checks in place to stop the popular and powerful Franklin Roosevelt.

IMAGE 5.2
President Franklin D. Roosevelt prepared to throw the first pitch of the opening day game between the Washington Senators and the Boston Red Sox in Washington on 16 April 1940. Despite his immense popularity, Roosevelt's ambitious legislative agenda was constrained by the constitutional system of checks and balances. © George R. Skadding/AP/Corbis.

Case Three: The Presidential Elections of 1980 and 1984

TABLE 5.3
Case Three: 1980

1980 National Vote Percentages
  Republican: Ronald Reagan, 50.7%
  Democratic: Jimmy Carter, 41.0%
  Independent: John Anderson, 6.6%
Makeup of 97th Congress
  House: Democrats 244, Republicans 191
  Senate: Republicans 53, Democrats 46, Other 1

Turning now to an examination of the 1980 and 1984 elections, we find that although President Reagan had different legislative priorities than President Franklin Roosevelt, he faced similar institutional obstacles.

In 1980 Ronald Reagan defeated the incumbent Jimmy Carter in a campaign that promised to return America to greatness by building up its defenses, cutting taxes and the bureaucracy, and balancing the budget. The Republican Party also won control of the Senate in 1980. For their part, the Democrats retained control of the House of Representatives and were strongly opposed to the president's program. In 1984, Reagan was reelected president by a large margin, and the Republicans maintained the Senate.

Once elected, President Reagan sought immediate tax relief from "big government" by pushing Congress to cut New Deal programs. By the time the 1984 election took place, the vote was considered a referendum on Reagan's legislative agenda in his first four years. It was ratified overwhelmingly. The difference between the two major political parties, which was clearly delineated in 1932, stayed the same: Republicans wanted weak national government, and Democrats wanted strong national government. This time, however, the proponents of small government had the upper hand in the executive branch, but were somewhat checked by a Democratic majority in the House of Representatives.

Reagan faced a Democratic-controlled House of Representatives. Tip O'Neill, the liberal Democratic Speaker of the House, along with a majority of the representatives, did not support the president's legislative package. O'Neill made it clear that they would block any measure they disagreed with. Reagan tried to outmaneuver O'Neill and the rest of his Democratic opposition by frequently claiming that the American people had granted him a national electoral "mandate" to implement his conservative legislative program.

Eventually, Reagan convinced Tip O'Neill not to block everything he was attempting to do, including tax cuts and increases in defense spending. O'Neill justified his cooperative position by stating that since the American people had voted for Reagan, he ought to let some of the right-wing agenda have a chance to work (or fail). O'Neill also gained some significant concessions from the president, who agreed not to slash spending on Social Security and on other human services programs. In sum, and as we discussed in chapter 1, Reagan and O'Neill decided to implement a legislative package that cut taxes, ended some governmental programs, maintained spending on Social Security, and increased defense spending—the combination of which significantly increased the national debt.

Both Republicans and Democrats have acknowledged that the national debt rapidly increased during the Reagan presidency; they blame each other for it. So what actually happened? Who was at fault for the increased debt? And what would have happened under the Westminster Compromise (see text box 1.2 for a discussion)?

Under a parliamentary system, the Republicans would have gained control of the National Assembly, and Reagan would have become the prime minister. There would have been no endless debates between Democrats and Republicans on the matter: the chief of state under the Westminster Compromise is responsible for the government and accountable for its policies. Since the burden of governing would be in the hands of the majority party under our parliamentary system, the success or failure of Reagan's policies would be his. Governmental responsibility and accountability would have been squarely in Reagan's hands.

Consequently, it is possible that the national debt would not have increased under a Prime Minister Reagan at all. That is, as prime minister, he would not have had to make costly compromises with his opposition in the legislature and so could have pursued his legislative goals in a more cost-efficient manner. Of course, we must also take into account that Reagan's electoral "mandate" was really not that commanding for the first four years. The Democrats, allied with the Independents, would have totaled close to 49 percent of the representative body in 1980. In such a scenario, Reagan would have presided over a razor-slim majority, and might have been more hesitant in his legislative initiatives. However, after the landslide election of 1984, Reagan would have had a commanding majority that could have been interpreted as a mandate.

Indeed, the very checks and balances that kept Franklin Roosevelt from implementing a large-scale welfare state on the European model also prevented Reagan from paring down government to the extent that he would have liked. Both Reagan and Roosevelt faced opposition from Congress. A Republican minority was able to slow down Roosevelt significantly in the 1930s; a Democratic majority was able to slow down Reagan in the 1980s.

Case Four: The Elections of 1992, 1994, and 1996

TABLE 5.4
Case Four: 1992, 1994, 1996

1992 National Vote Percentages
Democratic: Bill Clinton, 43%
Republican: George Bush, 37.5%
Independent: Ross Perot, 18.9%

Makeup of 103rd Congress
House: Democrats 257, Republicans 176
Senate: Democrats 56, Republicans 44

1994 Midterm Elections: Makeup of 104th Congress
House: Republicans 234, Democrats 198, Independents 1, Vacant 2
Senate: Republicans 53, Democrats 47

1996 National Vote Percentages
Democrat: Bill Clinton, 49.2%
Republican: Bob Dole, 40.7%

Reform: Ross Perot, 8.4%
Green: Ralph Nader, 1%
Libertarian: Browne, 1%
Makeup of 105th Congress
House: Republicans 223, Democrats 211, Independents 1
Senate: Republicans 55, Democrats 45

We will now examine the three national elections of the 1990s (two presidential and one midterm) together. As in all the other cases, the presidential vote can be considered a proxy for a national vote in a parliamentary system. In this case, however, the midterm congressional election, in an unusual turn of events, can also be considered a proxy for a national vote.

In the United States, most congressional elections turn on the maxim coined by House Speaker Tip O'Neill, that "all politics is local." In 1994, Newt Gingrich succeeded in gaining a Republican majority in the House by nationalizing the elections. Although the elections clearly had a regional focus (Republican dominance of Congress came mostly from elections in the south), the 1994 congressional elections are the closest thing this country has seen to a national, parliamentary-style election. The Contract with America was the platform on which the party ran, and Representative Newt Gingrich, as the party's national leader, would have been its prime minister.

In 1992, Clinton clearly received no mandate (gaining substantially less than 50 percent of the vote), and yet he faced a Congress with his party in the majority. Had the 1992 presidential election been a national election, the hypothetical National Assembly would have had nearly as many Republicans as Democrats, and almost 20 percent of its membership would have been Independent. The Independents, led by Ross Perot (who then founded the Reform Party in 1996), would have been a powerful force in creating a coalition government, exacting compromises and holding out the power of their numbers as a prize to the party they eventually aligned themselves with. Throwing their weight with the Republicans would have created a coalition with 57 percent of the membership, a powerful majority, rivaling the 60 percent majority the Democrats actually had in the House, and exceeding the 56 percent Democratic majority in the Senate.

It is not clear which party the Independents would have aligned themselves with, and who would have ended up prime minister in 1992. It is likely that they would have aligned with the Republicans, focusing on fiscal conservatism and balancing the budget. On the other hand, had the Independents aligned with the Democrats, and Clinton been elected prime minister, national healthcare might well have become the law of the land a decade and a half earlier, and the more liberal welfare reform expected of Clinton in the early part of his first term might still have been in place.

In actuality, Clinton pursued a more liberal agenda with mixed results from 1993 to 1994. Congress passed his proposal to increase taxes and cut spending to reduce the federal budget deficit in 1993. Later that year he won passage of the North American Free Trade Agreement, and lost on a proposal to implement a sweeping national healthcare system, which had envisioned a strong role for the federal government. After the Republicans won control of Congress in 1994, Clinton adopted a more centrist position. He supported an anticrime bill in 1995 and ended federal guarantees of support to the poor in his 1996 welfare reform program.[28]

So, who is the real Clinton? The one who proposed a large federal government involvement in his 1993 healthcare proposal, or the one who in 1996 eliminated a significant role for the federal government in welfare? It is difficult to know. And what would he have done had he been prime minister? The Republican Party and the Independents were clearly unhappy with President Clinton by 1994 (both groups were upset with his liberalism, his "waffling," and his inability to work with Congress, particularly in hammering out a budget package), so a Prime Minister Clinton would likely have faced a vote of confidence in 1994, and as likely would have lost it. The 1994 congressional election thus serves hypothetically as an example of both a vote overthrowing the existing government and the subsequent vote to elect a new government.

Had the 1994 election actually been a national election under a parliamentary system, the result would not have been the gridlock that caused so much voter disgust from 1992 to 1994; instead, the Republican Contract with America would have become law of the land. If we assume that a Prime Minister Clinton would have emerged as the coalition leader after the 1992 elections, then we could possibly have seen a national healthcare program pass in 1993, only to be overturned in 1995. Similarly, a liberal welfare program might have been passed in 1993, only to be replaced by a block grant in 1995. Such a scenario illustrates the instability of a parliamentary system, which can easily result in rapid and repeated systemic change.

The 1996 election also presents an interesting hypothetical for our imaginary system. The president received just under half of the national vote. The combination of votes garnered by the Reform Party, Green Party, and Libertarian Party adds up to 10 percent, which, together with the 41 percent that the Republicans received in the national election, could have created a slim majority. However, if the third parties had aligned themselves with the Democrats, they could have achieved a strong 58 percent majority in the National Assembly. As in 1992, it is unclear who would have ended up prime minister in a parliamentary system after the 1996 election. Given that the voters sent back a Republican Congress (although voter decisions in Congressional elections are more local than in presidential elections), the public clearly was ambivalent about the two political parties.

Although Newt Gingrich himself was reelected, and the Republicans maintained a majority in Congress, the presidential vote has been viewed as representing, if not a repudiation of the Republican Congress, then at least a message that the excesses of the Republicans should be balanced by the Democrats (and vice versa). It is possible under a parliamentary system that a Prime Minister Clinton could have been voted out of office and replaced by a Prime Minister Gingrich, only to have his party returned to power two years later. In that case, policies easily passed by the Republican majority could just as easily be swept away by a Democrat majority, resulting in rapid and significant policy swings.

Case Five: The Presidential Election of 2000

TABLE 5.5
Case Five: 2000

2000 National Vote Percentages
Democratic: Al Gore, 48.38%
Republican: George W. Bush, 47.87%
Green: Ralph Nader, 2.74%
Makeup of 107th Congress
House: Republicans 221, Democrats 211, Other 2, Vacant 1
Senate: Democrats 50, Republicans 50

The historic election of 2000 is a fascinating case of how a parliamentary system could have changed the final outcome. Most Americans recall the drama of the 7 November 2000 elections with a high degree of stress and pain—even years later. Early in the evening, Al Gore had reason for confidence. The Voter News Service (which delivers election results to the major television networks and the Associated Press [AP]) declared at 8 p.m. that Florida had voted for Al Gore, sending its entire electoral vote (twenty-five votes) to him. One hour later, the networks declared that Gore had won the key states of New York, Pennsylvania, and Michigan. For his part, George Bush won most of the south, including Virginia, Georgia, and Texas. But he was behind in the electoral count, and a state with a large number of electoral votes would help.

It is important to remember that the framers set up an unusual method for electing the president. They could have chosen to elect him from the legislature, creating a parliamentary system, as discussed earlier. They could also have chosen popular election. The framers did neither, instead setting up a complicated system whereby states would select electors who would in turn vote for the president. Each state would get a number of electors equal to the size of its congressional delegation (the number of representatives in that particular state plus two senators). The electors, who were expected to be individuals of high merit with good judgment, would then vote for president and vice president. In case of a tie, the election results would be sent to the House for a decision (as happened in the election of 1800). As time went on, several changes to the process were made, and eventually we ended up with the current system, in which American voters vote for electors pledged to a particular candidate (sometimes that fact is noted in small print on the ballot). It is not technically a direct election of the president, nor is it exactly what the framers intended.

On that November evening in 2000, things changed dramatically at 10:13 p.m., when the Voter News Service changed its mind, declared that the vote was too close to call in Florida, and moved the state back into the "toss-up" category. Suddenly, Bush was back in the race. Florida, whose governor was Jeb Bush, George W. Bush's brother, was potentially attainable. Gore won California at 11 p.m., but neither of the candidates had managed to reach the required 270 electoral votes at that time. The drama seemed to come to an end at 2:16 a.m., when Fox News projected that Florida was won by Bush. CNN made the same announcement at 2:18 a.m. It looked like Bush had won 271 electoral votes against Gore's 266. So Al Gore conceded the race at 2:30 a.m. and wished Bush good luck.

That is when things got interesting. As additional electoral returns came in, Florida actually seemed to be leaning toward the Democrat. So one hour later, at 3:30 a.m., Gore retracted his concession; in his view, the Florida vote was too close to call. A candidate conceding and then retracting his concession had never happened before in an American presidential election. Americans woke up on Wednesday, 8 November, to learn that the presidential election was essentially a tie.

All eyes focused on Florida: Whoever won its electoral votes would become president. A recount of the state election was immediately initiated; evening news shows were replete with images of election workers studying ballots, examining so-called hanging chads—which are incompletely punched holes from a punched card ballot—to ensure that each ballot was accurately registered to reflect the intention of the voter. The recount went on for almost six weeks. After several court battles over whether the recount would be statewide, or just of selected counties, the official, final Florida Division of Elections result certified that Bush had won Florida by 537 votes, out of a total of close to six million votes cast—less than the 1,784 vote margin of victory reported on 8 November 2000, but enough for victory.

The difficulty for many Americans was that Al Gore had actually won the popular vote—by a hair. Gore received 48.38 percent of the vote; Bush, 47.87 percent of the vote, giving Gore a lead of just over *half a percentage point* nationwide. Although most Americans believe that presidential elections are (or should be) direct national directions, they are not. The winner of the Electoral College votes is the winner. But the fact that the election was so close meant that a slight change in the vote of a state with a large Electoral College vote could have sent the election to the other candidate. So Al Gore had a very large incentive to keep the recount going in Florida, especially in light of inaccuracies and mistakes in the vote counting in a state governed by a Bush.

At that point, the battle went to the courts. The Gore campaign asked for a statewide manual recount, and on 8 December the Florida Supreme Court, by a 4–3 vote, ordered the same; the United States Supreme Court then stayed that decision the very next day by a 5-4 margin. Three days later, the United States Supreme Court decided in *Bush v. Gore*—in support of the argument offered by the Bush campaign—that there was no legal requirement for an additional recount in Florida. As such, this decision allowed the final certified results to stand, making George Bush president. Al Gore did not agree with this judgment, but decided that it was in the best interest of the nation to accept the decision of the Supreme Court. He conceded on 13 December 2000, and George Bush finally became president. It took six weeks to settle the election, and the process opened many questions. A *US News* story usefully observed in the aftermath of the battle:

> At that moment [election night], few foresaw the political roller coaster ride that would raise unprecedented questions about how the country elects its president. For 36 days, who won the White House was in limbo, as Bush and Gore were separated by a razor-thin margin, complicated by voting difficulties in Florida and the complexities of election law. Ultimately, 47 lawsuits related to the election were filed in Florida, and a ruling from the U.S. Supreme Court decided the matter. "Elections are a messy business," says Barry Richard, a Democrat who was Bush's lead trial litigation attorney. "There have probably been hundreds of thousands of mistakes [in past elections], but they were not noticed before 2000 because they didn't have such an impact." Since then, reform efforts have only somewhat improved how elections are run.[29]

How could these electoral results have played out under the terms of the Westminster Compromise? Certainly, a close election would create plenty of political intrigue in any democratic system, but a parliamentary system might have been able to provide much quicker resolution of the split national election. For instance, a proportional representation system would have allocated seats in the National Assembly in proportion to the votes received. Therefore, as the head of the party receiving a plurality of votes, Gore could have presided over a minority government with 48.38 percent of the seats. Gore might also have tried to form a coalition government with Ralph Nader's Green Party, for a 51.12 percent governing majority. In that case, Gore would certainly have had to accept environmental portions of the Green Party's platform in his own legislative agenda in exchange for their support. In such a case, Ralph Nader could also have negotiated a deputy prime minister position. There is also a scenario in which George Bush might have become prime minister in 2000. He might have tried to form a government with Ralph Nader; their combined electoral results would reach a total of 50.61 percent. In either case, Ralph Nader would have been the most powerful political player in Washington, and been in a position to demand legislative concessions from both sides, before he made a decision. It is not difficult to imagine that Gore would have readily accepted conditions requiring him to pursue more environmental protection legislation in the American National Assembly; however, if Bush made that type of deal, it could have fractured his Republican coalition, throwing that potential Bush-Nader coalition government into a crisis.

IMAGE 5.3
Election workers hand-check ballots for hanging, pregnant, or dimpled chads at the Miami Dade County Government Center on 20 November 2000. The counting is a three-person process, with classifications of challenge, overvote, and undervote, and with an official counter, a Democratic observer, and a Republican observer on hand. © Reuters/CORBIS.

However the governing accommodation might have been reached, any coalition government built on a split national vote would certainly have its political struggles. The opposition would be in a strong position to block outcomes; questions of a weak electoral mandate would surround the government. One might even wonder if the chief executive would have been in a position to respond effectively to the attacks of 11 September 2001. The current presidential system required that the 2000 election be determined by one undecided state after the electoral results in the other forty-nine states had been inconclusive (because neither candidate had yet won a sufficient number of electoral votes); the process was finally decided by the courts. In contrast, the Westminster Compromise would not have seen any court involvement in the process; instead, it would have required that the leading parties negotiate among each other to form a governing coalition following the close national vote. As such, it would have allowed for greater compromise, coalition building, and responsiveness—and, perhaps, a greater sense of legitimacy surrounding the results of the election.

Case Six: The Elections of 2008, 2010, and 2012

TABLE 5.6
Case Six: 2008, 2010, 2012

2008 National Vote Percentages
  Democratic: Barack Obama, 52.93%
  Republican: John McCain, 45.6%
  Independent: Ralph Nader, 0.56%
Makeup of 111th Congress
  House: Democrats 255, Republicans 180
  Senate: Democrats 58, Republicans 40, Independents 2
2010 Midterm Elections: Makeup of 112th Congress
  House: Republicans 242, Democrats 193
  Senate: Democrats 53, Republicans 45, Independents 2
2012 National Vote Percentages
  Democratic: Barack Obama, 51%
  Republican: Mitt Romney, 47%
  Libertarian: Gary Johnson, 1%
Makeup of 113th Congress
  House: Republicans 234, Democrats 201
  Senate: Democrats 54, Republicans 45, Independents 1

The three national elections beginning in 2008 (two presidential and one midterm), taken together, have some interesting similarities with the three national elections of the 1990s. As in the other cases, the presidential vote can be considered a proxy for a national vote in a parliamentary system. In this case, as was the case in 1994, the midterm congressional election might also be considered a proxy for a national vote.

President Barack Obama rode into office on a wave of goodwill and widespread popular support. The public was tired of war in Iraq and Afghanistan, the economy was on the downswing, and President George W. Bush's popularity was at a low. Senator Barack Obama easily defeated Senator John McCain with his message of hope and change, and his coattails gave the Democratic Party control of the House and the Senate. Similar to the first day of the new Republican-led Congress in 1994, there was a sense of euphoria and optimism surrounding the inauguration of President Barack Obama. This was the first time the Democrats had had that much power since the 1992 election of President Bill Clinton, when Democrats also controlled Congress. It seemed that Obama had a mandate to reform the healthcare system and change the way Washington did business. Had the 2008 presidential election been a national election, the mandate would not have been so evident: the hypothetical National Assembly would have been more closely balanced between Democrats and Republicans, given that Obama won 53 percent of the popular vote. It would have been enough to give him a parliamentary majority, however, and allow him to pass his legislative program easily. In actuality, Obamacare passed without a single Republican vote; there is every reason to believe that there would have been a similar outcome in the fictional National Assembly.

What would be the implications for the hope-and-change agenda of the Obama administration if the United States adopted a British-style parliamentary system? Looking at healthcare from that perspective, it might have been easier to get legislation institutionalizing hope and change passed in a parliamentary system. The fact that no Republicans voted for healthcare reform is a problem in our system, which is structured to encourage legislative compromise; in our Westminster Compromise, there would be no expectation that the majority coalition would bring the minority along to vote for legislation. Remember that in a parliamentary system coalitions are built prior to governing, while in our presidential system, coalitions are built one policy at a time. The passage of a bill without a broad-based legislative coalition—including the opposition—tends to erode its political legitimacy in a presidential system.

The 2010 national elections would have had a much greater impact under the terms of our Westminster Compromise than they had under the current institutional arrangement. As we saw in chapter 4, House Republicans voted almost forty times to repeal Obamacare, all to no avail. Republicans were left spinning their wheels: the Senate and the president were an effective brake on the will of the House, regardless of how much public opinion was on the Republicans' side. Had the 2010 election actually been a national election under the terms of our Westminster Compromise, the result would not have been gridlock; instead, the Republican-affiliated Tea Party movement would have seized the reins of the legislature, focused on decreasing taxes and government spending, and easily repealed Obamacare and replaced it with such legislation as they saw fit. In such a scenario, and as accurately described by Fareed Zakaria in his quote at the beginning of this chapter, the ongoing battles between Obama and Congress over raising the debt ceiling, and the associated disagreements over the proper size and function of government, the level of government spending, and its impact on the economy, would also be easily remedied by an act of the American National Assembly. They could simply vote to limit spending and to reduce the size of government. In such a system, the role of the Supreme Court would also be diminished: election results, rather than court decisions, become the final arbiter of policy choices.

Of course, the 2012 electoral results swung back in the opposite direction. Though the public was frustrated with big government and broad-based healthcare reform in 2010, in 2012 the public showed that it was not yet ready to give up on Obama and his healthcare reform. Although not as big a "wave" as the elections of 2008 and 2010, the 2012 election did demonstrate that the American public had a tendency to change its mind. Such a scenario in regard to Obamacare helps to demonstrate just how unstable a parliamentary system can be: it responds almost immediately to the voice of the people, and then alters in response to the demands of new voices in the public square. This kind of rapid systemic change is something the framers feared.

Arguably, this exploration of how American politics could function without checks and balances reveals in each case that the government in power could have been much more responsive to the demands of its constituency. Our proposed Westminster Compromise might have strengthened third parties, given better representation to minorities, and left the Republican and Democratic parties weakened, if indeed they managed to continue in their current forms. In addition, the blame game, in which Democrats and Republicans each blame the other side for the deficit and debt, would not be possible. In fact, the federal debt might not be as large, since spending and taxing compromises would not have been necessary, with one party controlling both the presidency and the legislature. Either way, the Westminster Compromise could lead to greater governmental accountability than is presently the case.

Further, under the fictional Westminster Compromise, it is quite possible that a European-style welfare state could have been created in the early 1900s by a Prime Minister Theodore Roosevelt, or during the Depression under a Prime Minister Franklin Roosevelt. If a national healthcare system had not been created then it is possible that a Prime Minister Bill Clinton could have been able to pass such legislation with a Democratic majority in the National

Assembly in 1993. Prime Minister Obama, then, would not have had to create a national healthcare system from scratch, but instead could have worked to improve an existing program. What cost would these changes have had? It is difficult to say. Perhaps the current American presidential form of government would have become less stable. That is, as American sentiment seems to shift from a preference for big government in times of crisis to much more limited government in times of prosperity, the legislature and the laws passed therein could have lurched back and forth from one extreme to another. In addition, the minority out of power would not be in a position to act as a check on the majority in power in passing legislation, which is unquestionably in opposition to what the framers of the Constitution actually intended.

American policy formation could certainly be different if the United States were on another ideational and institutional path. While we acknowledge that it is extremely risky business to make predictions about what might have been, we hope to have provided some food for thought regarding the question of how ideas and institutions might influence policy.

Notes

1. Joy Esberey, "What if There Were a Parliamentary System?" in *What if the American Political System Were Different?*, ed. Herbert M. Levine et al., 95–148 (Armonk, NY: M.E. Sharpe, 1992).

2. Ibid., 103.

3. Robert A. Dahl, *Democracy in the United States: Promise and Performance*, 2nd ed. (Chicago: Rand McNally, 1972), chapter 10. Reprinted in *Parliamentary versus Presidential Government*, ed. Arend Lijphart (Oxford: Oxford University Press, 1992), 57–65. Quote is from page 63.

4. Ibid., 95–147.

5. See Ralph Segalman, "The Protestant Ethic and Social Welfare," *Journal of Social Issues* 24 (1968): 123–30. Also see Max Weber, *The Protestant Ethic and the Spirit of Capitalism*, trans. Stephen Kalberg (New York: Oxford University Press, 2010).

6. Esberey, "What if There Were a Parliamentary System?," 109.

7. When President Bill Clinton nominated lawyer Lani Guinier to be assistant attorney general in charge of the Justice Department's Civil Rights Division in 1993, the issue of representation of all segments of the population was raised in a particularly contentious and adverse way. Due to the vociferousness of her opponents, President Clinton withdrew Guinier's nomination before the Senate started its consideration. Consequently, Guinier never was afforded the opportunity to spell out in public her view of how a single-member district plurality system, which allocates 100 percent of the power to 51 percent of the people, is fundamentally unfair to those minority groups in the population. See Lani Guinier, *The Tyranny of the Majority* (New York: Free Press, 1994).

8. Esberey, "What if There Were a Parliamentary System?," 130–31.

9. Ibid., 132.

10. For a list of the scandals facing the Obama administration, see communities. washingtontimes.com/neighborhood/tygrrrr-express/2013/jun/10/updated-obama-scandals-user-handbook/#ixzz2VrlHQcxl. Also see www.time.com/time/magazine/article/0,9171,2143562,00.html.

11. To complicate matters, on 16 September 2012, the administration sent United Nations Ambassador Susan Rice to explain the Benghazi situation on all five national Sunday talk shows. She suggested that the attack was a spontaneous response to an anti-Muslim film. See transcript from "Meet the Press," 16 September 2012, at www .nbcnews.com/id/49051097/ns/meet_the_press-transcripts/t/september-benjamin -netanyahu-susan-rice-keith-ellison-peter-king-bob-woodward-jeffrey-goldberg -andrea-mitchell/#.UbZ7zeeG1Y4. Also see "John King: Benghazi Investigation Both Legitimate and Partisan," www.cnn.com/2013/05/09/politics/king-benghazi.

12. Read more: www.foxnews.com/politics/2013/06/03/something-to-hide-repub licans-reject-doj-explanation-holder-testimony/#ixzz2Vru5SPV9.

13. www.time.com/time/magazine/article/0,9171,2143562-2,00.html.

14. Associated Press, "Sen. John McCain Wants Watergate-Style Panel to Probe Libya," 14 November 2012, www.realclearpolitics.com/articles/2012/11/14/mccain_ wants_watergate-style_panel_to_probe_libya_116157.html; "Sen Lindsey Graham Wants Watergate-Style Panel for IRS," www.ipolitics.ca/2013/05/26/with-irs-justice -department-scandals-gop-keeping-obama-on-hot-seat/.

15. www.archives.gov/federal-register/electoral-college/provisions.html.

16. One could also try this hypothetical exercise by reference to the aggregate congressional vote.

17. The Miller Center, "Campaigns and Elections: The Campaign and Election of 1904," millercenter.org/president/roosevelt/essays/biography/3.

18. Roosevelt's entire speech is available at ehistory.osu.edu/osu/mmh/1912/ 1912documents/TheLeaderandtheCause.cfm.

19. David M. Kennedy, Lizabeth Cohen, and Thomas Bailey, *The American Pageant*, vol. 2, 15th ed. (Boston: Wadsworth Cengage Learning, 2010), 662.

20. Theodore Roosevelt, "Address to National Progressive Party, Chicago, 6 August 1912," in *History of American Presidential Elections*, vol. 3, ed. Arthur M. Schlesinger and Fred L. Israel (New York: Chelsea House Publishers), 2220–26. Quote is from page 2222.

21. Ibid.

22. George E. Mowry, "The Election of 1912," in Schlesinger and Israel, *History of American Presidential Elections*, 2160–66.

23. Ibid., 2163.

24. See William Leuchtenburg, *Franklin Roosevelt and the New Deal: 1932–1940* (New York: Harper and Row, 1963).

25. The 1936 election is known as a *realigning* election, because millions of voters changed their party loyalty from Republican to Democrat, and remained Democrats for the rest of their lives.

26. Frank Freidel, "The Election of 1932," in Schlesinger and Israel, *History of American Presidential Elections*.

27. William E. Leuchtenburg, "Election of 1936," in *History of American Presidential Elections, 1789–1968*, ed. Arthur M. Schlesinger Jr. (New York: McGraw-Hill, 1972), 2851–57.

28. See Anne Marie Cammisa, *From Reform or Rhetoric? Welfare Policy in American Politics* (Boulder, CO: Westview, 1998).

29. See Samantha Levine, "Hanging Chads: As the Florida Recount Implodes, the Supreme Court Decides Bush v. Gore," www.usnews.com/news/articles/2008/01/17/the-legacy-of-hanging-chads.

6

Conclusion

Ideas and Institutions Matter

Over the past decade, a broad consensus has emerged that "institutions matter."

—Francis Fukuyama

A free government is a complicated piece of machinery, the nice and exact adjustment of whose springs, wheels, and weights, is not yet well comprehended by the artists of the age, and still less by the people.

—John Adams

T HIS BOOK HAS EXAMINED THE ideational and institutional tension of the American system of government, and argued that ideas and institutions matter to policy development. Many observers of American politics—tired of the current institutional arrangement that produces divided government and gridlock—have argued that the political system must be reformed to enable effective democratic governance. For instance, in their work, *It's Even Worse Than It Looks: How the American Constitutional System Collided with the New Politics of Extremism,* congressional experts Thomas E. Mann and Norman J. Ornstein argue that the recent rise of political extremism has moved national politics in the United States away from its tradition of compromise.[1] According to Mann and Ornstein, political extremism, combined with an institutional structure favoring incremental change, has turned Washington into a dysfunctional political capital, noting that "as voter disgust with political dysfunction grows in intensity, the market for ideas like public financing or even mandatory attendance at the polls will also grow."[2]

Critics have argued that the net result of gridlock has been a growing belief among the citizenry that it is not possible to change government, and a consequent development of apathy or even antigovernmental activities in some extreme cases. The previous chapters have identified three central problems with the current institutional design of the American system of government. These are:

- divided government,
- gridlock, and
- a lack of any mechanism for quickly replacing a failed or deadlocked government.

This concluding chapter will restate and review these three main problems associated with the constitutional system, and then examine some ideas for institutional reform.

Problem One: Divided Government

Many Americans are frustrated that Congress and the president have been slow to pass and implement legislation supported by a majority of people. Their reproach has focused on divided government, which occurs when there is an executive of a different party than the dominant party in the legislative branch. Although this situation nicely corresponds to the framers' intent that power be divided and separated, critics have noted that this very structure is responsible for a host of governmental problems. The Englishman Walter Bagehot argued in his 1867 work titled *The English Constitution* for the necessity of unified government (i.e., fused executive and legislative powers) to avoid the problems intrinsic to a divided power arrangement. He admonished the American system for its fixed and inelastic nature, which imperils its citizens, given its long and protracted procedures to respond during an unforeseen crisis. Further, Bagehot contended that the division of legislative and executive powers gives rise to the corollary problems of gridlock and lack of governmental accountability. Many contemporary observers echo Bagehot's critiques, and have demanded that this situation be reformed.

The American system of divided powers naturally generates a related problem: the lack of governmental accountability. Since there is no central nucleus of power in Washington, it is quite possible for presidents and representatives to "pass the buck," informing concerned citizens that they had very little to do with almost any measure. Or, on the other hand, there is also nothing to keep a political leader from claiming full responsibility for a popular measure, when, in fact, the law-making process involves many people. For example, even though both the executive and legislative branches had a hand in the increase in the national debt in the 1980s, or in the implementation of sequestration or the government shutdown in 2013, neither side accepted responsibility, and both have plausibly denied their role. This problem has led to poor policy making and an erosion of people's confidence in the democratic process. Former president Harry S. Truman did his best to deal with the lack of governmental responsibility by proudly displaying a sign on his desk in the Oval Office that proclaimed, "The buck stops here." Although the sentiment is commendable, the problem of accountability is institutional, and only institutional changes will overcome it.

Problem Two: Gridlock

The problem of divided government is profoundly linked to the problem of gridlock, which may be defined as an impasse within or between the branches of government over legislative priorities. Gridlock transpires at numerous points—between the president and Congress, between the president and one of the legislative houses, between the Senate and the House, or within each legislative branch among the majority and minority parties—and prevents Congress from moving on legislative programs. There is a school of thought that does not consider gridlock a problem. As discussed in chapter 1, neither divided government nor gridlock is necessarily incompatible with effective governance, in terms of getting important legislation passed.

Yet there are at least two dangers in the current constitutional arrangement. The first is that Congress and the president will simply be unable to bring the national debt under control, leading the country to an economic disaster at some point in the not-too-distant future. Second, the divided power arrangement can prevent the president from effective action during a time of crisis somewhere in the world.[3]

Further, it is important to note that gridlock can occur under certain parliamentary arrangements as well. For example, in parliamentary systems with bicameral parliaments, one house may fall into one party's hands and the other house into the hands of another party, creating gridlock. Another problem might arise if no one party has a majority in parliament, and the leading parties cannot form a majority coalition. If the United States were to adopt a parliamentary system, perhaps it too would face the peril of minority governments and gridlock. There are simply no easy solutions.

Problem Three: No Means to Quickly Replace
a Failed or Deadlocked Administration

The American presidential system has been constitutionally unable to quickly remove a failed or deadlocked administration. As we saw in chapter 5, given the separation of powers doctrine, Congress was unable to deal with the "long national nightmare" of Watergate swiftly and decisively by immediately instituting a new government. Similarly, the congressional investigation into the Iran-Contra scandal in the 1980s lasted for several years and cost the government millions of dollars. Debates over several Obama-era scandals have followed a similar path. The current institutional arrangement in the United States leaves policy makers little choice: whenever there are serious questions raised about an administration, congressional investigation into the executive branch may last for years. Even though a special prosecutor has been occasionally appointed to lend impartiality to the inquiry and speed up the process, the results have been less than satisfactory. Critics hold that short of institutional reform, we can look forward to more situations like these three well into the future.

Some Possible Solutions?

There have been attempts over the years to reform the American system of government. One notable effort took place just before the bicentennial of the signing of the Declaration of Independence in the spring of 1976, when the American Academy of Political and Social Science invited a group of distinguished scholars, lawyers, judges, political leaders, and representatives of various interest groups to gather in Philadelphia to reexamine the Constitution, including how well the separation of power mechanisms were working.

   Conference participants met in various historical settings throughout Philadelphia during their 5–8 April 1976 discussions. Papers were delivered to four separate committees (on values and society in revolutionary America, effectiveness of governmental operations, shaping of public policy, and the United States and the world), and subsequent discussions led to a consensus that several reforms, and some constitutional amendments, be adopted. In particular, Charles E. Gilbert's paper titled "Shaping of Public Policy" suggested a series of institutional reforms, including adding a legislative vote of confidence against the executive, and a procedure whereby the executive could dissolve the legislature. Yet, in the years since the conference, no significant progress has been made on these recommendations. In more recent times, James L. Sundquist, an original participant in the 1976 Bicentennial

Convention Meeting in Philadelphia, has suggested several remedies to the institutional problems associated with presidential government. Drawing on the suggested reforms offered by the members of the 1976 Bicentennial Committee on the Constitution and by Sundquist, we have identified some ideas that may serve as a starting point for a discussion about remedies to the problems listed earlier. These three possible solutions are:

- merge executive and legislative powers
- restore governmental accountability
- abandon fixed terms

We will now examine each one of these in turn.

Idea One: Merge Executive and Legislative Powers

The problem of divided government could possibly be modified if the executive and legislative branches were brought closer together. This solution envisions that the president would regularly attend legislative sessions with members of his cabinet, similar to the case of the British prime minister. Regularized executive-legislative contact could improve both communication and collegiality between the two branches of government. As suggested by both Gilbert and Sundquist in their respective works, it would also be a good idea to repeal Article I, Section 6, Clause 2 of the Constitution, so that cabinet officials might also simultaneously be members of Congress.[4] The net result of this change might be first that the executive and legislative branches would better understand each other, and second, that the House Speaker could emerge as a sort of congressional prime minister, focusing power and simplifying the law-making procedure. Or, as George Gilbert notes, "the American system fragments 'powers' and confuses 'functions'; parliamentary systems consolidate 'power' and provide a more sophisticated institutionalization of functions . . . in which policy-shaping power in legislation and administrative coordination is more effective governmentally and more responsible politically."[5] Of particular interest, Gilbert further remarks that perhaps some experimentation with the separation of powers be tried at the state level before any such reform be brought to Washington, noting that "if Pennsylvania could function with parliamentary government then, I suppose, so could any state."[6]

At the very least, removing the constitutional ban on members of Congress serving in the executive branch could lead to "constructive experimentation,"[7] resulting in a much less confrontational relationship between the two branches.

Idea Two: Restore Governmental Accountability

With the Democrat Barack Obama in the White House and Democratic majorities in both the Senate and the House following the 2008 elections, many observers cheered the return of governmental accountability. Everyone knew who was in charge (the Democrats) and whom to blame if things went bad (the Democrats). The key question was whether this election would finally end the bickering between the executive and legislative branches, or if Washington would return to the gridlock of the previous administrations. Then, almost without warning, the anti–big government Tea Party movement stormed the country in 2010, won back the House for the Republicans, and divided government was back. We can see a similar pattern in the recent past: 1992 presidential and congressional elections restored unified party government in Washington under the Democrats and President Bill Clinton, as did the 2004 presidential and congressional elections under the Republicans and President George W. Bush. For a variety of reasons, divided rule quickly returned in each case: in 1994 the Republicans won the House back from the Democrats, and in 2006 the Democrats won the House from the Republicans. Why do Americans seem to vote for divided government? What happened to the high hopes for unified government?

Many reasons have been offered for the failure of single party–controlled, unified government. Some have claimed that the Democrats overestimated their electoral strength after their presidential and congressional victories in 1992 and in 2008, and were not prepared for the Republican attacks. Others have argued that both the 1994 and 2010 legislative elections were a well-managed, effective Republican attack on the Democrats. Similarly, the Republicans may have overestimated their electoral strength after their presidential and congressional victories in 2004, and were unprepared for the 2006 elections, when the Democrats won back the House. Perhaps the most prescient explanation, however, was offered by former Reagan White House chief of staff Kenneth M. Duberstein. At a meeting of the Committee on the Constitutional System and the Brookings Institution on 24 February 1993, he gave an institution-based explanation for why the 1992 elections, which produced a Democratic president and Democratic majorities in the House and Senate, might not end gridlock and improve governmental accountability. In his view, gridlock and divided government is inevitable in our separated power situation:

> The good news is that on 3 November [1992] the American people clearly demonstrated that they wanted an end to gridlock, they want change, they want more accountability in our government—no excuses. The bad news is that now is about as best as it gets. . . . I hope that the American people will not be disap-

pointed, but I am concerned that the end of gridlock is unlikely. The system is biased toward gridlock, not toward action. It is far, far easier to block something on Capitol Hill than it is to pass something affirmatively.[8]

Duberstein turned out to be correct. Even though he was speaking in the aftermath of the 1992 presidential elections, his observations are not time bound: subsequent events have demonstrated that gridlock remains a pronounced feature of American government. Although gridlock may occur when the presidency and the majority in Congress are held by the same party, James Sundquist has argued that there is a greater likelihood of gridlock when the branches of government are divided between parties. To guard against party-based gridlock, he suggests that a so-called team-ticket reform be adopted. In Sundquist's view, the team-ticket would combine each party's candidates for president, vice president, Senate and House, into a slate that would be voted for as a unit. This method would "eliminate ticket splitting that produces divided government."[9] This method of voting was used in the United States before the advent of secret balloting, and some form of the party ballot was used up to the 1970s in several states, including Maine and Connecticut.

Alternatively, the United States could adopt a version of the d'Hondt system of proportional representation for national elections. An American variation of this system could see political parties presenting a closed list of candidates to the voters for all of the positions in government, including the executive and legislative branches. Voters would choose a party list, and could not divide their votes between particular candidates from opposing parties. Once the vote totals were announced, the d'Hondt system would allocate seats in the legislative assembly on the basis of a formula to determine the highest average of votes cast per party. This method of allocating seats in a legislature tends to favor larger parties, and so, arguably, the United States would continue to have two major parties. The advantage would be to oblige the voter to make a clear choice about national legislative priorities by freeing national elections from the narrower and more local "pork-barrel" concerns.

A corollary to this proposal would be to lengthen the terms of office for representatives and senators. In this regard, Sundquist has aptly observed:

Even a united government is constantly distracted by the imminence of the next election, which is never more than two years away. The two-year life of the Congress—shortest of any national legislature in the world—normally limits an incoming president to barely a year as his "window of opportunity" to lead his party in enacting the program for which it sought its victory. To eliminate the midterm election and thereby lengthen the period of relative freedom from election pressure would require four-year House terms and either four-year or eight-year Senate terms, with the latter more in accord with the staggered-term tradition of the Senate. Presidents and Congresses alike would be better able to undertake short-term measures that might be unpopular, in order to achieve a greater long-run good, and the legislative process would benefit from a more deliberate tempo.[10]

A unified government with a clear electoral mandate and undistracted by the next election would certainly be better equipped to avoid the dangers of gridlock and provide effective governance than the current situation allows. Other useful proposals envision the implementation of a line-item presidential veto, changing the Senate's filibuster and hold rules, the restoration of legislative veto, and a redefinition of governmental "powers." Each reform seeks to place clear responsibility in the hands of those making the decisions.

Idea Three: Abandon Fixed Terms

Perhaps some of the most frustrating political situations facing the American public result from the development of a lame-duck president or of an ineffective Congress. According to the current constitutional structure, all members of Congress and the president have the right to complete their term of office, regardless of their performance in those roles, save for dire circumstances. Congress can remove the president from office through the rare and difficult process of impeachment only if he or she is found to have violated the Constitution during his or her term of office. The president may also be removed from office if he or she is found to be incapacitated and unable to perform the job per the terms of the Twenty-fifth Amendment to the Constitution. Otherwise, for good or ill, the public is stuck with their president.

As we examined in chapter 2, the American presidential system is a form of democratic government in which the executive branch is distinct and separated from the legislative branch. The chief executive, or president, is directly elected by the people (through the mechanism of the electoral college) and is granted independent power and authority by the Constitution. In general, the president may not be appointed nor dismissed by a legislative vote, because executive power derives from the people and not from the legislature.[11] Further, the fixed nature of executive and legislative terms leads to a certain inflexibility of the American system, because, no matter how ineffective or incompetent a president or Member of Congress may be, they have the right to stay in office until the end of their electoral term.[12]

Perhaps it would be useful to reform this aspect of our presidential system with the introduction of a method for special elections to reconstitute a failed government. Certainly, if the United States were to adopt this so-called parliamentary safeguard (i.e., governments can be dissolved at any time, and new elections can be scheduled quickly), weak or ineffective governments in office for long periods of time would become a thing of the past. This reform could promote effective governance.[13]

The organizing principle behind this sort of reform is that a constitutional amendment implementing a parliamentary mechanism for elections would free the current American presidential system from its confinement to the elections timetable. Rather, political leaders in Washington would be able to turn to new elections whenever faced with a legislative-executive impasse. Arguably, there are many ways to arrange a new electoral procedure. In general, this type of constitutional amendment would have two central provisions: it would allow the president to dissolve Congress and call for new elections, if, in his view, Congress had lost the support of the people, and, conversely, it would subject the president to a congressional vote of no confidence, if, at any time, the legislature seriously doubted the continuing ability of a president to lead. These reforms would make the presidential system considerably less stable, but would certainly result in a closer executive-legislative partnership, as both sides could face dissolution by the other.[14]

Ideas and Institutions Matter

This book argues that ideas and institutions matter to policy formation: The Constitution creates a complex system of checks and balances among the three branches of government, and it also protects the rights of the minority out of power. The system tends to produce divided government and gridlock, and does not provide a mechanism for quickly replacing a failed or deadlocked government.[15] We also saw in chapters 3 and 4 how the foundational ideational and institutional tension in the United States impedes majority rule.

To conclude, let us revisit the Constitutional Convention. As we discussed in chapter 2, the origins of the tension of majority rule versus minority rights in American politics may be traced to the very founding of the nation in 1787. Having defeated British King George III in the War of Independence, the framers debated about the form and shape of their new democratic government at the Constitutional Convention in Philadelphia. As there were no other viable functioning democratic models in the world to emulate, their deliberations were charting an unknown territory. And their solution to the tension was to wager that it was better to have executive-legislative gridlock than to risk the tyranny of one person or of the majority. In that way, the framers launched an experiment in government predicated on divided and separated powers. We continue to live with this experiment.

Would a parliamentary system work better or worse in a context such as the current one, in which the parties seem completely bifurcated? The book

IMAGE 6.1
Washington as Statesman at the Constitutional Convention (1856), by Junius Brutus
Stearns (American, 1810–1885). Virginia Museum of Fine Arts, Richmond. © CORBIS.

is not advocating for a change to a parliamentary system, but rather asking
why our system is the way it is. Bearing in mind that the American experiment began with a cry of "taxation without representation," we conclude that
the American system has been well suited to the American psyche. A country
that prefers limited government is, by definition, wary of expansive change.
Whether we have reached a point at which our system is broken and needs to
be fixed, or whether the system will eventually return to a state of equilibrium,
is a question that is not yet answerable. And, as the Declaration of Independence so aptly notes, "mankind are more disposed to suffer, while evils are
sufferable."[16] In other words, change is not likely to happen unless and until
the public and their elected officials decide that the difficulties associated with
changing the system are more bearable than the difficulties in the existing
system. We are not there yet.

Arguably, the threat of tyranny that so concerned the framers is as valid
today as ever. So should we really try to significantly alter this system of
government? Americans always have the option to alter or amend the Constitution; prior to any change, however, it is incumbent upon us to carefully
consider the pros and cons of the current arrangement, and of the proposed
change. The framers struggled with how to organize their new democracy at
the end of the eighteenth century, and made their determination. Now, the
decision is up to us. What should we do?

This book has demonstrated some ways that ideas and institutional arrangements influence the formation of public policy in the United States. In particular, the American presidential system has been designed to be antagonistic to majority rule, a design that has generated, among other difficulties, the problems of divided government, gridlock, and a lack of any mechanism for quickly replacing a failed or deadlocked government. Former President Woodrow Wilson understood these limitations of our constitutional structure, and suggested at the end of the nineteenth century that it would be better if the United States adopted a British-style parliamentary system to suit the changing times. The three ideas suggested in this chapter echo Wilson's very concerns. Taken in aggregate, these ideas could, perchance, permit governmental leaders to change the institutional structures of American democracy to allow for the quick passage of new laws and better enable the government to adapt to the changing times—if that is, indeed, what the people want. These ideas also help to illustrate our main contention in this book: that the foundational ideational and institutional tension has set American policy formation down a bumpy, cobblestoned path of checks and balances, which will continue to impede the development and passage of innovative and comprehensive policy unless and until the people of the United States decide to take another path.

Notes

1. Thomas E. Mann and Norman J. Ornstein, *It's Even Worse Than It Looks: How the American Constitutional System Collided with the New Politics of Extremism* (New York: Basic Books, 2012).

2. Ibid., 162.

3. James L. Sundquist, *Constitutional Reform and Effective Government*, rev. ed. (Washington, DC: Brookings Institution, 1992), 323.

4. Charles E. Gilbert, "Shaping of Public Policy," in *The Revolution, the Constitution, and America's Third Century: The Bicentennial Conference on the United States Constitution*, vol. 1, *Conference Papers* (Philadelphia: American Academy of Political and Social Science by the University of Pennsylvania Press, 1976), 163–215 (quote is from page 197). Also see Daniel Beland and Robert Henry Cox, *Ideas and Politics in Social Science Research* (New York: Oxford University Press, 2010); Peter A. Hall, "Conclusion: The Politics of Keynesian Ideas," in *The Political Power of Economic Ideas* (Princeton, NJ: Princeton University Press, 1989); John Campbell, "Institutional Analysis and the Role of Ideas in Political Economy," *Theory and Society* 27 (1998): 377–409; Frank Fischer, *Reframing Public Policy*, chapter 4, "Public Policy and Discourse Analysis" (New York: Oxford University Press, 2003); Alan M. Jacobs, "How Do Ideas Matter? Mental Models and Attention in German Pension Politics," *Comparative Political Studies* 42, no. 5 (February 2009): 252–79; Deborah A. Stone,

"Causal Stories and the Formation of Policy Agendas," *Political Science Quarterly* 104, no. 2 (1989): 281–300; V. A. Schmidt, "Does Discourse Matter in the Politics of Welfare State Adjustment?" *Comparative Political Studies* 35, no. 2 (2002): 168–93; Vivien A. Schmidt and Claudio M. Radaelli, "Policy Change and Discourse in Europe: Conceptual and Methodological Issues," *West European Politics* 27, no. 2 (2004): 183–210; Robert C. Lieberman, "Ideas, Institutions, and Political Order: Explaining Political Change," *American Political Science Review* 96, no. 4 (2002): 697–712.

    5. Gilbert, "Shaping of Public Policy," 198.

    6. Ibid., 200.

    7. Sundquist, *Constitutional Reform and Effective Government*, 324.

    8. Kenneth Duberstein, "The Prospects for Ending Gridlock," in *Beyond Gridlock? Prospects for Governance in the Clinton Years—And After*, ed. James Sundquist (Washington, DC: Brookings Institution, 1993), 17–18.

    9. Sundquist, *Constitutional Reform and Effective Government*, 323.

    10. Ibid.

    11. See Giovanni Sartori, *Comparative Constitutional Engineering: An Inquiry into Structures, Incentives and Outcomes* (New York: New York University Press, 1994), 101.

    12. Juan J. Linz and Arturo Valenzuela, *The Failure of Presidential Democracy: Comparative Perspectives* (Baltimore: Johns Hopkins University Press, 1994), 5–22.

    13. Sundquist, *Constitutional Reform and Effective Government*, 199.

    14. Ibid., 196–97.

    15. There is much useful literature on the role of ideas in comparative public policy. See Mark Blyth, "Powering, Puzzling, or Persuading: The Mechanisms of Building Institutional Orders," *International Studies Quarterly* 51 (2007): 761–77; John L. Campbell, "Institutional Analysis and the Role of Ideas in Political Economy," *Theory and Society* 27, no. 3 (June 1998): 377–409; John L. Campbell and Ove Kaj Pedersen, "Knowledge Regimes and Comparative Political Economy," in *Ideas and Politics in Social Science Research*, ed. Daniel Beland and Robert Henry Cox, 234–70 (New York: Oxford University Press, 2011); Peter A. Hall, "Historical Institutionalism in Rationalist and Sociological Perspective," in *Explaining Institutional Change: Ambiguity, Agency, and Power*, ed. James Mahoney and Kathleen Thelen, 204–20 (Cambridge: Cambridge University Press, 2010); and Robert Lieberman, "Ideas, Institutions, and Political Order: Explaining Political Change," *American Political Science Review* 96, no. 4 (December 2002): 697–712.

    16. A transcription of the Declaration of Independence is available at www.archives.gov/exhibits/charters/declaration_transcript.html.

Bibliography

Adams, Rebecca. "Health Care Overhaul Still in 'Happy Talk' Stage." *Congressional Quarterly Weekly Reports*, 19 January 2009. library.cqpress.com/cqweekly/document .php?id=weekly report111-000003012941&t.

Adler, Jonathan. *The Promise: Obama, Year One*. New York: Simon and Schuster, 2010.

Alexander, G. "Institutions, Path Dependence, and Democratic Consolidation." *Journal of Theoretical Politics* 13, no. 3 (2001): 249–70.

Almond, Gabriel A., G. Bingham, J. Powell Jr., Russell J. Dalton, and Kaare Strom. *Comparative Politics Today: A World View*. 9th ed. New York: Longman, 2009.

Alter, Jonathan. *The Promise: Obama, Year One*. New York: Simon and Schuster, 2010.

Anderson, James. *Public Policymaking*. 7th ed. New York: Wadsworth, 2010.

Armstrong, Drew. "Senate Passage of Health Bill Sets Stage for Talks with House." *Congressional Quarterly Weekly Reports*, 24 December 2009. www/cq.com/doc/news-3273233?print=true.

Armstrong, Drew, and David Clarke. "Panels Advance Health Care Overhaul." *Congressional Quarterly Weekly Reports*, 20 July 2009. library.cqpress.com/cqweekly/document.php?id=weekly report111-0000031705090&t.

Armstrong, Drew, and Alex Wayne. "Debate Gets Off to a Rocky Start." *Congressional Quarterly Weekly Reports*, 22 June 2009.

Armstrong, Drew, and Alex Wayne. "Tentative First Steps Toward a Deal on Health Care." *Congressional Quarterly Weekly Reports*, 11 January 2010.

Baaklini, Aldo I., and Helen Desfosses, eds. *Designs for Democratic Stability: Studies in Viable Constitutionalism*. Armonk, NY: M.E. Sharpe, 1997.

Bagehot, Walter. *The English Constitution*. London: Fontana, 1993. (Originally published by Chapman and Hall in 1867.)

Bailey, Michael A. "Comparable Preference Estimates across Time and Institutions for the Court, Congress, and Presidency." *American Journal of Political Science* 51, no. 3 (2007): 433–48.

Beck, Paul Allen, and Frank J. Sorauf. *Party Politics in America.* New York: Harper Collins, 1992.

Beland, Daniel, and Robert Henry Cox. *Ideas and Politics in Social Science Research.* New York: Oxford University Press, 2010.

Benson, Clea. "A New Kind of Abortion Politics." *Congressional Quarterly Weekly Reports,* 29 March 2010. www.cq.com/doc/weeklyreport-3634203?print=true.

Berns, Walter, ed. *After the People Vote: A Guide to the Electoral College.* Washington, DC: AEI Press, 1992.

Bettelheim, Adriel. "Overhaul Hard to Steer Using Hands-Off Approach." *Congressional Quarterly Weekly Reports,* 10 August 2009. library.cqpress.com/cqweekly/document.php?id=weekly report111-000003189437&t.

Bill, James A., and Robert L. Hardgrave Jr. *Comparative Politics: The Quest for Theory.* Washington, DC: University Press of America, 1981.

Blondel, Jean. *Comparative Legislatures.* Englewood Cliffs, NJ: Prentice Hall, 1973.

Blyth, Mark. "Ideas, Uncertainly and Evolution." In *Ideas and Politics in Social Science Research,* edited by Daniel Beland and Robert Henry Cox. New York: Oxford University Press, 2011.

Blyth, Mark. "Powering, Puzzling, or Persuading: The Mechanisms of Building Institutional Orders." *International Studies Quarterly* 51 (2007): 761–77.

Blyth, Mark. "The Transformation of the Swedish Model." *World Politics* 54, no. 1 (October 2001): 1–26.

Brady, David W. "The Causes and Consequences of Divided Government: Toward a New Theory of American Politics?" *American Political Science Review* 87, no. 1 (1993): 183–94.

Brady, David W., and Craig Volden. *Revolving Gridlock: Politics and Policy from Jimmy Carter to George W. Bush.* 2nd ed. Boulder, CO: Westview, 2005.

Broder, David S. "Vote May Signal GOP Return as Dominant Party." *Washington Post,* 10 November 1994.

Brown, Carrie Budoff. "Dems Seek Deal as Senate Debate Begins." *Politico,* 29 November 2009.

Brown, Carrie Budoff, and Patrick O'Connor. "Fallout: Dems Rethinking Health Bill." *Politico,* 21 January 2010.

Burnham, David. *Above the Law: Secret Deals, Political Fixes, and Other Misadventures of the U.S. Department of Justice.* New York: Scribner, 1996.

"Cabinet Government in the United States." *International Review* 7 (August 1879): 146–63.

Cammisa, Anne Marie. *From Rhetoric to Reform? Welfare Policy in American Politics.* Boulder, CO: Westview, 1998.

Cammisa, Anne Marie. *Governments as Interest Groups.* Westport, CT: Praeger, 1995.

Campbell, Colin, Harvey Feigenbaum, Ronald Linden, and Helmut Norpoth. *Politics and Government in Europe Today.* Boston: Houghton Mifflin, 1995.

Campbell, John L. "Institutional Analysis and the Role of Ideas in Political Economy." *Theory and Society* 27, no. 3 (1998): 377–409.

Campbell, John L., and Ove Kaj Pedersen. "Knowledge Regimes and Comparative Political Economy." In *Ideas and Politics in Social Science Research*, edited by Daniel Beland and Robert Henry Cox. New York: Oxford University Press, 2011.

Cassata, Donna. "Republicans Bask in Success of Rousing Performance." *Congressional Quarterly Weekly Reports*, 8 April 1995.

Center for Budget and Policy Priorities. "Where Do our Tax Dollars Go?" 12 April 2013. www.cbpp.org/cms/index.cfm?fa=view&id=1258.

Chaddock, Gail Russell. "Inside Pelosi's Realm." *The Christian Science Monitor*, 19 July 2010.

Chilcote, Ronald. *Theories of Comparative Politics: The Search for a Paradigm Reconsidered.* 2nd ed. Boulder, CO: Westview, 1994.

Chong, Dennis, and James N. Druckman. "Framing Public Opinion in Competitive Democracies." *American Political Science Review* 101, no. 4 (November 2007): 637–55.

Clingermayer, James C., and Richard C. Feiock. *Institutional Constraints and Policy Choice: An Exploration of Local Governance.* Albany: SUNY Press, 2001.

Cloud, David S. "GOP, to Its Own Great Delight, Enacts House Rules Changes." *Congressional Quarterly Weekly Reports*, 7 January 1995.

Cloud, David S. "House GOP Shows a United Front in Crossing 'Contract' Divide." *Congressional Quarterly Weekly Reports*, 22 February 1995.

Cloud, David S. "House Speeds Pace on Contract." *Congressional Quarterly Weekly Reports*, 11 February 1995.

Conaghan, Catherine. Remarks made at a conference titled "Presidential or Parliamentary Democracy: Does it Make a Difference: A Research Symposium on Stable Democracy." Organized by Juan Linz and Arturo Valenzuela, Georgetown University, Washington, DC, 14–16 May 1989.

Conley, Tom. "Globalisation as Constraint and Opportunity: Reconceptualising Policy Capacity in Australia." *Global Society: Journal of Interdisciplinary International Relations* 16, no. 4 (October 2002): 377–99.

Conolly, Ceci. "61 Days from Near-Defeat to Victory: How Obama Revived his Health Care Bill." *Washington Post*, 23 March 2011.

Conradt, David, and Eric Langenbacher. *The German Polity.* 10th ed. Lanham, MD: Rowman and Littlefield, 2013.

Constituição da República Portuguesa: As Três Versões Após 25 de Abril 1989/1982/1976. Lisbon: Porto Editora, 1990.

Cooper, Kenneth J., and Helen Dewar. "100 Days Down, but Senate to Go for Most 'Contract' Items." *Washington Post*, 9 April 1995.

Corkill, David. "The Political System and the Consolidation of Democracy in Portugal." *Parliamentary Affairs* (October 1993): 517–32.

Curtis, Michael. *Introduction to Comparative Government.* 4th ed. New York: Longman, 1997. (5th ed. New York: Longman, 2006.)

Dahl, Robert A. *Democracy in the United States: Promise and Performance.* 2nd ed. Chicago: Rand McNally, 1972, chapter 10. Reprinted in *Parliamentary versus*

Presidential Government, edited by Arend Lijphart. Oxford: Oxford University Press, 1992.

Dahl, Robert A. *Pluralist Democracy in the United States: Conflict and Consent*. Chicago: Rand McNally & Company, 1967.

Davidson, Roger H. "The 104th Congress and Beyond." In *The 104th Congress: A Congressional Quarterly Reader*, edited by Roger H. Davidson and Walter J. Oleszek. Washington, DC: CQ Press, 1995.

Davidson, Roger H., and Walter J. Oleszek, eds. *The 104th Congress: A Congressional Quarterly Reader*. Washington, DC: CQ Press, 1995.

Davis, John. "The Economic Stimulus, Health Care and Financial Reform: Evaluating President Obama's Legislative Agenda." In *The Barack Obama Presidency: A Two-Year Assessment*, edited by John Davis. New York: Palgrave Macmillan, 2012.

Davis, John, ed. *The Barack Obama Presidency: A Two-Year Assessment*. New York: Palgrave Macmillan, 2012.

de Smith, S. A., and Rodney Brazier. *Constitutional and Administrative Law*. 7th ed. Harmondsworth, UK: Penguin, 1994.

Dicey, A. V. *Introduction to the Law of the Constitution*. 10th ed. London: Macmillan, 1959.

Dillon, C. Douglas. "The Challenge of Modern Government." In *Reforming American Government: The Bicentennial Papers of the Committee on the Constitutional System*, edited by Donald L. Robinson. Boulder, CO: Westview: 1985.

Dionne, E. J. *Why Americans Hate Politics*. New York: Touchstone, 1995.

Donaghy, Peter J., and Michael T. Newton. *Spain: A Guide to Political and Economic Institutions*. Cambridge: Cambridge University Press, 1987.

Downs, Anthony. *An Economic Theory of Democracy*. New York: Harper and Row, 1957.

Duberstein, Kenneth. "The Prospects for Ending Gridlock." In *Beyond Gridlock? Prospects for Governance in the Clinton Years—And After*, edited by James Sundquist. Washington, DC: Brookings Institution, 1993.

Dunn, Charles W. *American Exceptionalism: The Origins, History, and Future of the Nation's Greatest Strength*. Plymouth, UK: Rowman & Littlefield, 2013.

Dye, Thomas. "A Full Plate: The Obama Policy Agenda." In *Obama, Year One*, edited by Thomas Dye. New York: Longman, 2010.

Dye, Thomas, ed. *Obama, Year One*. New York: Longman, 2010.

Easley, Jonathan. "GOP Support Grows to Force Shutdown over Funding Obama Care." The Hill, 22 July 2013. thehill.comvideosenate312497-sen-lee-threatens-shutdown-to-block-obamacare-#ixzz2a4MH2kNF.

Epstein, Leon D. "Changing Perceptions of the British System." In "Presidential and Parliamentary Democracies: Which Work Best?" Special Issue, *Political Science Quarterly* 109, no. 3 (1994): 483–98.

Esberey, Joy. "What if There Were a Parliamentary System?" In *What if the American Political System Were Different?*, edited by Herbert M. Levine et al. Armonk, NY: M.E. Sharpe, 1992.

Etzioni, Amitai. *Capital Corruption: The New Attack on American Democracy*. 2nd ed. New Brunswick, NJ: Transaction Books, 1988.

Fahrenthold, David A. "Once Again, the House Votes to Repeal Obamacare." *Washington Post*, 17 May 2013.

Fiorina, Morris P. *Divided Government*. Boston: Allyn & Bacon, 1996.

Fischer, Frank. *Reframing Public Policy*. New York: Oxford University Press, 2003.

Forestiere, Carolyn, and Christopher Allen. "The Formation of Cognitive Locks in Single Party Dominant Regimes." *International Political Science Review* 32, no. 4 (September 2011): 380–95.

Freedman, Leonard. *Politics and Policy in Britain*. New York: Longman, 1996.

Freidel, Frank. "The Election of 1932." In *History of American Presidential Elections*, vol. 3, edited by Arthur M. Schlesinger and Fred L. Israel. New York: Chelsea House Publishers, 2002.

Frenzel, Bill. "The System Is Self-Correcting." In *Back to Gridlock? Governance in the Clinton Years*, edited by James L. Sundquist. Washington, DC: Brookings Institution, 1995.

Fukuyama, Francis. "Do Defective Institutions Explain the Gap between the United States and Latin America?" *The American Interest*, November/December 2006. www.the-american-interest.com/article.cfm?piece=198.

Gilbert, Charles E. "Shaping of Public Policy." In *The Revolution, the Constitution, and America's Third Century: The Bicentennial Conference on the United States Constitution*, vol. 1, *Conference Papers*. Philadelphia: American Academy of Political and Social Science by the University of Pennsylvania Press, 1976.

Gillespie, Ed, and Bob Schellhas, eds. *Contract with America: The Bold Plan by Rep. Newt Gingrich, Rep. Dick Armey and the House Republicans to Change the Nation*. New York: Times Books, 1994.

Gitelson, Alan R., Robert L. Dudley, and Melvin J. Dubnick. *American Government*. 4th ed. Boston: Wadsworth, Cengage Advantage Books, 2011.

"GOP Agenda Hits Snag in Senate." *Congressional Quarterly Weekly Reports*, 4 February 1995.

"GOP Plan for a Marathon January." *Congressional Quarterly Weekly Reports*, 31 December 1994.

Graham, Lawrence S., et al. *Politics and Government: A Brief Introduction to the Politics of the United States, Great Britain, France, Germany, Russia, Eastern Europe, Japan, Mexico, and the Third World*. Chatham, NJ: Chatham House, 1994.

Greener, Ian. "The Potential of Path Dependence in Political Studies." *Politics* 25, no. 1 (February 2005): 62–72.

Gross, Martin L. *A Call for Revolution: How Government Is Strangling America—and How to Stop It*. New York: Ballantine, 1993.

Gruenwald, Juliana. "Shallow Tactics or Deep Issues: Fathoming the GOP Contract." *Congressional Quarterly Weekly Reports*, 19 November 1994.

Gugliotta, Guy. "Breakneck Pace Frazzles House." *Washington Post*, 7 March 1995.

Guinier, Lani. *The Tyranny of the Majority*. New York: Free Press, 1994.

Hall, Peter A. "Conclusion: The Politics of Keynesian Ideas." In *The Political Power of Economic Ideas*. Princeton, NJ: Princeton University Press, 1989.

Hall, Peter A. *Governing the Economy: The Politics of State Intervention in Britain and France*. Oxford: Oxford University Press, 1986.

Hall, Peter A. "Historical Institutionalism in Rationalist and Sociological Perspective." In *Explaining Institutional Change: Ambiguity, Agency, and Power*, edited by James Mahoney and Kathleen Thelen. Cambridge: Cambridge University Press, 2010.

Hamann, Kerstin. "The Creation of Regional Identities and Voting Behavior in Spain." Paper presented to the Iberian Study Group, Center of European Studies, Harvard University, 17 February 1998.

Hamann, Kerstin. "Federalist Institutions, Voting Behavior, and Party Systems in Spain." In "Federalism and Compounded Representation in Western Europe." Special issue, *Publius* 29, no. 1 (Winter 1999): 111–37.

Heilemann, John, and Mark Halperin. *Game Change: Obama and the Clintons, McCain and Palin and the Race of a Lifetime*. New York: HarperCollins, 2010.

Hook, Janet. "Republicans Step Up to Power in Historic 40-Year Shift." *Congressional Quarterly Weekly Reports*, 7 January 1995.

Hook, Janet. "Republicans Vote in Lock Step, But Unity May Not Last Long." *Congressional Quarterly Weekly Reports*, 18 February 1995.

Horowitz, Donald L. "Electoral Systems: A Primer for Decision Makers." *Journal of Democracy* 14, no. 4 (October 2003): 113–27.

Huntington, Samuel P. *Political Order in Changing Societies*. New Haven, CT: Yale University Press, 1968; reissued 2006.

Immergut, Ellen M. "Institutional Constraints on Policy." In *The Oxford Handbook of Public Policy*, edited by Michael Moran, Martin Rein, and Robert E. Goodin. New York: Oxford University Press, 2006.

Immergut, Ellen M., and Karen M. Anderson. "Historical Institutionalism and West European Politics." *West European Politics* 31, nos. 1/2 (January–March 2008): 345–69.

Jacobs, Alan M. "How Do Ideas Matter? Mental Models and Attention in German Pension Politics." *Comparative Political Studies* 42, no. 5 (February 2009): 252–79.

Jacobs, Lawrence R., and Theda Skocpol. *Health Care Reform and American Politics: What Everyone Needs to Know*. New York: Oxford University Press, 2012.

Jennings, Ivor. *The British Constitution*. 5th ed. Cambridge: Cambridge University Press, 1966.

Jones, Charles O. *The Presidency in a Separated System*. Washington, DC: Brookings Institution, 1994.

Jones, David R. *Political Parties and Policy Gridlock in American Government*. Lewiston, NY: Edwin Mellen Press, 2001.

Karl, Terry Lynn. *The Paradox of Plenty: Oil Booms and Petro-States*. Berkeley: University of California Press, 1997.

Katz, Jeffrey L. "GOP Faces Unknown Terrain without 'Contract' Map." *Congressional Quarterly Weekly Reports*, 8 April 1995.

Kemp, B. *King and Commons, 1600–1832*. New York: Macmillan, 1957.

Kennedy, David M., Lizabeth Cohen, and Thomas Bailey. *The American Pageant*, vol. 2. 15th ed. Boston: Wadsworth Cengage Learning, 2010.

Kernell, Sam. *Going Public: New Strategies Of Presidential Leadership*. 4th ed. Washington, DC: CQ Press, 2006.

Killian, Linda. *The Freshman: What Happened to the Republican Revolution?* Boulder, CO: Westview Press, 1998.

King, Desmond S. "The Establishment of Work-Welfare Programs in the United States and Britain: Politics, Ideas, and Institutions." In *Structuring Politics: Historical Institutionalism in Comparative Perspective*, edited by Sven Steinmo, Kathleen Thelen, and Frank Longstreth. Cambridge: Cambridge University Press, 1992.

Kingdon, John. *Agendas, Alternatives, and Public Policies.* 2nd ed., with an epilogue on health care. New York: Longman Classics in Political Science, 2010.

Kingdon, John. *America the Unusual.* New York: Worth Publishers, 1999.

Klein, Ezra. "The Unpersuaded: Who Listens to a President?" *The New Yorker*, 19 March 2012. www.newyorker.com/reporting/2012/03/19/120319fa_fact_klein#ixzz1qzYA96Pf.

Krauthamer, Charles. "Republican Mandate." *Washington Post*, 11 November 1994.

Langdon, Steve. "'Contract' Dwarfs Senate GOP Pledge." *Congressional Quarterly Weekly Reports*, 25 February 1995.

Larson, Edward J. *A Magnificent Catastrophe: The Tumultuous Election of 1800, America's First Presidential Campaign.* New York: Free Press, 2007.

Laundy, Philip. *Parliament and the People: The Reality and the Public Perception.* Surrey, UK: Ashgate, 1997.

Laundy, Philip. *Parliaments in the Modern World.* Hafts, Canada: Dartmouth Publishing Company, 1989.

Leuchtenburg, William E. "Election of 1936." In *History of American Presidential Elections, 1789–1968*, edited by Arthur M. Schlesinger Jr. New York: McGraw-Hill, 1972.

Leuchtenburg, William. *Franklin Roosevelt and the New Deal: 1932–1940.* New York: Harper and Row, 1963.

Levine, Herbert M. *Political Issues Debated: An Introduction to Politics.* 4th ed. Englewood Cliffs, NJ: Simon and Schuster, 1993.

Levine, Samantha. "Hanging Chads: As the Florida Recount Implodes, the Supreme Court Decides Bush v. Gore." www.usnews.com/news/articles/2008/01/17/the-legacy-of-hanging-chads.

Lichbach, Mark Irving, and Alan S. Zukerman. *Comparative Politics: Rationality, Culture, and Structure.* Cambridge Studies in Comparative Politics. Cambridge: Cambridge University Press, 2009.

Lieberman, Robert C. "Ideas, Institutions, and Political Order: Explaining Political Change." *American Political Science Review* 96, no. 4 (December 2002): 697–712.

Light, Paul. *The President's Agenda: Domestic Policy Choice from Kennedy to Clinton.* 2nd ed. Baltimore: Johns Hopkins University Press, 1998.

Lijphart, Arend. *Democracies: Patterns of Majoritarian and Consensus Government in Twenty-one Countries.* New Haven: Yale University Press, 1984.

Lijphart, Arend. *Patterns of Democracy.* 2nd ed. New Haven, CT: Yale University Press, 2012.

Lijphart, Arend. *Thinking about Democracy: Power Sharing and Majority Rule in Theory and Practice.* London: Routledge, 2007.

Lijphart, Arend, ed. *Parliamentary versus Presidential Government*. New York: Oxford University Press, 1992.

Lijphart, Arend, and Bernard Grofman, eds. *Choosing an Electoral System: Issues and Alternatives*. New York: Praeger, 1984.

Linz, Juan J., and Arturo Valenzuela. *The Failure of Presidential Democracy: Comparative Perspectives*. Baltimore: Johns Hopkins University Press, 1994.

Lipset, Seymour Martin. *American Exceptionalism: A Double-Edged Sword*. New York: Norton, 1996.

Lipset, Seymour Martin, and Gary Wolfe Marks. *It Didn't Happen Here: Why Socialism Failed in the United States*. New York: W. W. Norton & Company, 2001.

Lockhart, Charles. *The Roots of American Exceptionalism: Institutions, Culture and Policies*. New York: Palgrave Macmillan, 2003.

Lowi, Theodore. "Presidential and Parliamentary Democracies: Which Work Best?" *Political Science Quarterly* 104, no. 3 (Special Issue 1994): 414.

Lowi, Theodore. "Presidential Democracy in America: Toward the Homogenized Regime." *Political Science Quarterly* 109, no. 3 (1994): 401–38.

Lowi, Theodore J., Benjamin Ginsberg, and Kenneth A. Shepsle. *American Government*. 12th ed. New York: W. W. Norton, 2012.

Lux, Mike. "One More Step." *Huffington Post*, 9 November 2009. www.huffington post.com/mike-lux/one-more-step_b_351269.html.

Mackenzie, G. Calvin, and Saranna Thornton. *Bucking the Deficit: Economic Policymaking in America*. Boulder: Westview, 1996.

Madison, James, John Jay, and Alexander Hamilton. *The Federalist Papers*. Edited by Clinton Rossiter. New York: New American Library, 1961.

Mahler, Gregory S. *Comparative Politics: An Institutional and Cross-National Approach*. 2nd ed. Englewood Cliffs, NJ: Prentice Hall, 1995. (5th ed. Englewood Cliffs, NJ: Pearson, 2007.)

Mahler, Gregory S. *Principles of Comparative Politics*. New York: Pearson, 2012.

Mahoney, James. "Path Dependence in Historical Sociology." *Theory and Society* 29, no. 4 (2000): 507–48.

Mahoney, James, and Kathleen Thelen, eds. *Explaining Institutional Change: Ambiguity, Agency, and Power*. Cambridge: Cambridge University Press, 2010.

Mahtesian, Charles, and Patrick O'Connor. "GOP at Risk of Becoming Party in the No." *Politico*, 26 February 2009. www.politico.com/news/stories/0209/19346.html.

Mainwaring, Scott, and Arturo Valenzuela, eds. *Politics, Society, and Democracy: Latin America. Essays in Honor of Juan J. Linz*. Boulder, CO: Westview, 1999.

Mann, Thomas E., and Norman J. Ornstein. *It's Even Worse Than It Looks: How the American Constitutional System Collided with the New Politics of Extremism*. New York: Basic Books, 2012.

Mannin, Michael L. *British Government and Politics: Balancing Europeanization and Independence*. Plymouth, UK: Rowman & Littlefield, 2010.

Mansfield, Harvey Claflin. *America's Constitutional Soul*. Baltimore: Johns Hopkins University Press, 1991.

Manuel, Paul C. *The Challenges of Democratic Consolidation in Portugal, 1976–1991: Political, Economic and Military Issues*. Westport, CT: Praeger, 1996.

Manuel, Paul Christopher, and Anne Marie Cammisa. *Checks and Balances: How a Parliamentary System Could Change American Government.* Boulder, CO: Westview Press, 1998.

Maraniss, David. "Clinton and Obama: Presidential Parallels." *Washington Post*, 25 March 2012.

Marcet, Joan, and José Ramon Montero, eds. *Roads to Democracy: A Tribute to Juan J. Linz.* Barcelona: Institut de Ciencies Politiques I Sociais, 2007.

Marshall, Geoffrey. *Constitutional Theory.* Oxford, UK: Clarendon Press, 1971.

Mayhew, David R. "Divided Party Control: Does It Make a Difference?" *PS: Political Science and Politics* 24, no. 4 (December 1991): 637–640.

Mayhew, David. *Divided We Govern.* New Haven, CT: Yale University Press, 1991.

Mayhew, David R. *Divided We Govern: Party Control, Lawmaking, and Investigations, 1946–2002.* 2nd ed. New Haven, CT: Yale University Press, 2005.

McGurn, William. "Let's Face It: Obama is No Post-Partisan." *Wall Street Journal*, 21 July 2009.

Mezey, Michael L. *Comparative Legislatures.* Durham, NC: Duke University Press, 1979.

Milbank, Dana. "Sweeteners for the South." *Washington Post*, 22 November 2009. www.washingtonpost.com/wp-dyn/content/article/2009/11/21/AR20091121 02272.html.

Mill, John Stuart. *Considerations on Representative Government.* London: Parker, Son and Bourn, 1861.

Montesquieu, Charles de Secondat, Baron de. *The Spirit of the Laws.* New York: Cambridge University Press, 1989.

Morin, Richard. "Voters Repeat Their Simple Message about Government: Less Is Better." *Washington Post*, 13 November 1994.

Mowry, George E. "The Election of 1912." In *History of American Presidential Elections*, vol. 3, edited by Arthur M. Schlesinger and Fred L. Israel. New York: Chelsea House Publishers, 2002.

Norton, Philip. *The British Polity.* 3rd ed. New York: Longman, 1994. (5th ed. New York: Pearson, 2010.)

Nye, Joseph S., Jr., Philip D. Zelikow, and David C. King, eds. *Why People Don't Trust Government.* Cambridge, MA: Harvard University Press, 1997.

"Obama Begins Fresh Health Care Push." *Politico.com*, 10 May 2013.

"Obama Gives Senate Democrats Another Push on Health Care." *Congressional Quarterly Weekly Reports*, 15 December 2009. www.cq.com/doc/nes-3267710?print=true.

O'Connor, Karen. *No Neutral Ground.* Boulder, CO: Westview, 1996.

O'Connor, Karen, and Larry Sabato. *American Government: Continuity and Change, 1997.* Boston: Allyn and Bacon, 1997.

Ornstein, Norman J., and Amy L. Schenkenberg. "The 1995 Congress: The First Hundred Days and Beyond." *Political Science Quarterly* 110, no. 2 (1995): 183–206.

Ostrom, Elinor. "Coping with Tragedies of the Commons." *Annual Review of Political Science* 2 (1999): 493–535.

Owens, John E. "A 'Post-Partisan' President in a Partisan Context." In *Obama in Office*, edited by James Thurber. Boulder, CO: Paradigm Publishers, 2011.

Patterson, Thomas E. *We the People*. 4th ed. New York: McGraw-Hill, 2004.

Pearce, Malcolm, and Geoffrey Stewart. *British Political History, 1867–2001: Democracy and Decline*. 3rd ed. London: Routledge, 2001.

Pearson, Drew. *The Case against Congress: A Compelling Indictment of Corruption on Capitol Hill*. New York: Pocket Books, 1969.

Peele, Gillian. *Governing the UK*. 3rd ed. Oxford, UK: Blackwell, 1995. (*Governing the UK: British Politics in the 21st Century*, 4th ed. London: Wiley-Blackwell, 2004.)

Penny, Timothy J., and Steven E. Schier. *Payment Due: A Nation in Debt, A Generation in Trouble*. Boulder: Westview, 1996.

Peters, B. Guy, Jon Pierre, et al. "The Politics of Path Dependency: Political Conflict in Historical Institutionalism." *The Journal of Politics* 67, no. 4 (2005): 1275–300.

Peters, Jeremy. "House Votes Again to Repeal Health Law." *New York Times*, 17 May 2013.

Phillips, Kevin P. *Arrogant Capital: Washington, Wall Street, and the Frustration of American Politics*. Boston: Little, Brown and Company, 1994.

Pierson, Paul. "Increasing Returns, Path Dependence and the Study of Politics." *American Political Science Review* 96, no. 2 (June 2000): 697–712.

Pierson, Paul. *Politics in Time: History, Institutions, and Social Analysis*. Princeton, NJ: Princeton University Press, 2004.

Pierson, Paul. "When Effect Becomes Cause: Policy Feedback and Political Change." *World Politics* 45, no. 4 (July 1993): 595–628.

Pole, J. R. *Political Representation in England and the Origins of the American Republic*. New York: St. Martin's Press, 1966.

Pontusson, Jonas. "From Comparative Public Policy to Political Economy: Putting Political Institutions in their Place and Taking Interests Seriously." *Comparative Political Studies* 28, no. 1 (April 1995): 117–47.

Raju, Manu, and Chris Frates. "Lincoln's Long Walk to 60th Vote." *Politico*, 22 November 2009. www.politico.com/news/stories/1109/29824_Page2.html.

Reich, Simon. "The Four Faces of Institutionalism: Public Policy and a Pluralistic Perspective." *Governance* 13, no. 4 (October 2000): 501–22.

Riker, William H. "Federalism." In *Handbook of Political Science: Governmental Institutions and Processes*, vol. 5, edited by Fred I. Greenstein and Nelson W. Polsby. Reading, MA: Addison-Wesley, 1975.

Robertson, David. *Class and the British Electorate*. New York: Basil Blackwell, 1985.

Robinson, Donald L., ed. *Reforming American Government: The Bicentennial Papers of the Committee on the Constitutional System*. Boulder, CO: Westview, 1985.

Roosevelt, Theodore. "Address to National Progressive Party, Chicago, 6 August 1912." In *History of American Presidential Elections*, vol. 3, edited by Arthur M. Schlesinger and Fred L. Israel. New York: Chelsea House Publishers.

Rouquié, Alain. *The Military and the State in Latin America*. Translated by Paul Sigmund. Berkeley: University of California Press, 1987.

Safran, William. *The French Polity*. 7th ed. Englewood Cliffs, NJ: Prentice Hall, 2008

Salant, Jonathan D. "Gingrich Sounds Familiar Themes." *Congressional Quarterly Weekly Reports*, 8 April 1995.

Salant, Jonathan D. "Senate Altering Its Course in Favor of Contract." *Congressional Quarterly Weekly Reports*, 29 April 1995.

Samuels, David. "Separation of Powers." In *The Oxford Handbook of Comparative Politics*, edited by Carles Boix and Susan Stokes. New York: Oxford University Press, 2007.

Sartori, Giovanni. *Comparative Constitutional Engineering: An Inquiry into Structures, Incentives and Outcomes*. New York: New York University Press, 1994.

Scharpf, Fritz W. "Institutions in Comparative Policy Research." *Comparative Political Studies* 33, nos. 6–7 (September 2000): 762–90.

Schick, Allen. *The Capacity to Budget*. Washington, DC: The Urban Institute Press, 1990.

Schier, Steven. "Obama's "Big Bang' Presidency." *The Forum* 8, no. 3 (October 2010): doi:10.2202/1540-8884.1392.

Schmidt, V. A. "Does Discourse Matter in the Politics of Welfare State Adjustment?" *Comparative Political Studies* 35, no. 2 (2002): 168–93.

Schmidt, Vivien A. "Discursive Institutionalism: The Explanatory Power of Ideas and Discourse." *Annual Review of Political Science* 11 (2008): 303–26.

Schmidt, Vivien A., and Claudio M. Radaelli. "Policy Change and Discourse in Europe: Conceptual and Methodological Issues." *West European Politics* 27, no. 2 (2004): 183–210.

Schmitter, Philippe C., and Terry Lynn Karl. "What Democracy Is . . . and Is Not." *Journal of Democracy* 2, no. 1 (Summer 1991): 75–89.

Schumpeter, Joseph. *Capitalism, Socialism and Democracy*. 2nd ed. New York: Harper and Row, 1947.

Segalman, Ralph. "The Protestant Ethic and Social Welfare." *Journal of Social Issues* 24 (1968): 123–30.

Shugart, Matthew Soberg. "Presidentialism, Parliamentarism, and the Provision of Collective Goods in Less-Developed Countries." *Constitutional Political Economy* 10 (1999): 53–88.

Shugart, Matthew Soberg, and John M. Carey. *Presidents and Assemblies: Constitutional Design and Electoral Dynamics*. Cambridge: Cambridge University Press, 1992.

Sinclair, Barbara. "Congressional Leadership in Obama's First Two Years." In *Obama in Office*, edited by James Thurber. Boulder, CO: Paradigm Publishers, 2011.

Sinclair, Barbara. *Unorthodox Lawmaking: New Legislative Processes in the U.S. Congress*. 4th ed. Washington, DC: CQ Press College, 2011.

Social Security Advisory Board. *The Unsustainable Cost of Health Care*. September 2009. www.ssab.gov/documents/TheUnsustainableCostofHealthCare_508.pdf.

Somashekhar, Zachary A. "Health-Care Rule Is Delayed a Year." *Washington Post*, 3 July 2013.

Stepan, Alfred. *Rethinking Military Politics*. Baltimore: Johns Hopkins University Press, 1988.

Stone, Deborah A. "Causal Stories and the Formation of Policy Agendas." *Political Science Quarterly* 104, no. 2 (Summer 1989): 281–300.

Stone, Geoffrey R. "The Supreme Court and the 2012 Election." *Huffington Post*, 13 August 2012.

Streeck, Wolfgang, and Kathleen Thelen. "Introduction: Institutional Change in Advanced Political Economies." In *Beyond Continuity: Institutional Change in Advanced Political Economies*, edited by Wolfgang Streeck and Kathleen Thelen. Oxford: Oxford University Press, 2005.

Sundquist, James L. *Constitutional Reform and Effective Government*. Rev. ed. Washington, DC: Brookings Institution, 1992.

Sundquist, James L., ed. *Back to Gridlock? Governance in the Clinton Years*. Washington, DC: Brookings Institution, 1995.

Sundquist, James L., ed. *Beyond Gridlock? Prospects for Governance in the Clinton Years—And After*. Washington, DC: Brookings Institution, 1993.

Thelen, Kathleen. "Historical Institutionalism in Comparative Politics." *Annual Review of Political Science* 2 (1999): 369–404.

Thelen, Kathleen. *How Institutions Evolve: The Political Economy of Skills in Germany, Britain, the United States and Japan*. New York: Cambridge University Press, 2004.

Thelen, Kathleen, and Sven Steinmo. "Historical Institutionalism in Comparative Politics." In *Structuring Politics: Historical Institutionalism in Comparative Perspective*, edited by Sven Steinmo, Kathleen Thelen, and Frank Longstreth. Cambridge: Cambridge University Press, 1992.

Thompson, E. P. *The Making of the English Working Class*. New York: Pantheon Books, 1964.

Thurber, James. "An Introduction to an Assessment of the Obama Presidency." In *Obama in Office*, edited by James Thurber. Boulder, CO: Paradigm Publishers, 2011.

Thurber, James, ed. *Obama in Office*. Boulder, CO: Paradigm Publishers, 2011.

Toner, Robin. "GOP Blitz of First 100 Days Now Brings Pivotal Second 100." *New York Times*, 9 April 1995.

Tsebelis, George. "Decision Making in Political Systems: Veto Players in Presidentialism, Parliamentarism, Multicameralism, and Multipartyism." *British Journal of Political Science* 25 (1995): 289–325.

Wald, Kenneth D. *Crosses on the Ballot: Patterns of British Voter Alignment since 1885*. Princeton, NJ: Princeton University Press, 1983.

Wayne, Alex, and Drew Armstrong. "Overhaul Debate Put Off Until Fall." *Congressional Quarterly Weekly Reports*, 3 August 2009. library.cqpress.com/cqweekly/document.php?id=weeklyreport111-000003184517&a.

Wayne, Alex, and Drew Armstrong. "Overhaul Struggles on Hill, Back Home." *Congressional Quarterly Weekly Reports*, 10 August 2009. library.cqpress.com/cqweekly/document.php?id=weeklyreport111-000003189448&t.

Wayne, Alex, Kathleen Hunter, and Jennifer Scholtes. "Senate Passes Reconciliation, Returning It to House for Final Vote." *CQ Today Online News*, 25 March 2010. www.cq.com/doc/news-3622652?print=true.

Weaver, R. Kent, and Leslie Pal, eds. *Government Taketh Away: Political Institutions and Loss Imposition in Canada and the United States*. Washington, DC: Georgetown University Press, 2003.

Weaver, R. Kent, and Bert A. Rockman. *Do Institutions Matter? Government Capabilities in the United States and Abroad*. Washington, DC: Brookings Institution, 1993.

Weber, Max. *The Protestant Ethic and the Spirit of Capitalism.* Translated by Stephen Kalberg. New York: Oxford University Press, 2010.

Weir, Alison. *The Six Wives of Henry VIII.* New York: Grove Press, 1992.

Wiarda, Howard J., and Harvey F. Kline. *Latin American Politics and Development.* 7th ed. Boulder, CO: Westview, 2010.

Wilson, Bradford P., and Peter W. Schramm, eds. *Separation of Powers and Good Government.* Lanham, MD: Rowman and Littlefield, 1994.

Wilson, Frank L. *Concepts and Issues in Comparative Politics.* 2nd ed. Upper Saddle River, NJ: Pearson, 2001.

Wilson, Graham K. *Only in America? American Politics in Comparative Perspective.* Chatham, NJ: Chatham House, 1998.

Wilson, James Q. *American Government.* 3rd ed. Lexington, MA: D. C. Heath, 1994. (6th ed. Lexington, MA: D. C. Heath, 2002.)

Wilson, Woodrow. "Cabinet Government in the United States." *International Review* 7 (August 1879): 146–63.

Wilson, Woodrow. *The Politics of Woodrow Wilson. Selections from His Speeches and Writings.* 1st ed. New York: Harper and Brothers, 1956.

Young, Kerry. "Health Care Bill Could Hinge on Byrd Rule." *Congressional Quarterly Weekly Reports,* 14 September 2009. library.cqpress.com/cqweekly/document.php?id=weekly report111-000003200762&t.

Index

accountability: Affordable Care Act and, 146; in Congress, 95; divided government and lack of, 10–13; gridlock preventing, 10, 190, 194; as an institutional problem, 191; in parliamentary system, 111–12; political parties and, 10, 12–13, 111, 194; prime ministers and, 14, 63, 112; restoration ideas, 194–97; under Westminster Compromise scenario, 176, 185

Affordable Care Act (ACA): bipartisan bill as goal, 127, 134; broad comprehensive change, as example of, 85–86; congressional committee work, 128–30; Contract with America, comparison, 117–18, 142, 147; Democratic votes, winning, 4, 146; difficulties passing into law, 2, 6, 86, 126; Health, Education, Labor and Pensions (HELP) committee, 123, 129–30, 135, *137, 138;* healthcare committees, *121;* healthcare reform, early attempts at implementing, 2, 107, 118, 178; House of Representative and, 2–3, 130, 132–33, 135–40, 142, 147, 184; law, becoming, textbook version *vs.* real story, 137, 138–39; minority rights and, 144; parliamentary system, faring in, 4, 5, 143, 146, 147, 177–78, 184–86; Nancy Pelosi championing, 133, 136–37; policy entrepreneurs, involvement of, 122–24; policy window opening, 119, 122, 147; public opinion, 3, 135, 185; Republican opposition, 2–3, 24–25, 118, 131, 140–42, 145, 147, 184; single payer solution, 120

African-American political influence, 159–60

air traffic controllers furlough, 10, 12–13

Articles of Confederation, 24, 26, 66–67, 68, 69, *77*

Bachmann, Michelle, 2

Bagehot, Walter, 13–14, 59, 190

Baucus, Max, 2, *121,* 130–32, 135, *138*

Benghazi scandal, 164–65, 187n11

bicameral legislature, 26–28, 68, 145, 154

Boehner, John, 5, 40n6, 101

Brown, Scott, 123, 135, *136*, 139, 148n9
Bull Moose party, 169, 170, 171
Bush, George W., 179–82, 184, 194

Carter, Jimmy, 11, 162, 175
checks and balances: as uniquely American, 73; blame game resulting from, 165; dramatic change, preventing, 10, 171; among government branches, 17, 87, 141, 145, 197; as a means of impediment, 64, 86, 89, 91, 117, 142, *174*, 176, 199; law passage requirements, 135; parliamentary system, absent in, 57, 63, 78, 109; Senate, role of, 104; Supreme Court, role of, 74; tyranny of the majority, as a means of avoiding, 3, 6, 71, 79
Clinton, Bill: 1992 election, 32, 177, 184, 194; healthcare reform attempt, 107, 118, 119, 178; impeachment, 43n31, 163–64; political personality, 128; as fictional prime minister, 164, 177–79, 185; single-member district plurality system and, 31–32, 186n7; vetoes and, 103, 106–107
Clinton, Hillary, *107*, 118, 119, 121, 122, 123, 128, 163
cloture votes, 126, 133–34, 137, 139
coalitions: in parliamentary system, 33–34, 36, 62, 86, 111, 143, 184, 191; in presidential system, 4, 86, 111, 127, 138, 143–44, 146, 184; in Westminster Compromise scenario, 156, 170–71, 173, 177–78; 182–83, 184
cognitive locks, 17–23, 23–26, 26–29, 29–30, 30–36, 36–38
confederal system, 26, 66, 67
Constitution: amendments, 76, 96; Bill of Rights, 67; British Constitution, 57–59, 64; defining, 49, 73; divided power, encouraging, 8, 72, 89, 124, 126, 186, 197; elector selection, 74–75, 166; federalism and, 23–24;

flexibility of, 77; impeachment due to violation of, 196; legislative branch and financial responsibility, *11;* misperceptions, 17, 36–37, 38; political settlements, as a result of, 16; population representation, 155; reexamination of, 192–93, 198; Spanish Constitution, 25; tyranny of the majority, designed to block, 6, 64, 78–79, 90, 105
Constitutional Convention: confederal system, finding solutions for, 26, 67; events of, 77; parliamentary system consideration, 68–69; philosophical influences, 72; political settlements during, 16, 197; George Washington, attendance at, *198;* in Westminster Compromise scenario, 154–55
Contract with America (Republican): Affordable Care Act, comparison, 117–18, 142, 147; difficulties passing into law, 2, 6, 85, 86, 91; Newt Gingrich and, 86, *88*, 93, 94, 102, 106; House of Representatives and, 5, 86, 88, 91, 92–94, 97, 98–104, 104–08, 110, 113, 142; first hundred days, 98–100, 100–102, 102–04, 108, 112; as a mandate, 88–89, 93; parliamentary system, how it would have fared in, 5, 178; British parliament system, similarities, 109–11, 143, 177; ten-point agenda, 87, 95–97; tyranny, and fear of, 90–91, 105
Cromwell, Oliver, 54, *57*
Cromwell, Thomas, 53

Daschle, Tom, 129, 149n22
Debs, Eugene, 170–71
debt, national, *11*, 12, 175–76, 185, 191
Declaration of Independence, 64, 65–66, 72, *77*, 198
Democratic Party: Affordable Care Act, supporting, 4, 118, 127, 146, 147; Blue Dog Democrats, 122, 130, 131, 138, 148n7; Republican

Contract with America and, 89–90, 92–94, 97; crossover voting, 100, 101, 110–11, 142; divided government and accountability, *11*, 12–13, 111, 194; Health Care Reform Bill passage, role in, 2, 4, 132–35, 135–39, 140–41; in 104th Congress, 87–88, 98–100, 101, 102, 104, 109; Ted Kennedy as unifying force, 123–24; party loyalty switch, 187n25; public good, belief in government as a vehicle for providing, 120; political scandals, involvement in, 160–66; in Westminster Compromise scenario, 159–60, 166–68, 168–71, 172–73, 174–76, 176–79, 183–86

devolution, 25–26

dual-executive (semi presidential) system, 19–21, *22*, *23*, 29–30

electoral college, 69, 74–75, 166–67, 181, 196

Emanuel, Rahm, 122, 128, 131

Esberey, Joy, 154, 158, 160

federalism, 8, 23–25, 67, 141, 145

filibusters, 105, 126, 136, 196

Florida, role in 2000 election, 179–81

Gaulle, Charles de, 19

Gephardt, Richard, 98–99, 110

Gingrich, Newt: Republican Contract with America, 86, *88*, 93, 94, 102, 106; elections, nationalizing, 177; as fictional prime minister, 5, 179; as Speaker of the House, 5, 98–99, *107*

Gore, Al, 179–82

Grassley, Charles, 130–32

gridlock: defense of, 9–10; defined, 9, 191; dissatisfaction with term, 42n20; as a feature of American government, 197, 199; frustration with, 87, 142, 178, 189, 190; governmental accountability, preventing, 11, 190, 194; as inevitable, 194–95;

parliamentary system, less prominent in, 185; presidentialism, as a feature of, 37–38, 166; tyranny, as a means of preventing, 90, 197; unified government minimizing, 196

hanging chads, 180, *182*

healthcare reform. *See* Affordable Care Act (ACA)

d'Hondt, Victor, 34–35, 195

Hoover, Herbert, 172

House of Representatives: Affordable Care Act and, 2–3, 130, 132–33, 135–40, 142, 147, 184; Constitution specifications, 155; Republican Contract with America and, 5, 86, 88, 91, 92–94, 97, 98–104, 104–08, 110, 113, 142; divided government and, *11*, 87, 94, 175, 191, 194; as a driving force in the system, 73–74; election schedules, 74, 105, 114n15, 195; healthcare committees, *121;* House of Commons as British equivalent, 4, 5; impeachment process involvement, 43, 163, 164; as part of legislative branch of government, 27; as reactive to the will of the people, 141; reform proposals, 92–93, 95–96; Senate, differences, 104–5; Senate acting as a brake to actions of, 89, 91, 101, 131, 184; Speaker of the House, leadership function, 4, 43n7, 81n34, 193; as tiebreakers in an election, 180; 104th Congress: as an anomaly, 113, 147; British parliament system, imposing characteristics of, 108; coalition building, not favoring, 111; first day of, 95, 98–99; legislative agenda, 93; party-line voting, 110, 145; policy window, taking advantage of, 112; Republican party domination, 101, 109; separated system, blocked by, 2, 6, 142; Speaker of the House, expanding role of, 100; tax cuts, pushing, 105; time periods of, 114n15. *See also* Contract with America

impeachment, 18, 43, 161, 163–64, 196
Iran-Contra affair, 161–63, 192
IRS targeting scandal, 2, 165

judicial review, *23*, 74, 75–76, 145

Kennedy, Edward (Ted), *121*, 123–24, 129, 132, 134, 135, 139, 140
Kingdon, John, 112, 119, 121, 122

Landrieu, Mary, 131, 133, 134
Latin American democracy, 37–38
Lincoln, Blanche, 133, 134, 140
Locke, John, 70–71, 72, 77, 82n45 82n50
Lowi, Theodore, 13, 42n20

Madison, James, 71, 90–91, 126
Magna Carta, 50–52, 53, 54, *57*, 58
Mahoney, James, 48, 78
majority rule *vs.* minority rights: Congress favoring minority rights, 173; foundational tension, 1, 6, 39, 197; in healthcare reform, 118, 141; James Madison on majority factions, 90–91, 126; minority reassertion of rights, 144; governmental obstruction, 3, 8, 38, 85, 199; philosophical influences, 70–72; in Westminster Compromise scenario, 158. *See also* tyranny
Mayhew, David, 9–10
monarchy: American rejection of, 64, 68, 69; divine right of kings, 50–51; Henry VIII, King of England, 52–53, 54, *57*, 80n13; Magna Carta challenge, 51–52, 58; monarch as head of state, 29, *31*, 60; parliament, monarch as part of, 59, 61, 82n52; power seized from, 49; Stuart monarchs, 53–55, *57*, 82n45; as symbolic, 56, 58, 60; tyranny and, 71

Montesquieu, Charles de Secondat, Baron de, 70, 71–72, 77

Nader, Ralph, 182
New Deal, 112, 172, 173, 175
Nixon, Richard, 161, *162*, 164

Obama, Barack: 2008 election, 142, 184; 2012 election, 40n6, 76; congressional strategy, 127–28, 129–30; Congressional support, calling for, 134, 140; healthcare reform as campaign theme, 118, 121, 122, 138; Ted Kennedy and, 123, 124; mother, struggle with healthcare, 148n5; Nancy Pelosi, her frustration with, 135; photos, *30*, *124*, *144*; policy window, taking advantage of, 119, 122; as fictional prime minister, 4–5, 186; scandals of administration, 164–65, 192; Obamacare. *See* Affordable Care Act
O'Neill, Tip, *11*, 175, 177

parliamentary system: backbenchers, 62, 63, 109, 111; British parliament background, 50–52, 52–55, 55–56, 56–57, 57–59, 82n45; central government domination, 25, 44n42; coalition building, 33–34, 36, 62, 86, 111, 143, 184, 191; Constitutional Convention, considering adoption of, 68–69, 153, 154; Republican Contract with America, comparison, 109–11, 143, 177; countries implementing, *23*; electoral system, 31, 33, 94; first-past-the-post electoral system, 31, 61; American healthcare reform, how it would have fared in, 4, 5, 143, 146, 147, 177–78, 184–86; House of Commons, 3–4, 19, 28, 50, 55–57, 59, 61–63, 81n33–34, 113; House of Lords, 4, 28, *51*, 55–57, 59, 60–61, 74, 80n12, 81n32; majority and minority parties, 4, 19, 20, 33, 43n35, 60, 61–63, 81nn33–34, 97, 108–09, 111, 113; no confidence votes, 5, 14, 97, 161, 163, 164, 166, 197; power consolidation, 193; presidential system, differences, 6–7, 43n32, 108, 142, 145–46; Westminster model, 19, *20*, 28, 43n35, 59–63. *See also* prime minister; Westminster Compromise

path dependency, 48, 79nn3–4, 85, 118, 167

Patient Protection and Affordable Care Act. *See* Affordable Care Act (ACA)

Pelosi, Nancy, 4, 123–24, *125*, 129, 130, 132–33, 135–38, 140, *144*

policy entrepreneurs, 119, 122–24

policy windows of opportunity, 112–13, 119, 122, 124, 147, 195; American presidential system: coalition building, 111, 127, 143, 184; cognitive locks preventing reform consideration, 17; creation of, 63–65; electoral votes, 183; as flawed, 13, 199; Latin American countries, adoption of, 37; parliamentary system, differences, 108–13, 145–47; reform suggestions, 192–97

presidential democracy, 18–19, *20*

presidentialism, 37–38, 166

prime minister: accountability, 14, 63, 112; budget approval as swift, 145; in coalition governments, 33, 36; in dual-executive regimes, 19–22, 30; executive decisions, 58, 61; as head of government, 29, 30, *31*, 60, 61; legislation and, 28, 193; majority party selection, 4, 5, 19, *20*, 29, 61, 81n34, 155, 156, 163; no confidence votes as method of removal, *5*, 163, 164, 166; non-democratic version, 68–69; photo, *30;* powers of, 109; presidents as fictional prime ministers, 4–5, 161, 163–64, 176, 177–79, 182, 185–86

proportional representation electoral system, 32–36, 155–56, 159–60, 167–68, 170, 171, 181, 195

public good, 8, 90, 120

Reagan, Ronald, 5, *11*, 93–94, 101, 161–63, 175–76

reconciliation bills, 126–27, 136–37, 139

Reid, Harry, 4, 134, 140, *144*

Republican Party: Affordable Care Act, opposition to, 2–3, 24–25, 118, 131, 140–42, 145, 147, 184; divided government and accountability, *11*, 12–13, 111, 194; government intrusion, desire to limit, 120; Health Care Reform Bill passage, role in, 134, 138–39; House of Representatives and, 4, 141, 148n9; party loyalty switch, 187n25; political scandals, involvement in, 160–66; Tea Party faction, 2, 132, 135, 141, 146, 159, 165, 185, 194; In Westminster Compromise scenario, 166–68, 168–71, 172–73, 174–76, 176–79, 183–86. *See also* Republican Contract with America; 104th Congress

Romney, Mitt, 5, 40n6, 76, 148n9, 164

Roosevelt, Franklin Delano, 112, 122, 172–73, *174*, 176

Roosevelt, Theodore, 167–71

rotten-borough system, 55, 56

Sandinistas, 162

political scandals, 2, 160–66; 187n11, 192

Schumpeter, Joseph, 17

Senate: checks and balances, role in, 91, 104, 142; Republican Contract with America and, 89, 101–04, 104–06; filibusters, 105, 126, 136, 196; geographical interests, representing, 28; healthcare reform and, 3, *121*, 129–32, 133–35, 135–40; House of Representatives, differences, 74, 104–05; impeachment trials, roles in, 43n31, 164; improvement proposals, 195–96; as part of legislative branch of government, 27

sequestration, 12–13, 191

single-member district plurality voting system, 30–32, 34, *36*, 145, 155, 159, 186n7

Snowe, Olympia, 130–31, 134, 138, 149n27

Sundquist, James, 10, 72, 192–93, 195–96

Supreme Court: Affordable Care Act and, 6, 118, 141–42; appointments as controversial, 76; *Bush v. Gore* electoral decision, 181; in checks and balances system, 74; role in government, 23–24, 73; Watergate tapes decision, 161; in Westminster Compromise scenario, 185

Taft, William Howard, 168, 169–70

Tea Party, 2, 132, 135, 141, 146, 159, 165, 185, 194

Thatcher, Margaret, 62, 109, 113, 116n47

Truman, Harry S., 146, 191

tyranny: checks and balances system preventing, 3, 6, 71, 78–79; Republican Contract with America

and fear of, 90–91, 105; framers of the Constitution, fear of, 68–69, 91, 197, 198; of the majority, 8, 38, 70, 92, 105, 126, 144, 158, 167, 171

vetoes: checks and balances, as a means of ensuring, 142, 145; Bill Clinton, not using frequently, 106, 107; line-item veto, 89, 96, 97, 100, 102, 103, 104, 196; in Portuguese political system, 22; veto overrides, 74, 89, 91

Virginia Plan, 64, 68–69, 77, 153, 154

Watergate scandal, 160–61, 163, 165, 192

welfare states, 113, 167, 169, 171, 173, 176, 185

Westminster Compromise: coalition forming, 156, 170–71, 173, 177–78; 182–83, 184; alternative Constitutional Convention, 154–55; election outcome scenarios, 166–68, 168–71, 172–73, 174–76, 176–79, 179–83, 183–86; majority *vs.* minority power, 155–60, 176–79; American political development as modified, 156–58; political scandal handling, 160–66

Whitewater scandal, 163

Wilson, Woodrow, 14–15, *16*, 39, 170–71, 199

About the Authors

Anne Marie Cammisa is a visiting professor at the McCourt School of Public Policy at Georgetown University. Previously, she taught at Suffolk University in Boston and at Saint Anselm College. Cammisa directed the Center for the Study of New Hampshire Politics and Political Traditions at the New Hampshire Institute of Politics at Saint Anselm. She has also taught at the University of New Hampshire. Cammisa is the author of four books and numerous scholarly articles. One of her books, *From Rhetoric to Reform: Welfare Policy in American Politics*, was named by *Choice Magazine* as an "outstanding academic book." Cammisa has also served on the executive council of the New England Political Science Association, and was a visiting scholar at the Radcliffe Institute, Harvard University. She holds a BA from the University of Virginia, an MPP from the McCourt School, and a PhD in government from Georgetown University.

Paul Christopher Manuel is professor of political science at Mount Saint Mary's University in Maryland, where he directs the Institute for Leadership. Previously, he was professor of politics and department chair at Saint Anselm College. He cofounded the New Hampshire Institute of Politics at Saint Anselm and served as its executive director. Manuel has also taught at the McCourt School of Public Policy at Georgetown University and at the School for Public Policy at the University of Maryland–College Park. He has authored or coauthored seven books and numerous scholarly articles. He has served on the executive council of the New England Political Science Association, and was a visiting scholar at the Minda de Gunzburg Center for European Studies at Harvard University. Manuel holds a BA and an MA from Boston University, an MTS from the Weston Jesuit School of Theology in Cambridge, Massachusetts, and a PhD in government from Georgetown University.